Library of
Davidson College

FROM VILLAGE TO STATE IN TANZANIA

The Politics of Rural Development

FROM VILLAGE TO STATE IN TANZANIA

The Politics of Rural Development

CLYDE R. INGLE

Cornell University Press | ITHACA AND LONDON

Copyright © 1972 by Cornell University

All rights reserved. Except for brief quotations in a review, this book, or parts thereof, must not be reproduced in any form without permission in writing from the publisher. For information address Cornell University Press, 124 Roberts Place, Ithaca, New York 14850.

First published 1972 by Cornell University Press.
Published in the United Kingdom by Cornell University Press Ltd., 2-4 Brook Street, London W1Y 1AA.

International Standard Book Number 0-8014-0733-8
Library of Congress Catalog Card Number 72-4570
PRINTED IN THE UNITED STATES OF AMERICA
BY VAIL-BALLOU PRESS, INC.

Librarians: Library of Congress cataloging information appears on the last page of the book.

FOR EVA

Preface

One of the most crucial questions for Tanzania and other undeveloped countries is: How can the national political system effectively promote modernization in the rural areas? My study, based on field research in 1967–1968, analyzes the linkages between selected village political systems and the national system in two districts of Tanzania—Tanga and Handeni—in order to show how these intermediate political systems are used to bring national goals into the village communities. In 1967, President Julius K. Nyerere introduced a potentially revolutionary break with previous policy in the Arusha Declaration. In that document, as well as in subsequent documents, Tanzanian leadership has stressed independent, self-reliant development in the rural areas, where at least 90 per cent of Tanzanian citizens live and die. After first tracing earlier Tanzanian development policy, during both the colonial and early independence periods, I am here concerned with capturing the essence of politics and development as displayed by the interaction between village, district headquarters, and national government during the period immediately following the Arusha Declaration, and with showing some of the implications for the people involved, both peasants and officials.

I am grateful to Fred G. Burke, who provided inspiration for this work and gave counsel and criticism during the field research and the writing. My initial field work in Tanzania was made possible by grants from the Ford Foundation and the Program of

Eastern African Studies of the Maxwell School of Citizenship and Public Affairs, Syracuse University. Subsequent grants from the Research Foundation of the State University of New York and the Joint Committee on African Studies of the Social Science Research Council and the American Council of Learned Societies facilitated preparation of the final manuscript and allowed me to carry out additional field work in East Africa in 1971. None of these institutions bears any responsibility for my findings or conclusions.

Many individuals have knowingly or unknowingly aided my research. In particular I wish to thank my research assistant, safari companion, and friend, Lukemelye S. K. Sadatale, for his assistance and advice. My work in Tanzania was made possible only by the cooperation and patience of countless Tanzanians, both official and unofficial; to them, I am most grateful. The interpretation and analysis that follow are made with the deepest respect for the idealism of the Tanzanian leaders and their dedication to the task of improving the life of their countrymen.

The Office of Sponsored Research, State University of New York, Geneseo, provided generous assistance in the preparation of the manuscript, facilitated by the director of that office, Richard Hale; and I am grateful for the diligent and cheerful typing of Judy Worden and Shirley Schmidt. Nancy Steen of the Department of Political Science also assisted in preparing the manuscript, and the department chairman, Edward G. Janosik, gave unlimited professional support to my scholarly endeavors. Brian Lynch ably assisted me in the final editing of the manuscript.

I wish to express my appreciation to the editors for permission to use material that appeared earlier in my articles "Compulsion and Rural Development in Tanzania," *Canadian Journal of African Studies,* IV (Winter 1970), and "The Ten-House Cell System in Tanzania," *Journal of Developing Areas,* VI (January 1972). I also gratefully acknowledge the permission granted by East African Publishing House Ltd. to quote selected statistics from tables published in William Tordoff, *Government and Politics in Tanzania* (Nairobi, 1967), and R. G. Penner, *Financing Local Government in Tanzania* (Nairobi, 1970). I also acknowledge and express my appreciation to President Julius K. Nyerere and to Oxford University Press for permission to quote from the collected writings and speeches of President Nyerere contained in *Freedom and Unity* (Dar es Salaam: Oxford University Press, 1966), © Oxford University Press 1966, and *Freedom and Socialism* (Dar es Salaam: Oxford University Press, 1968), © Julius K. Nyerere, 1968.

Finally, I acknowledge my indebtedness to Eva Purdom Ingle, a persistent critic and supporter of this study from its conception and through many rewritings to its completion, and to Katherine and Brian who endured this process.

CLYDE R. INGLE

Geneseo, New York

Contents

    Preface   vii

I.   Introduction: The Arusha Declaration   1
    An End and a Beginning   3
    The Imperative of Rural Development   11
    The Arusha Declaration and the Rural Areas   16

II.   Local Political Systems: A Theoretical Comment   19
    Immediate, Intermediate, and National Political Systems   20
    System-to-System Relationships   22
    The Approach and the Methods   35

III.   Rural Development in Tanzania   39
    German Period   40
    British Period   42
    Postindependence Efforts to Promote Rural Development: Continuity and Change   48

IV.   The Developmental Environment   79
    The Physical Environment   79
    The Cultural Environment   84

V.   The District *Boma:* National Outpost   107
    Colonial Intrusions   109
    The District *Boma*   113
    District Officers: Technicians   120
    District Council   122
    The Political Party: Instrument of Fusion   131

	District Development and Planning Committee	138
	Summary 142	
VI.	From *Boma* to Village	145
	Division 145	
	Ward 154	
	Village 166	
	Ten-House Cell 169	
VII.	Village and State: Systems in Action	185
	Sharing of Functions 185	
	Intersystem Roles: The Question of Dominance 209	
	The District Councilor: Perceptions of Roles 213	
	Intersystemic Inputs and Outputs 229	
VIII.	The Village, the State, and Rural Development	251
	The Interim Result: Accommodation, Acquiescence, Withdrawal 253	
	The Center-Periphery Nexus: An Assessment 257	
	The Development of Subsystems: A Threat to National Direction? 259	
	Selected Bibliography	261
	Index	275

Charts and Tables

Chart 1. Political organization: From region to district   115
Chart 2. Political organization: From division to village   146

Table 1. Comparative yearly rainfall   80
Table 2. Rainfall for month of May, 1922–1935, showing irregularity of rainfall in Tanga District   81
Table 3. Methods of dispute settlement in a small village   177
Table 4. The district council's main sources of revenue   245
Table 5. Main items of district expenditure   246

FROM VILLAGE TO STATE IN TANZANIA | The Politics of Rural Development

CHAPTER I

Introduction: The Arusha Declaration

On December 9, 1961, Tanganyika became an independent sovereign state in the world community. Thus a half century of foreign domination of nearly 363,000 square miles and some 10 million people in Eastern Africa came to an end. Control of Tanganyika had been granted to the victorious British by the League of Nations Trusteeship Council at the end of World War I. Before the British, Germany had ruled the area, in accordance with the decision at the Congress of Berlin in 1885, when European powers chose arbitrary boundaries to enclose the diverse lands and peoples which are Tanzania today. While the unfurled flag on top of Mount Kilimanjaro symbolized newly won independence from the British, Tanzania's real independence is perhaps more accurately dated from February 8, 1967. On that day President Julius K. Nyerere, the leader of the independence movement and the nation's first leader of government, presented the Arusha Declaration, a document that has since become the basis of the national creed. That document emphasized self-reliant development. "Independence," declared the President, "means Self-Reliance. Independence cannot be real if a Nation depends upon gifts and loans from another for its development." [1]

The Arusha Declaration is a turning point in Tanzania's brief

[1] Julius K. Nyerere, "The Arusha Declaration," in Julius K. Nyerere, *Freedom and Socialism: A Collection from Writings and Speeches 1965–1967* (London, 1968), pp. 231–251.

postcolonial history. During the five transitional years between independence and the Arusha Declaration, the Republic of Zanzibar and Tanganyika united in the new national entity of the United Republic of Tanzania in 1964.[2] A military mutiny in the same year, though unsuccessful, revealed the fragility of the political institutions of the new nation, and in 1965 the party of Tanganyikan independence, the Tanganyika African National Union (TANU), was made by law the single governing party.[3] During this period of adjustment the new rulers of Tanzania sought ways to promote the objectives that had been articulated by the nation's leaders during the drive for independence. The Arusha Declaration was, as I shall show, a logical result of the lessons learned during these first years.

This book is a study of the relationship between the ideals of the Arusha Declaration and the behavior of the peasants in selected village communities in Tanzania.[4] By using available source materials and by field research in these villages, I have attempted to illuminate the complex problem one African government faced and continues to face in linking the political center with outlying villages. This problem, a crucial one for all developing nations, was cogently stated by President Nyerere in 1961:

[2] While the term Tanzania formally refers to both the island of Zanzibar and the mainland of Tanganyika, I will adopt the more widely accepted practice of using Tanzania throughout this study even though my research was confined to the mainland.

[3] For treatments of both developments see Henry Bienen, *Tanzania: Party Transformation and Economic Development* (Princeton, N.J., 1967). Hereafter the Tanganyika African National Union will be referred to as TANU.

[4] Throughout this study, I use the term peasant to refer to the small-scale, usually subsistence farmer and do not enter the debate over whether the African farmer is to be called a peasant. For a discussion of this question and appropriate bibliographic references see David Brokensha and Charles Erasmus, "African 'Peasants' and Community Development," in David Brokensha and Marion Pearsall (eds.), *The Anthropology of Development in Sub-Saharan Africa*, Society for Applied Anthropology Monograph No. 10 (Lexington. Kentucky, 1969).

INTRODUCTION: THE ARUSHA DECLARATION

"While other countries aim to reach the moon," he said, "we must aim for the time being, at any rate, to reach the village."[5] My effort here is to show in selected areas how the Tanzanian government has attempted to reach the villages to implement the Arusha Declaration and how these villages have responded.[6]

An End and a Beginning

President Nyerere presented the Arusha Declaration to the annual meeting of the national conference of TANU in the town of Arusha in February 1967. At least as early as June 1966, the President had articulated the major theme of the Arusha Declaration. Before the national legislature, he had assessed the first two years of the First Five-Year Development Plan and noted: "We can accept the fact that although outside events will affect our achievement, only we ourselves will determine our endeavour. We can rely on ourselves, and what we achieve will ultimately depend on that more than on any other factor. For the man who shoots an arrow at a target is the man who really determines whether the target is hit."[7] Nyerere then concluded by calling on the National Assembly to "let our motto for the coming year be 'self-reliance,' and in that spirit let us pursue our goal of economic betterment for our country and all its people."[8]

The Arusha Declaration placed the principle of self-reliance at the center of future development efforts. For Nyerere, the lessons of the first years of development efforts were clear: "Our Five Year Development Plan aims at more food, more education and better health; but the weapon we have put emphasis upon is

---

[5] Quoted in Stanley Dryden, *Local Administration in Tanzania* (Nairobi, 1968), p. 42.

[6] Excellent studies that pursue a similar theme in other regions of Tanzania include Goran Hyden, *Political Development in Rural Tanzania* (Nairobi, 1969), and G. Andrew Maguire, *Toward Uhuru' in Tanzania: The Politics of Participation* (Cambridge, 1969).

[7] Nyerere, *Freedom and Socialism*, p. 174.   [8] *Ibid.*

money. . . . We think and speak as if the most important thing to depend upon is MONEY and anything else we intend to use in our struggle is of minor importance." [9] For the future, Tanzania in the President's view should not depend upon money, which could only be obtained from outside sources, as the principal weapon for securing development:

> It is stupid to rely on money as the major instrument of development when we know only too well that our country is poor. It is equally as stupid, is even more stupid for us to imagine that we shall rid ourselves of our poverty through foreign financial assistance rather than our own financial resources. . . . We made a mistake in choosing money—something we do not have—to be the big instrument of our development. We are making a mistake to think that we shall get the money from other countries; first, because in fact we shall not be able to get sufficient money for our economic development; and secondly, because even if we could get all that we need, such dependence upon others would endanger our independence and our ability to choose our own political policies.[10]

The President concluded in a later elaboration of the self-reliance theme: "Self-reliance in development is merely an application of something we knew in 1954—that only Tanzanians are sufficiently interested to develop Tanzania in the interests of Tanzanians, and only Tanzanians can say what those interests are." [11]

The principle of self-reliance logically led to an increased concern for the rural areas of the nation, where at least 90 per cent of the population lived and where the vast majority of Tanzania's limited resources were located. The Arusha Declaration expounded upon this fact: "The mistake we are making is to think that development begins with industries. It is a mistake because we do not have the means to establish many modern industries in our country. We do not have either the necessary finances or the technical know-how." [12]

Nyerere then called for a shifting of primary emphasis to the

[9] *Ibid.*, p. 235. [10] *Ibid.*, p. 238. [11] *Ibid.* [12] *Ibid.*, p. 241.

INTRODUCTION: THE ARUSHA DECLARATION

rural areas and to the peasant farmer, since it was the peasant farmer who ultimately had to pay back through his production the loans that would be used for the developed areas.[13] The obvious conclusion based on this reasoning was that the future of national development in Tanzania lay in promoting development in the agricultural sector. Surveying these prerequisites of development in the Tanzanian context, the President concluded that agriculture was the basis of development in the nation:

Because the main aim of development is to get more food, and more money for our other needs, our purpose must be to increase production of these agricultural crops. This is in fact the only road through which we can develop our country—in other words, only by increasing our production of these things can we get more food and more money for every Tanzanian.[14]

The conclusion that agriculture had to be the basis of Tanzania's development did not originate with the Arusha Declaration in 1967. As early as 1965, President Nyerere had warned:

Agriculture progress is the basis of Tanzanian development. This truth is said so often that people forget it. They almost don't listen; the words become part of the atmosphere, and have no impact any more. To talk of the importance of agriculture is like playing a record which has been heard too often.

Yet it remains true. Agricultural progress is indeed the basis of Tanzanian Development—and thus of a better standard of living for the people of Tanzania.[15]

A third major theme articulated in the Arusha Declaration was a reaffirmation of the national elite's intent to strive toward the achievement of a socialist society. African socialism has had varied interpretations. In the Tanzanian case, from the earliest period, the ideology of African socialism has, at the least, assumed two

[13] *Ibid.*, p. 242. [14] *Ibid.*, p. 244.
[15] *Ibid.*, p. 104. This comment was made in an address at the opening of the Morogoro Agricultural College, November 18, 1965.

objectives—the prevention of exploitation of one group of people by others, and the people's control over the major means of production. In speaking of "Principles and Development" in 1966, President Nyerere had noted that the purpose of African socialism remained the same as in traditional society, that is

> the welfare of every individual in the context of the needs of the society of which he is a member. It was to build this kind of society that we wanted independence; to build a kind of society in which a few were very rich and the masses desperately poor would be a betrayal of the people. This would be true even if the total wealth of a different kind of society were greater, for our purpose is not the production of wealth for its own sake, or for display, or "national prestige," but for the benefit of all the people.[16]

In the Arusha Declaration of 1967, policies were defined more specifically than ever before for the implementation of socialism. It provided that

> 1. Every TANU and Government leader must be either a Peasant or a Worker, and should in no way be associated with the practices of Capitalism or Feudalism.
> 2. No TANU or Government leader should hold shares in any Company.
> 3. No TANU or Government leader should hold Directorships in any privately-owned enterprises.
> 4. No TANU or Government leader should receive two or more salaries.
> 5. No TANU or Government leader should own houses which he rents to others.[17]

At the same time, Nyerere announced the nationalization of major sectors of the economy including the banks, major processors of raw materials, and wholesalers of consumer products.[18] Thus the

[16] *Ibid.*, p. 199.   [17] *Ibid.*, p. 249.
[18] See the survey discussion in United Republic of Tanzania, *Background to the Budget—1968–69* (Dar es Salaam, 1968), p. 3.

Arusha Declaration set about putting teeth into what had been hitherto vague statements of ideology. In summing up the events of Arusha a few days later, President Nyerere noted:

> Tanzania has defined the economic implications of her socialist policies, and in doing so has specified the areas of Public and the areas of Private enterprise. In the division the key positions of the economy have been secured for the nation in the same way as, during a war, an army occupies the sites which dominate the countryside. Our war is a war against poverty, and for the freedom and self-government of our people. In this fight we can now welcome the enterprise of private investors without reservations, because we no longer have any cause to fear the effect of their activities on our social purpose.[19]

Thus the Declaration "re-examined, updated, and clarified Tanzania's development strategy following the initial consolidation of political independence and the first experiences in coherent national development planning." And it marked the beginning of a new phase in Tanzania's search for independence and successful development strategies.[20]

In the following months, the speeches of the President and the ministers and several position papers elaborated on the principles of the Arusha Declaration. The first such paper was "Education for Self-Reliance," which outlined changes in the colonially inherited educational system such as a new emphasis on cooperative efforts and agricultural techniques in keeping with the needs of the rural areas and the concept of self-reliance.[21]

His second major policy paper, "Socialism and Rural Development," aimed at reconciling the ideal of African socialism with the goal of rural development.[22] Here Nyerere sought to point out that

[19] *Sunday News,* February 12, 1967, reprinted in Julius K. Nyerere, *The Arusha Declaration* (Dar es Salaam, 1967), p. 25.

[20] *Background to the Budget—1968–69,* p. 3.

[21] Julius K. Nyerere, "Education for Self-Reliance," in *Freedom and Socialism,* pp. 267–290.

[22] Julius K. Nyerere, "Socialism and Rural Development," in *Freedom and Socialism,* pp. 337–366.

contemporary society in Tanzania was breaking away from the traditional values of the society.

> Our society, our economy, and the dominant ambitions of our own people are all very different now from what they were before the colonial era. There has been a general acceptance of the social attitudes and ideas of our colonial masters. We have got rid of the foreign government, but we have not yet rid ourselves of the individualistic social attitudes which they represented and taught. For it was from these overseas contacts that we developed the ideas that the way to comfort and prosperity which everyone wants is through selfishness and individual advancement.[23]

Thus individual Tanzanians had accepted the goal of individual wealth, and in the all important rural areas, where land and wealth had traditionally been held in common, a rural capitalist class had begun to emerge even though the government had tried to stem this trend with a law in 1963 which sought to reaffirm the traditional principle that land belonged to society and not to the individual and to establish the government as caretaker or "trustee" for the land.[24] President Nyerere continued:

> The small-scale capitalist agriculture we now have is not really a danger; but our feet are on the wrong path, and if we continue to encourage or even help the development of agricultural capitalism, we shall never become a socialist state. On the contrary, we shall be continuing the break-up of the traditional concepts of human equality based on sharing all the necessities of life and on a universal obligation to work.[25]

To reverse this trend, Nyerere proposed the establishment of socialist villages (*ujamaa vijiji*) in the rural areas. These ujamaa villages constituted the ideal society envisaged by Nyerere:

---

[23] *Ibid.*, p. 340.
[24] R. W. James, *Land Tenure and Policy in Tanzania* (Nairobi, 1971), p. 21.
[25] Nyerere, *Freedom and Socialism*, p. 344.

Our agricultural organization would be predominantly that of co-operative living and working for the good of all. This means that most of our farming would be done by groups of people who live as a community and work as a community. They would live together in a village; they would farm together; market together; and undertake the provision of local services and small local requirements as community. Their community would be the traditional family group, or any other group of people living according to ujamaa principles, large enough to take account of modern methods and the twentieth century needs of men.[26]

At the national conference of TANU delegates in October 1967, Nyerere gave further attention to the concept of self-reliance that had been the source of considerable discussion since its emphasis in the Arusha Declaration. The President noted that self-reliance ultimately meant that Tanzanian development and Tanzanian independence were possible only if Tanzania was dependent upon its own resources for its development: "Self-reliance is a positive affirmation that we shall depend upon ourselves for the development of Tanzania and that we shall use the resources we have for that purpose, not sit back and complain because there are other things we do not have."[27]

For Tanzania this then meant "that the emphasis of our development will be in the rural sector, and particularly in agriculture." For a community, the President elaborated, "self-reliance means that they will use the resources and the skills they jointly possess for their own welfare and their own development. They will not take the attitude that the Government, or Local Council, or anyone else, must come and do this or that for them before they can make any progress."[28]

During the course of the interpretation of the Arusha Declara-

[26] *Ibid.*, p. 351.
[27] Julius K. Nyerere, "After the Arusha Declaration" in *Freedom and Socialism*, p. 388.
[28] *Ibid.*

tion, the role of the local community received more and more emphasis in the whole process of national development. The ujamaa village concept aimed at revitalizing the traditional village along lines that were compatible with African socialism and traditional values. Subsequent statements by various ministers and a final major paper in the Arusha sequence reiterated the importance of the locality and local participation in development efforts. "Freedom and Development," presented by the President in October 1968, stressed the importance of securing voluntary, enthusiastic participation from local communities in the development effort.

Development brings freedom, provided it is development *of people*. But people cannot be developed; they can only develop themselves. For while it is possible for an outsider to build a man's house, an outsider cannot give the man pride and self-confidence in himself as a human being. Those things a man has to create in himself by his own actions. He develops himself by what he does; . . . he develops himself by making his own decisions, by increasing his understanding of what he is doing, and why; by increasing his own knowledge and ability, and by his own full participation—as an equal—in the life of the community he lives in . . . he is not being developed if he simply carries out orders from someone better educated than himself without understanding why those orders have been given. A man develops himself by joining in free discussion of a new venture, and participating in the subsequent decision; he is not being developed if he is herded like an animal into the new venture. Development to [*sic*] a man can, in fact, only be effected by that man; development of the people can only be effected *by the people*.[29]

Greater production in the rural areas depended upon the ability of the national leadership to penetrate the countless village communities and bring about a change in the patterns of village life that would encourage the peasant farmer to adopt new techniques,

[29] Julius K. Nyerere, "Freedom and Development," *Standard,* October 18, 1968.

seeds, and tools, and most important, to work more. At the same time the leadership of Tanzania hoped to bring about rural change within the context of what were described as traditional African values embodying a spirit of community and not individual gain. These difficult goals were to shape all policies and actions of the Tanzanian government.

The Imperative of Rural Development

Tanzania shares with the rest of the African continent the dominance of the agricultural sector. While most new African nations accepted the importance of the rural sector, their early development plans tended to understress rural development.[30]

Even before these nations became independent, numerous observers had stressed the need to concentrate on the development of the rural areas as a basis for all other development. Prominent among those offering such advice was the well-known economist and development planner, Arthur Lewis, who as early as 1953 advised officials in what was to become Ghana that "the most certain way to promote industrialization in the Gold Coast is to lay the foundation it requires by taking vigorous measures to raise food production per person engaged in agriculture." [31] While many others also stressed the imperative of rural development, Tanzania, in the Arusha Declaration of 1967, was the first African nation to officially dedicate her primary development efforts to that task.

The arguments for emphasizing the rural areas in African development efforts stressed two cardinal facts about the continent. First, Africa is predominantly rural, with at the least 80 per cent of its inhabitants engaged in subsistence agriculture. In Tanzania

[30] Consider the Report of the Commission on International Development, *Partners in Development* (New York, 1969), p. 270. (Commonly referred to as the Pearson Report.)

[31] A good survey of the views supporting the priority of the rural area by a major proponent of this view is found in Guy Hunter, *The Best of Both Worlds?* (London, 1967), pp. 49 ff.

at least 90 per cent of the population were dependent upon the land for their income.[32] Second, Africa is poverty stricken by virtually anyone's standards. The per capita gross national product in 1967 for all of the continent excluding South Africa was approximately $130. This figure is startling if compared to a similar statistic of $145 for East Asia, $135 in the Near East and South Asia, $425 in Latin America, and $3,966 in the United States. In Tanzania, the per capita gross national product was $73,[33] which President Nyerere has graphically described as follows:

> If all the wealth of all the people in this country were put into one big heap, and then divided equally between all the people who live in Tanzania, each person would receive goods to the total value of Shs. 525/–[about $75.00, the Tanzanian shilling = U.S. $0.14]. That is all he would have for a year. Not a month, but a year. This means that the total wealth of the country is valued at about Shs. 5,455,000,000/–. Out of that amount, nearly 10½ million people have to eat and clothe themselves; we have to run our schools, our hospitals, maintain our roads and our houses, pay for our administration, pay our Army and police Forces, pay for our Government, and do every other single thing which we want to do in this country. But in addition it is from this same amount that we have to invest for a better life in the future by building new roads and communication, by building factories, houses, new schools, and so on. In fact, the total wealth available to be spent by all the people of Tanzania during one year is much less than America spends on its military forces in one week.[34]

Because of this poverty, African domestic markets simply could not provide markets for local industries even if they developed. Thus, in Tanzania the capacity to produce cotton cloth outstrips the effective domestic market for it. The only way to provide effec-

---

[32] From the Government's White Paper on Wages and Incomes, *Standard*, December 5, 1967.

[33] U.S. Agency for International Development, Statistics and Reports Division, *Selected Economic Data for the Less Developed Countries*. (Washington, D.C., June 1969).

[34] Nyerere, *Freedom and Socialism*, p. 397.

tive demand for the efficient operation of the industrial sector, small though it is, is to increase the productivity of and therefore the income of the farmer.

The scarcity of capital resources and the reluctance to become dependent upon external aid that characterize many African independent states have led to an increased concern for the most efficient use of the few resources available. Here, again, rural development seems the only solution. Some experts refer to agriculture as the "bargain sector."[35] The nature of the bargain has been cogently stated by President Nyerere. During a teach-in on the Arusha Declaration at the University of Dar es Salaam, the President noted that providing one job in a highly mechanized industry could cost over $5,000. "On the other hand," he went on, "it is possible to double the output of cotton on a particular acre by spending Shs. 130/ [approximately $18.50] on fertilizer and insecticide; it is possible to double a farmer's acreage under crops by the provision of an ox-plough at a cost of Shs. 250/ [approximately $35.70] or less. . . ."[36]

Nyerere's stress on the cost of providing a job for one person brings into focus another strong argument in favor of stressing the development of the rural sector that was increasingly heard during the last half of Africa's first decade of independence. Unemployment is so significant as to be described by Guy Hunter as the "dominant problem of Africa in the 1970's." The unemployment rate for much of Africa may be as high as 20 per cent and the percentage of the population that is underemployed is probably even greater. The nature of the problem and some of its implications have been concisely stated by Hunter:

When a two and one-half percent population growth is applied to a 75 percent rural population, the resulting increase in absolute rural numbers will far exceed the natural growth [two and one-half per cent

[35] S. R. Sen, *The Strategy of Agricultural Development* (London, 1962), quoted in Hunter, *The Best of Both Worlds?* p. 49.
[36] Nyerere, *Freedom and Socialism*, p. 319.

on 25 per cent] in towns; it will exceed it even if growth *plus* immigration to towns adds up to six percent per annum. Thus, in the sharpest contrast to Western experience, the rural areas in Africa and Asia will have to give a livelihood to greatly increased absolute numbers for a generation or more. Even with a seven percent per annum growth in gross national product, in modern experience salaried employment seldom increases faster than two to three percent per annum. Thus, the towns will not be able to absorb their own growth; and the country will face ever-mounting pressure on lands and jobs.[37]

Specific examples make the unemployment problem even more menacing. Only one-third of those who sought employment in the modern sector of Nigeria in 1968 were able to find jobs. In Kenya, while the annual output of secondary schools in 1968 was 150,-000, only 50,000 jobs were available.[38] During 1970, 20 to 35 per cent of the labor force in Ghana were unemployed, and the figure grows as from 70,000 to 80,000 middle-school pupils leave school each year.[39] And in Tanzania, with a population of over 12 million, for 250,000 of an age group entering the labor force, only 25,000 jobs were available in the modern sector.[40] Only in the rural areas is there a potential solution to the problem of unemployment in Africa. There, with relatively little input, employment can be provided in a way that also contributes to the total productivity of the society.

In addition to these arguments favoring a primary emphasis upon the development of the rural areas, two other considerations have increasingly influenced policy decisions during the first decade of African independence. First, the results of efforts to promote economic development have on the whole been poor. For the period 1960–1966 in countries representing 22 per cent of the population of Africa, the per capita gross domestic product actu-

[37] Guy Hunter, "The New Africa," *Foreign Affairs*, XLVIII (July 1970), 719.
[38] Arthur T. Porter, "Africa-Crisis in Education," *AAUW Journal*, LXI (March 1968), 110.
[39] *Africa Digest*, October 1970, p. 90.
[40] Porter, "Africa-Crisis in Education."

INTRODUCTION: THE ARUSHA DECLARATION 15

ally fell; it increased by more than 2 per cent annually in countries representing only 27 per cent of the population of the continent. For the continent as a whole, excluding the white-minority-ruled areas of southern Africa, per capita GDP went from $103 in 1955 to only $112 in 1966. More specifically, for the continent as a whole the increase in agricultural productivity per annum from 1950–1967 did not exceed 2 per cent. The importance of this gross statistic is highlighted by the fact that the per annum growth in population during the same period was 2.3 per cent.[41] While such gross statistics mask exceptional increases in agricultural productivity,[42] they also mask dismal failures. On the average they clearly show that for the continent as a whole, agricultural productivity is not keeping up with the number of mouths that have to be fed. In the specific case of Tanzania, the output in the subsistence sector of the economy increased at 2.1 per cent during the period 1960–1967 while the population was increasing at a rate of 2.7 per cent.[43] In short, for Africa and for Tanzania it is imperative even for the most minimal of goals—that of keeping consumption at its present level—to increase the productivity of the rural areas.

Second, most African leaders have an ideological commitment to majority rule that necessitates at least lip service to the concerns of the areas where the vast majority of the population lives. This consideration is of particular importance in Tanzania, where national leadership has taken the tenets of African socialism quite seriously.

In the face of the realities of these arguments, the 1970's seemed

[41] Samir Amin, "Development and Structural Change: The African Experience 1950–1970," *Journal of International Affairs*, XXIV (1970), 210, *passim*, and *Partners in Development*, p. 358.

[42] Compare Amin, *ibid.*, p. 213.

[43] United Republic of Tanzania, *Background to the Budget; 1968–69* (Dar es Salaam, 1968), p. 10, *passim*, and United Republic of Tanzania, *Tanzania Second Five-Year Plan for Economic and Social Development, 1st July, 1969–30th June, 1974*, Volume I: *General Analysis* (Dar es Salaam, 1969), p. viii.

to find an increasing awareness throughout the continent of the imperative of placing the rural areas at the center of development efforts. Fragmentary evidence suggests that the national development plans of the second decade of African independence will place a greater proportion of government resources in the development of the rural sector. Tanzania's innovative approach to national development efforts spelled out in the policies of Arusha has led one observer to describe this development program as "an ideology for Africa." [44]

The Arusha Declaration and the Rural Areas

From the Arusha Declaration, it is clear that Tanzanian leaders in the national capital accepted the imperative of rural development. My concern here was to study the response of local communities to national policies and principles. In order to examine the various levels of government that transmit policy from Dar es Salaam to the villages, I conducted field work from May 1967 to July 1968 in two settings, Tanga and Handeni districts, both of which are located in Tanga Region of northeastern Tanzania, and in selected groups of communities within these two districts.

Although the administrative and political institutions in Handeni and Tanga districts were similar in a formal sense, the contrasts in their functioning were severe, due in part to the difference in the levels of modernization of the two districts. Even though the data for strict statistical comparisons of relative levels of socioeconomic development was scarce, enough was available to suggest the contrast between Handeni and Tanga. Tanga District has within its borders Tanga, the second largest city in the nation and the second most important port and transportation center. The headquarters of the district are located in the city, which can be reached by air, hard-surfaced road, rail, or sea under virtually any weather

[44] Henry Bienen, "An Ideology for Africa," *Foreign Affairs*, XLVII (April 1969).

conditions. Travel to Handeni, where the Handeni district headquarters are located, on the other hand, is possible only by a dirt road that may be impassable during the rainy season.

A more precise indicator of the contrasting levels of economic development is the fact that in 1966 Handeni had a total of 1,054 regular salaried employed citizens, representing less than one per cent (.7 per cent) of its total population while Tanga had a total of 31,999 such employees representing 15 per cent of the district's total population.[45]

The population densities of the two districts also differ greatly. In 1967, Handeni had a population of 132,300 in a land area of 5,100 square miles and, thus, had a population density of 25.9 per square mile. Tanga, in contrast, had a population of 197,353 in an area of 1,900 square miles for a density of 135.9.[46] The Handeni population density is not noticeably affected by concentrations in specific densely settled areas, while the Tanga figures understate the actual density since a large proportion of the district is covered with sisal fields, forcing the inhabitants into relatively more dense settlement patterns.

What happens to national plans, goals, and procedures as the capital seeks to apply them in these markedly different districts? The success of the national leadership in achieving these plans lies in its ability to penetrate the countless villages in the nation and to make national goals the goals of the villager and his family. The success of this effort or the causes of its failure must be assessed in the village.

[45] Calculated from United Republic of Tanzania, Central Statistical Bureau, *Employment and Earnings 1966* (Dar es Salaam, July 1966), p. 35, and United Republic of Tanzania, Ministry of Economic Affairs and Development Planning, Central Statistical Bureau, *Preliminary Results of the Population Census Taken in August, 1967* (Dar es Salaam, December 1967).
[46] *Preliminary Results*, pp. 22–23.

CHAPTER II

Local Political Systems: A Theoretical Comment

This study assesses the phenomenon of political behavior from the perspective of systems analysis.[1] The employment of the concept of system stresses those actions which relate to the formation and enforcement of policies in any political community. For David Easton, the "political system can be designated as those interactions through which values are authoritatively allocated for a society." These interactions structure themselves into roles and structures which are identifiable and which are conceptually separate from other systems of activity such as religious and economic activity. The usual tendency in political science is to think of political systems in terms of the national political system. A central assumption of a system analysis approach to the study of political behavior is that the system will strive to maintain itself in the face of stress upon it. While the application of the concept to the new nations of Africa and Asia has tended to emphasize the "developing" nature of these societies where the national state system strengthens itself, in fact, as I shall stress in this study, systems lower than the national may also develop to counter stresses and demands upon them, the principal source of which may be the national system itself. In so doing they may jeopardize

---

[1] I am most indebted to David Easton's *A Systems Analysis of Political Life* (New York, 1965). In addition, however, see Gabriel A. Almond and G. Bingham Powell, Jr., *Comparative Politics: A Developmental Approach* (Boston, 1966), and Ernest B. Haas, *Beyond the Nation State* (Stanford, Calif., 1964).

the development of the larger systems of which they are a part. Thus the use of the concept of system in this study does not assume a strengthened national government or state. Instead the systemic conception is employed in this study as a useful tool for placing political behavior in meaningful perspective. More specific dimensions of the systemic concept are extracted to direct special attention to those aspects of system-to-system behavior which are of special interest. One caveat should be offered. "Concepts," as Easton has noted, "are neither true nor false; they are only more or less useful." [2]

Immediate, Intermediate, and National Political Systems

A basic assumption upon which this study proceeds is that in any time and place an individual is an actor in several political systems. These political systems are engaged in the authoritative allocations of values in the respective societies of which they are a part. The relative ability of the various political systems to allocate values independent of other systems depends upon a number of factors, ranging from the coercive capability of the respective systems, the degree of consent to these values, the importance of the issue in the view of the subjects, and many more. While precise cataloguing of these factors is unnecessary and, perhaps, impossible, a tentative classification of political systems is required.

The classification of political systems chosen for the purposes of this analysis is immediate, intermediate, and national. *Immediate* political systems are those most directly impinging upon the behavior of the individuals, and have generally been referred to as local political systems. Here, immediate has been chosen as a term of reference more useful for analysis than local political system

[2] David Easton, *A Framework of Political Analysis* (Englewood Cliffs, N.J., 1965), p. 33.

since there are at present at least four administrative and political systems in Tanzania that could accurately be referred to as "local" political systems. "Local," as it is used in this study, becomes a relative term; obviously some political systems are more local— that is, immediate to the individual—than are others.[3] "Localness" then becomes a characteristic that could be measured in greater to lesser terms for any political system one might wish to analyze. Discarding "local" political systems as a type of political system has the additional advantage of freeing our analysis from restrictions to an area focus.[4] Immediate political systems in this study refers to those structures exercising the political functions in village communities.

Intermediate political systems are those social systems involved in the making and implementation of decisions for political systems *intermediate* between the immediate political systems, the villages, and the national political system spreading outward from the capital city of Dar es Salaam. In Tanzania at this time there are four political structures intermediate between the village and the national political system (see Charts 1 and 2, below). From the village upward in the hierarchy, they are the ward, the division, the district, and the region. Each of these geographically based administrative units is involved in some form of allocation of values even if minimal. It is assumed here that although these systems may be creations of the national political system, they are functioning either with some independence or as appendages of the immediate systems. In either case, they are with varying degrees taking on the characteristics that are normally associated with political systems.

[3] For some actors, e.g., presidents, ministers, and possibly members of national legislatures, the national system may be the "most local" political system.

[4] See the important study of ethnicity as the principal base for a political system in Abner Cohen, *Custom and Politics in Urban Africa* (London, 1969).

The *national* political system is centered in the capital city and is the source of national authority. The essentially hierarchical classification is presented here to draw attention to the fact that the behavior of individuals is influenced by the attempted imposition of values from different sources in their environment. Individual responses to these influences will vary. The three classes of political systems differ not only in the *structures* through which political functions are performed but also in the relative *extent* to which these functions are performed. This analytic classification of political systems in Tanzania or in any national system will, I believe, simplify the consideration of linkages between these systems.

System-to-System Relationships

Efforts to conceptualize relationships between national political systems and their subsystems are few and inadequate. The anthropologist Julian H. Steward, has suggested that

national institutions are mediated to the local or traditional society by several different mechanisms and agencies. These agencies are logically distinguishable and in some cases represent developmental stages. Three categories are: first, individual agents who link the traditional society with a state institution; second, forced regimentation of the members of the society; and third, organizations or associations which represent local levels of national institutions.[5]

Charles P. Loomis, another student of linkages between systems, has commented that

systemic linkage may be defined as the process whereby the elements of at least two social systems come to be articulated so that in some ways they function as a unitary system. Systemic linkage is based

[5] Julian H. Steward, *Contemporary Change in Traditional Societies*, vol. I-III (Urbana, Ill.: University of Illinois Press, 1967); see especially vol. I, *Introduction and African Tribes*, p. 14, for above comment.

upon a model which may be conceived as two or more social systems as going concerns which come to be related in such a way that the two eventually, in some ways and on occasion, function as one.[6]

My attempt to create conceptual tools for the analysis of system-to-system relationships has led to the formulation of three propositions that will serve as foci for analysis and will illuminate the linkage between political systems. The first is that within any national society the political functions of that society are shared by a series of political systems. The second proposition is that political actors occupy political roles in the several political systems in the same fashion as they simultaneously occupy several roles within social systems. The third proposition is that an input-output exchange occurs between the several political systems in a "national" setting.

The Sharing of Political Functions

A major working hypothesis for the formulation of system-to-system relationships employed here is that in every society the political functions are shared by a variety of political systems in that society intermediate between the individual and the national political system. Although the hierarchy of systems could also include the international political system, for practical immediate purposes this formulation will arbitrarily postulate the national political system as the preeminent system.

It is theoretically possible that the immediate system may be unimpinged upon by other political systems; it would thus be the preeminent political system and would not share political functions with other political systems. In fact, however, this has seldom been the case. Usually several political systems share these functions. This sharing and the number of functions that each system takes on are results of the attempt of each political system

[6] Charles P. Loomis, "Systemic Linkage of El Cerrito," *Rural Sociology* XXIV (March 1959), 55.

to maintain itself—and the self-maintenance of each is threatened by the other political systems with which it must coexist. The central problem of every national political system both in the underdeveloped world and elsewhere is how to use immediate and intermediate political systems for the mobilization of the society's resources for the pursuit of the goals of the national political system. The national political system may go so far as to attempt a wholesale creation of new immediate and intermediate political systems, or it may choose to attempt to penetrate the existing systems so as to direct the actions of these systems toward the achievement of national goals. In both these cases, the proposition that the central objective of each political system is to maintain itself suggests that the existing systems will take measures to cope with this stress that is placed upon them by the national system. The degree to which this effort is successful may spell success or failure for the survival of the national system.

The state-building process in the new nations may be viewed primarily as the process of conflict and competition between the localities and a fledgling national state system that in most cases is a legacy of the colonial system and that must struggle to survive. The same struggle goes on in older, more developed nations, but there it is more likely the survival of the immediate and the intermediate systems that is threatened and not the national system.

To complete this formulation of a sharing of political functions between political systems, I have prepared a categorization of functions which will serve to direct attention to the structures that perform these functions in the political systems studied. If one accepts the postulate that the first objective of any political system is to maintain itself, the system will perform the following major functions.

The maintenance of order. Possibly the foremost demand in any society is for social order. Order maintenance, here, includes the resolving of personal disputes, providing security from external threats, and protecting personal rights and properties. Also included are the functions related to rule-keeping. In sum we are referring to the control element of the political system's performance.

It is possible to ascertain qualitatively if not statistically the extent to which individual and group behaviors are in fact subject to the control of the respective political systems to which they are subject. Different types of individual and group behavior may be controlled by different political systems. A divorce dispute may initially be subject to the workings of the village political system for resolution; under certain circumstances, however, the intermediate political systems may take part in the dispute. If the intermediate political systems are incapable of resolving the dispute, the resulting conflict may bring the national political system into the order-maintenance function. If the national political system is incapable of dealing with the dispute, violence may be the only alternative remaining. This sharing of the task of order maintenance by different political systems within a national system is not unique to the less developed nations. In the United States, conspiring to deprive one of certain rights because of his race is dealt with by the national political system while killing a person because of his race is dealt with by the state government, an intermediate political system. The nature of the sharing of political functions between political systems in both the highly developed societies and the less developed societies is an immensely complicated problem for analysis.

The communications function. Communications, for the purposes of this study, includes all flows of information within and between political systems. Communication within a village political system—the most local system for the purpose of this study—is a relatively simple function. The structures involved in this process are relatively undifferentiated, involving little more than the morning conversation between the occupants of adjacent huts. In the national political system, on the other hand, the communications function becomes complex. The structures engaged in communicating different types of information—from central government orders, to the warning that a tax collector is approaching, to the enunciation of the nation's foreign policy—can become very complicated. For this study of intersystem linkages, the communication function is an extremely useful dimension of the political process since an analysis of specific messages from the center reveals the specific nature of the nexus between the political systems under observation.

The political socialization function. Political socialization is the process by which individuals are taught what their attitude toward and role in the political system should be.[7] The end result of this process has been referred to as political culture: "Political culture is the pattern of individual attitudes and orientations towards politics among the members of a political system."[8] Political socialization has been defined as "the process by which political cultures are *maintained* and *changed*."[9] This dichotomy of the political socialization function is an accurate and useful one. On the one hand, the maintenance of political tradition is of central importance in guiding political actors and the general populace in their respective roles. On the other hand, political socialization is likely to be central to the capacity of a political system to *change* and thus to cope with the inevitable stresses upon the system. Thus the political socialization function must provide for both maintenance and change if a political system is to be able to cope with stress and to survive.

In this analysis of the relationships between political systems it will be seen that there is overlap between the socialization function as performed by the various intermediate political systems. This overlap may be cooperative; it may also bring about conflict. In

---

[7] See Richard E. Dawson and Kenneth Prewitt, *Political Socialization* (Boston, 1969).

[8] Almond and Powell, *Comparative Politics*, p. 50.

[9] *Ibid.*, p. 64, emphasis is mine.

this study it will be important to determine the structures that perform the socialization function in each political system and to note the basic features of the political culture that each system aims to instill.

The problem of political socialization is particularly acute in developing societies since the village political system may socialize its members into roles that are in direct contradiction to those demanded by the intermediate and national political systems. In addition, the developing nation not only has to socialize its youth, as does every system, but it also must resocialize its total population. While the socialization function is an ongoing concern in every society, the rapid and effective achievement of a change in political culture resulting from effective socialization is especially important to the new nations.

Extraction and mobilization. The ability of the system to extract resources from the society and its environment is the prerequisite of the system's survival and the achievement of established goals.

Closely related to extraction is the concept of mobilization, which refers to the ability of the political system to direct individual and group action toward the goals established for the political system. The function of extraction-mobilization goes on within political systems; it also goes on between systems. The between-systems extraction and mobilization process is of special interest to this study.

The immediate political system may mobilize resources in its environment for repairing a road or for dealing with a famine. In either case the problem and its solution may be accepted and coped with by the political system in which it falls, and the act of mobilization is seen as for the benefit of the members of that political system.

On the other hand, the village needing a better road may demand materials and labor from intermediate political systems such as the district political system. To the extent to which such a demand is accepted and responded to, the village political system is able to extract from a wider political system, conceivably from the national political system, and even from the international political system.[10]

Colin Leys has commented on this phenomenon in respect to the district in Uganda. "From the point of view of a district . . . the net inflow or outflow of resources would be one useful indicator of the performance of district politicians operating as a group vis à vis the rest of the country."[11] Leys further spells out one of the implications of this proposition: "If local politics can significantly reduce—perhaps, in some cases, even reverse—the flow of resources from the rural areas to the capital, what implications does such a political system have for the possibility of planned economic development?"[12] I would add: What implications does such a condition have for political development?

A central problem of every political system and a measure of its development is its capacity to extract and mobilize resources. This problem is particularly acute for most of the newly developing nations since they must extract from limited resources through new and often very weak structures. National systems often try to extract resources from areas under the jurisdiction of immediate and intermediate political systems that resist their efforts. An

[10] Village extraction from the international system is not only conceivable, it is a fact. In certain villages in Tanzania, for example, the village wells had been built by UNESCO, and when the pumps were in disrepair, the demands for repair went through various channels to UNESCO. In addition, any visitor to villages in Africa or Asia might be asked for assistance, either from himself personally, or from his country, church, and so on. And many have complied. Local groups in Tanzania have been able to make direct contact with the international political system for some time. Groups of people suffering injustice during the colonial period took their case directly to the United Nations (see Kirlo Japhet and Earle Seaton, *Meru Land Case* [Nairobi, 1967]), although they most often approached missionaries and international agencies at work throughout the country.

[11] Colin Leys, *Politicians and Policies* (Nairobi, 1967), p. 102.
[12] *Ibid.*, p. 103.

alternative is for the national political system to attempt to mobilize resources in and through the intermediate and immediate systems and to direct these resources to national goals. The national political system must then convince sufficient numbers of the actors in the more local systems that the national goals are their goals. This accomplishment is of first priority; but it is only a first step. The operational problem of either *creating new structures* to carry out this extraction and mobilization function throughout the nation or to use the *existing structures* of these systems persists.

These political functions are performed to a greater or lesser extent in all political systems. The totality of the nation and state-building process is directed toward the centralization of these functions under the direction of the national political system. Certain of these functions may be more crucial for the survival of political systems than others. As an extreme example, the nation's political system may demand that it control the right to cross its territory. On the other hand, the ultimate solution of a divorce dispute in a village may be of no immediate concern to the national political system. At any particular time in any national political system, in a developed or underdeveloped nation, these functional categories will be shared to a greater or lesser extent by all the component political systems—national, intermediate, immediate, and conceivably, even the international political system. If a basic postulate of the systems analysis of political behavior is that the system attempts to maintain itself, it can always be expected that each system responds to and resists the encroachment of other systems on the performance of its functions.

While it is theoretically possible to assess the extent to which each political function is performed by the various political systems to which the individuals are subject, in practice it is possible only to suggest the nature of this sharing in a very relative fashion. For example, in Tanzania order maintenance may be performed almost completely by the village political system. A village system might perform a hypothetical 50 per cent of the communication function, 75 per cent of the political socialization function, and 50 per cent of the extraction/mobilization function. The village political system would then share the political functions with the intermediate and the national systems.

As a function is taken over by wider political systems—by the district or nation, for example—the scale of the function increases. Functions that must be carried out by political systems wider in scope than the village political systems will require an immensely more complicated structure and operation. For example, if the national system is to perform the function of preserving order in the nation, it must be prepared to field a security establishment that is costly in finance and technical skills, while the same function may be performed in the village system by the elders receiving little or no compensation and who at the same time perform other functions in the system.

The scale of the extraction and mobilization function particularly increases if it is performed by wider political systems. It will then require larger and more specialized structures and its very upkeep will demand more extraction. In addition, as the national political system achieves the preeminent position vis-à-vis individuals, it almost inevitably enunciates goals for the nation that demand greater resources and therefore a substantial increase in the extraction and mobilization function.

When the national political system attempts to increase its share of the functions by penetrating the intermediate and immediate systems, these systems may respond to this stress by increasing their own capacity to carry out the political functions. This does not necessarily mean that they resist the national system that they confront. It may mean, however, that the village and district systems increase their capabilities to deal with the threat to their survival, in other words, they develop. Thus, the efforts of the national political system to develop may set in motion development in the immediate and intermediate systems that could threaten the development of the national system.

Alternately, the development of the intermediate and immediate systems may be turned to the same or similar goals pursued by the national political system. In this case the dominant political system will be reaching toward an optimum of development since it has managed, intentionally or otherwise, to direct the total of the political systems in the society toward similar ends. All political systems in the society may in effect function as a unitary system.

Intersystem Roles

Widespread agreement exists on the definition of a role. David Easton's is fairly representative: "The roles consist of regularized patterns of behavior and expectations about the ways in which the occupants of particular positions in society will behave and of how others ought to behave toward them." [13] While the particular concern here is with political roles, it must be recognized that individual occupants of political roles also occupy other roles in society, for example, family, religious, and economic roles. Each role demands particular behavior from the individual. An impressive literature demonstrates the utility of role analysis; it ranges from the complex and methodologically sophisticated study to the simple statement of focus.[14] Here I use the concept of role as a general statement of focus for illuminating the interrelationships between political systems.

A second aspect of role analysis useful for this study is its applicability to the analysis of political change or development. It has been noted, for example, that

[13] Easton, *A Systems Analysis*, p. 206.

[14] For an excellent bibliography on role analysis in all the social sciences see footnote 6 in J. C. Wahlke *et al.*, *The Legislative System* (New York, 1962), p. 7. Among the more outstanding applications of role analysis in political science are *The Legislative System, ibid.*, and Samuel J. Eldersveld, *Political Parties: A Behavioral Analysis* (Chicago, 1969).

a principal aspect of the development or transformation of the political system is what we call role *differentiation* or *structural differentiation*. By "differentiation" we refer to the processes whereby roles change and become more specialized or more autonomous or whereby new types of roles are created. . . . We refer not only to the development of new types of roles and the transformation of older ones: we refer also to changes which may take place in the relationship between roles, between structures, or between subsystems.[15]

Thus the introduction of new roles from whatever source can cause change and conflict within the political system. Of central concern to this study is the introduction of new roles by the national political system into the immediate and intermediate systems and the resulting response of these systems to the intrusion.

Four dimensions of the concept of role are important here. First, what are the political roles of the political systems under observation? Who are the occupants of these roles? Political scientists have pointed out that one of the characteristics of a less developed political system is a low level of role differentiation. Thus political roles in the Tanzanian village political system—or in small, less developed systems—may be few and unspecialized, and some may be filled only intermittently. Almond and Powell describe the ideal type of this political system as an *intermittent* political system: "It has no set of roles, no structure, which is specialized for political purposes. . . . It is one in which there are no differentiated political roles and no specialized political structure." [16]

A third aspect of role analysis that is revealing for the study of intersystem linkages is the extent to which an individual's intersystem political roles are shared among systems; under what conditions does his role in one system become dominant over that in another? The district councilor, for example, is a member of a

---

[15] Almond and Powell, *Comparative Politics*, p. 22; emphasis is Almond and Powell's.
[16] *Ibid.*, p. 43.

village political system and leader of the ward from which he is elected, and also, as a member of the district council, he is part of the district political system. Under what conditions and to what effect is his behavior in one of these roles likely to be determined or influenced by his simultaneous occupancy of the other political roles?

Some political roles are intentionally intersystemic in function. The district tax collector who was assigned to a particular subdivision of a district is a district actor whose role is performed in villages X and Y. The FBI agent is assigned to work in a county; there his role, in contrast to that of the county sheriff, is a national one to be performed in an intermediate political system. Which of these roles, the wider or the more local, is likely to be dominant and under what conditions? [17] When one system introduces a new role into its own or another political system, the response of the relevant system to that role will be of particular importance to the analysis of intersystem linkage. The establishment of the role of party cell-leader in Tanzania, for example, introduced an entirely alien role into the village political system, but in a few years that role became institutionalized by the village political system. Such a process raises important questions: To what extent has the impact of the existing roles in the village political system shaped the role of cell leader? Has the village political system simply made the traditional headman or an elder cell leader? If so, what is the effect upon the function that the cell leader was expected to perform for the national political system?

[17] An example of this type of role conflict has been reported in a study of the FBI's investigation of the shooting of thirty Black students at Orangeburg, South Carolina, in 1968. The authors reported that FBI agents had "disconcertingly close relations" with state law enforcement agents who were themselves subjects of the federal investigation. Further, they reported that the "agent in charge of the Columbus, South Carolina, office of the FBI was staying in the same room at the Orangeburg Holiday Inn occupied by [the] chief of the state police, himself one of the subjects of the Federal investigation." See the discussion in the *New York Times,* September 21, 1970.

Conversely, what has been the impact upon the headman, who is now cell leader and thereby has acquired new rights, obligations, and a role in other political systems? Have these changes markedly altered his political behavior within the village political system?

Such questions are crucial for the analysis of system-to-system relationships. Some answers to them are essential for the successful penetration of localities by the national political system, and in turn may be essential for the success of new nations' efforts to bring about rapid socioeconomic development. A study of the linkages between political systems may fruitfully focus on the concept of roles as well as functions.

Input-Output Analysis

Input-output analysis is a general concept that can be applied to one political system and its internal processes, to the transactions between any political system and its environment, and to the transactions that take place between political systems. In the last case, the range of political systems may include international political systems, a national political system's transactions with international political systems (e.g., member states' relations with NATO), or the transactions may be carried on with the more immediate political systems.

In this study, input-output analysis can usefully be applied to transactions between immediate, intermediate, and national political systems. What are the respective inputs and outputs of the political systems? In more concrete terms, what does the village political system do to or for the district political system? Conversely, what does the district political system do to or for the village political system? And, concurrently, what do they do *with* each other?

A comparison of the outputs of the village political system seen as inputs to the district political system, with the outputs of the district system seen as inputs into the village system, provides a useful approach to the analysis of the nature of the relationship between the two political systems. If these exchanges are measured in financial terms, for example, an accurate description of the extractive capacity of one system from another emerges. As noted above, this analysis provides an important indicator of the development of state systems in the underdeveloped world, as well as supplies a measure of the success of socioeconomic changes.

The Approach and the Methods

I determined to approach the nexus between center and periphery in Tanzania by examining the rural development program because it was the most prominent issue and would best reveal the relationship between the relevant political systems. The emerging national ethic of the nation's elite had made rural development their central concern. My findings suggest, in fact that it was becoming the central concern of the peasant, as well. The Swahili term for rural development, *maendeleo vijijini,* literally translated "development *in* the villages," states this ethic with precision. This choice of rural development as the major issue for analysis meant that I posed questions and framed statements in the terminology of rural development.

The tools used in gathering information for this research were essentially of four types. First, after securing permission to investigate each setting, I interviewed the relevant officials in two districts in order to identify the problems of rural development that the districts faced and the respondents' conception of their development role within the district political system. I then chose areas at the subdistrict level for more intensive investigation of the problems and techniques of promoting rural development. Finally, I asked similar questions at the village level. My primary concern was to determine the nature of the meshing between these sites, which, though primarily identifiable by geographical characteristics, were for the purposes of this study conceived as political systems. At the village level, I also attempted to identify individual conceptions of rural development efforts and, in the process, to illuminate the nature of the relationship between the individual and the political systems.

These interviews varied in formality. In several cases, for example, individuals refused to talk with me by themselves; this was true of the district working committee of TANU in one district and also of the officials in one division. While the people were generally suspicious of a researcher and his intent, their reluctance was also cultural. Local people, unaccustomed to responding as individuals, simply refused to speak their view as individuals. I had to learn their views of the developmental process by interpreting the consensus they reached at general meetings. In the field, particularly, both official and nonofficial spokesmen reacted in this manner to my questions. They felt that the best technique was to arrange a general meeting (*baraza*) so that I could sense the feeling of the people.

I conducted interviews with three types of officials: (1) the central government officials, all appointed by the national government; (2) the local government people, most elected in some fashion; and (3) the representatives of the political party, TANU, some of whom were elected and some appointed. The reluctance to talk varied with the three groups; generally the more local groups were the least willing to respond to questions.

A second tool was the questionnaire. I attempted a number of types of questionnaires with varying degrees of success. In one case, the party chairman of a ward took me to a village, called out the people, and ordered that the questionnaire be filled out. Three hours later thirty-five people—the entire adult population—had, with the assistance of my research assistant and another literate person, finished their questionnaires, and we departed.

A few days later, in the same ward, we arrived at another village accompanied by a government official. The party leaders were called to a general meeting to answer the questionnaire. While there should have been thirty leaders at the meeting, only nine elders arrived. With the greatest cordiality, they took the questionnaires and returned them empty, much to the embarrassment of the government officer. In other places, the officials refused to allow the use of the questionnaire. Instead, they held a *baraza* under a mango tree with the men and some women of the villages. I asked questions from the questionnaire; these were discussed by the assembled people, and then I "sensed" a communal answer. Despite these different approaches, the information gathered from the mass meeting technique was essentially the same as that derived from formal questionnaires. In most cases the mass meeting technique was the only possible technique to use.[18]

The third and in many ways the most useful information-gathering technique was observation and limited participation. I attended meetings from the village to the district level. What happened, what did not happen, and who did what constitute some of the more meaningful data in this study. There can be no doubt, however, that my presence did indeed alter the behavior of the participants in the gathering. I discussed problems of development, taxes, and government with anyone who would talk about these topics. In most cases, these conversations served to confirm or cast doubt upon information gathered by other techniques.

Last, I consulted the available documentary material. District records and minutes of district council and committee meetings proved useful, as did files from the colonial period now stored in the National Archives.

The realities of Tanzania often thwarted my attempts to be scientific and systematic in methodology. It became quite clear that I would have to use any technique, even gossip and direct participation, in order to gather the information I needed. I do not, however, apologize for the methodology employed in this study. It is scientific in the broader sense suggested by David Riesman, who defines "scientific" as "a canon of ethical scrupulousness and

---

[18] For a discussion of the "group interview" for the collection of historical data in Africa, see J. B. Webster, "Research Methods in Teso," *East Africa Journal,* VII (February 1970), 32.

choice of the most appropriate methods, not allowing these methods to be monopolized by any particular sect of methodologists."[19] Much of the descriptive material below was derived from my own impressions built upon interviews, surveys, participant observation, and discussions in each of the locales studied over the period of approximately one year.

[19] In the "Foreword" of Elenore Smith Bowen, *Return to Laughter* (Garden City, N.Y., 1964), p. xvi.

CHAPTER III

Rural Development in Tanzania

The principal public issue in contemporary Tanzania is rural development. The President, civil servants, party officials, and newspapers struggle with the question of how best to promote development in the villages. And rural development in the present terminology means more than an increase in the productivity of the individual farmer. President Nyerere has declared, "We are not simply trying to organize increased production; we are trying to introduce a whole new way of life for the majority of our people." [1] The problem of inducing change in the life style of the peasant is more complex than the introduction of new machinery or techniques. In a country where over 80 per cent of the population are subsistence farmers, their major tool is the hoe, and the major source of energy is their own backs,[2] President Nyerere has set a much more ambitious goal for his people than did any of the foreign powers who controlled Tanzania.

Before the Germans came to Tanganyika in the late nineteenth century, the population, which is largely Bantu, had contacts with the Greeks, Chinese, Arabs, and Portuguese. These peoples, however, made no attempt to change traditional behavior or agricultural patterns, the principal form of which was subsistence agri-

[1] Julius K. Nyerere, "After the Arusha Declaration," in *Freedom and Socialism,* p. 407.
[2] Tordoff, *Government and Politics in Tanzania,* p. 184. The 80 per cent is actually a conservative estimate, since only 4.5 per cent of the population were wage earners in 1963.

culture, which entailed using a plot of land for a few seasons and then shifting to new and often virgin land once the soil's fertility had been depleted. Land was held in common by tribal authorities, and individual ownership of land was virtually unknown. Agricultural activity was above all a quest for community survival, not for individual enrichment.

German Period

The German colonials were the first to attempt to enrich themselves by developing the agricultural potential of the area. Even they rather modestly assessed Tanganyika's future as an economic venture. One of the earliest of German pioneers, Carl Peters, noted that

> as a whole the colony may be described as a good agricultural country, and it has already been found fit for all sorts of tropical plantations. . . . Taken all in all German East Africa is perhaps not a colony of the first class, but it has splended openings in several directions, and if properly managed, it may be developed into a wide and very important field for German enterprise.[3]

The priorities of the German colonizing effort were to stamp out the slave trade and restore order to the countryside. The Germans were ruthless in achieving these ends. In Handeni District, for example, oldtimers recall that the Germans arrived to find the area torn by intratribal warfare aimed at securing slaves for the Arab market. The Germans hanged the first slavers they caught, publicly displayed the bodies in the Handeni town market, and proclaimed that other offenders would suffer a similar fate.[4]

After putting down the Maji Maji Rebellion in southeastern Tanganyika in similar fashion during 1905–1906, the Germans

---

[3] This quotation appears in R. F. Eberlie, "The German Achievement in East Africa," *Tanganyika Notes and Records,* LV (September 1960), 195.

[4] Interview, Sindeni Ward, Handeni District.

increased their attention in agricultural development, particularly in estate agriculture.[5] First they opened up vast stretches of uncultivated land; then they used European management and techniques and often unenthusiastic African labor to produce crops such as sisal, cotton, and rubber for export. A prominent feature of the estates effort was the use of compulsory labor, enforced by the use of the rhinoceros hide whip. A contemporary scholar has noted:

Without some form of compulsion the labour force could not be organized to play its part in the opening up of the country's economy. The work had to be done to till the settler's first plantations, to carry the crops to the waiting ships, to lay the railways and to construct the ports. It may be argued that, before the arrival of a cash economy, economic development was quite impossible without some form of compulsory labour.[6]

Although the welfare of the individual African farmer was definitely of secondary importance to the estate agriculture in the German colonial effort, it was not completely ignored. R. V. Pierard, for example, calls attention to the fact that the Colonial Secretary Dernberg

encouraged the Africans to engage in agriculture themselves. He maintained that they could produce a larger quality and a much more diversified range of goods than the plantations, and this would offer the additional benefit of making the population self-sustaining. Although Dernberg conceded that plantation culture could make a significant economic contribution, he was firmly convinced that peasant agriculture undertaken by the indigenous population was the backbone of East African economic life and that it could not be replaced by plantations.[7]

---

[5] See J. F. R. Hill and J. P. Moffett (eds.), *Tanganyika: A Review of Its Resources and Their Development* (Dar es Salaam, 1955), p. 358, for comment.

[6] Eberlie, "The German Achievement," p. 193.

[7] R. V. Pierard, "The Dernberg Reform Policy and German East Africa," *Tanzanian Notes and Records,* LXVII (June 1967), 37.

Further, memoranda such as the following from a 1907 document set the ever hopeful tone to be repeated hundreds of times by all the development officials in the regimes to follow: "The cultivation of cotton by the Africans . . . is experiencing continuous development. In many parts of the colony the Africans have already recognized the advantages of this crop, and one may assume that with further encouragement cotton planting will become a permanent practice." [8] World War I brought German rule to an end and led to the establishment of the British colonial regime, which had a greater impact upon the individual African producer.

British Period

During the early years of British administration there was little emphasis on rural development, as events outside the territory shaped policy. Recovery from World War I and the economic slump of the 1930's restricted efforts to promote development of the area. World War II further curtailed the number of men and resources available for developmental projects,[9] but the end of the war brought a period of fairly sustained effort on the part of the British to promote development in Tanzania.[10] In 1946, Tanganyika became a United Nations Trust Territory under British administration, and for all intents and purposes the efforts to promote rural development can be dated from about 1950.[11]

[8] Quoted in Hans Ruthenberg, *Agricultural Development in Tanganyika* (Berlin, 1964), p. 45.

[9] For a comprehensive account of the period see J. P. Moffett (ed.), *Handbook of Tanganyika*, 2d ed. (Dar es Salaam, 1958), pp. 89–145.

[10] For an assessment, see Cyril Ehrlich, "Some Aspects of Economic Policy in Tanganyika, 1945–1960," *Journal of Modern African Studies*, II (July 1964), 265–277.

[11] See the surveys in Ruthenberg, *Agricultural Development*, pp. 54 ff, and *The Economic Development of Tanganyika*, Report of a Mission organized by the International Bank for Reconstruction and Development at the Request of the Governments of Tanganyika and the United Kingdom (Baltimore, 1961), pp. 19–25; hereafter cited as World Bank Report.

Whether through British efforts or in spite of them, the economy as a whole seems to have made progress in the 1950's. The World Bank Report estimated the over-all growth rate at about 5 per cent.[12] During this period the growth rate of the production of African food crops and other subsistence products probably increased at about 2.5 per cent per year. Since the World Bank estimated a population growth rate of 1.7 per cent, the Report concluded that there had been a real increase in per capita income.[13]

British development efforts took three directions. First, the British encouraged the estate agricultural system initiated by the Germans, and considerable expansion of acreage occurred. Second, the colonial administration initiated a number of special development schemes aimed at substantial and fundamental changes in the agricultural development of the country, and third, the British promoted the increased productivity of the peasant farmer through extension methods.

Of these efforts to promote rural change, the British put a major emphasis on their special scheme approach. The most renowned of these efforts was the Groundnut Scheme, an attempt to grow peanuts—groundnuts in the parlance of the British—on a very large scale at the end of World War II. As conceived, the scheme was to cover 5,000 square miles of territory and produce 600,000 tons of peanuts a year. Fleets of bulldozers left over from the war years were shipped to East Africa to assist in the opening of the virgin land for the peanut fields. In the haste to get the project started, elementary considerations—including the amount of rainfall for the area which was recorded in the colonial records and the composition and potential of the soil—were overlooked. The effort, now notorious in colonial development efforts, ended as a colossal failure.[14] Many other special schemes less spectacular in nature were initiated during the 1950's, and some were continued

[12] World Bank Report, p. 25.   [13] *Ibid.*
[14] For an excellent treatment of the Groundnut Scheme, see Alan Wood, *The Groundnut Affair* (London, 1950).

into the early years of independence.[15] Ideally, these schemes were to revolutionize agriculture in a particular situation and would then serve as a model for similar situations in the country. Most of these projects were capital intensive, required a radical change on the part of the African farmers who participated, and were brainchildren of expatriate colonial officers whose idealism and enthusiasm often exceeded their knowledge of the regions and peoples that they sought to transform. Today the countryside is littered with the relics of these projects, which never seemed to fail completely enough to warrant an official report of failure, but which, instead, declined and were forgotten as the initiator was transferred or left the service. The impact upon the life of the peasant farmer appears to have been minimal. Melville J. Herskovits noted of the special schemes:

Conceived and executed in a large scale, they posed requirements in the way of land, capital equipment and technical direction that were far beyond the capacity, not merely of any single African participant, but even of any group of Africans and, later, of most African governments. . . . Their functioning as agents of cultural change was thus minimal.[16]

Another dimension of the British effort to promote rural change was the systematic use of compulsion. As early as 1901, the Colonial Secretary, Joseph Chamberlain, proclaimed to the House of Commons: "It is good for the native to be industrious. . . . Under all circumstances the progress of the native towards civilization is only secured when he should be convinced of the necessity and

---

[15] See the survey in Ruthenberg, *Agricultural Development*, pp. 45–103. Consider also treatments of a particular effort, the Sukamaland Development Scheme, in G. Andrew Maguire, *Toward 'Uhuru' in Tanzania: The Politics of Participation* (London, 1969), pp. 26 ff, and John C. de Wilde et al., *Experiences with Agricultural Development in Tropical Africa*, II (Baltimore, 1967), 415–451.

[16] Melville J. Herskovits, *The Human Factor in Changing Africa* (New York, 1967), p. 159.

dignity of labour, where this is not the case . . . , then we must make every effort to teach him to work." [17]

During World War II, the colonial officers had justified the use of compulsion by the refusal of Africans to volunteer to work in the local industries and on the estates whose activities had been stimulated by the war. Revealing the official British attitude of this period, Hill and Moffet note that this failure to volunteer to work, coinciding with a drought and famine in 1942 and 1943.

strained the food supply of the country, so that the requirements of the essential industries became steadily more pressing until resort to conscription for civil employment could no longer be avoided. The conscription was controlled by the Manpower Department which was set up in 1939 and that in all some 73,752 Africans were conscripted for essential industries, which included sisal, pyrethrum, mixed farming, sugar, rubber, mineral production, timber, essential public services, etc. Conscription finally ended in 1945.[18]

The full story of wartime labor conscription in Tanzania has not been told. Fragmentary evidence for Tanga Region suggests ill treatment of conscript labor by estate management and a primary role for estate management in the conscription process itself. An aide memoire on a meeting at the Office of the Provincial Commissioner, Tanga, in February 1944 noted that

exemplary sentences imposed in the Tanga District in the recent past on Deserters, in some cases as long as two years imprisonment, together with the other measures taken, have had—temporarily at all events—the deterrent effect aimed at. The Tanga prison now has 50% more inmates than is authorized and the Prison authorities find it necessary to transfer over 100 prisoners to other jails outside the Province.[19]

[17] R. F. Eberlie, "The German Achievement in East Africa, *"Tanganyika Notes and Records,* LV (September 1960), 193.
[18] Hill and Moffett, *Tanganyika,* p. 269.
[19] Tanga Province, "Aide Memoire. Meeting at Office of Provincial Commissioner, Tanga, on 20th February, 1944 to Discuss Certain Aspects

Under the enlightened colonial policy of the 1950's and the watchful eye of the United Nations, compulsion took the form of the enforcement of agricultural ordinances that attempted to govern the agricultural practices of the peasant farmer.[20] One British officer argued that "the African must be compelled to help himself" and suggested that an "understanding by those who govern that in place of the stress which forces Europeans to do things, the African must be compelled—and forcibly too—to improve the conditions under which he lives, with his own hands."[21] Hans Ruthenberg has described these ordinances:

> Administrative ordinances were considered the proper instrument to get peasant development. Local Authorities were instructed to issue agricultural regulations. The implementation of such regulations was supervised by officers of the Agricultural Department. Cases of non-observance were reported and punished by the Local Authorities. The increasing activities of the Department of Agriculture consequently meant more ordinances and more controls.[22]

If British colonial officers felt no qualms about using force to further agricultural development, they certainly needed no special justification to use compulsion to try to prevent famine. During the colonial days famine was a constant threat throughout Tanzania, and the ultimate protection against it was to attempt to force the peasant to plant sufficient, drought-resistant crops. Ruthenberg, for example, calls attention to the fact that

> a regulation requiring the cultivation of manioc on a specific area of land was already effective during the German colonial administration. Manioc was to serve as a protection against famine in case of poor maize or millet harvests. This regulation was revived in the late forties. The coastal strip of the Tanga Region had become an area of chronic

---

of the Conscript Labour Problem," National Archives, "Compulsory Labour File" (45/560).

[20] See Ruthenberg's treatment of ordinances in *Agricultural Development,* pp. 48 ff.

[21] Quoted in Maguire, *Toward 'Uhuru,'* p. 28.   [22] *Ibid.*

hunger, even though sufficient land was available for manioc cultivation. A change in the nutritional situation was brought about by forced cultivation. The farmer who did not plant was fined. Agricultural Officers exercised control. They often had to be accompanied by armed policemen when carrying out their duty. In the case of manioc cultivation in the Tanga Region success was achieved. Today surplus is produced, dried and exported.[23]

In accordance with the policy of indirect rule,[24] the British attempted to use indigenous institutions to initiate and enforce compulsory cultivation. In December 1951 the Provincial Office, Tanga, issued a list of functions to be performed by native authorities, as the indigenous institutions selected or appointed by the British for conducting colonial policy were called. The list suggested that native authorities, generally at this time in the form of a local council, might "require any person to cultivate land to such crops as will secure an adequate supply of food for the support of such person and of those dependent upon him." [25] Some of the Native Authorities took up the suggestion. The Native Authority in Handeni, for example, passed a bylaw of January 1, 1956, to the effect that "every house owner has to have one acre of cassava planted or two acres once a year of sorghum. He who fails to do so will have three months' imprisonment." [26]

During the second half of the decade before independence in 1961, the inherent resistance of the peasant to change was bolstered by the emergence of a nationalist movement that encouraged resistance to the colonial government. The emerging political leaders seized upon the tenacity of the peasant's conservatism to muster

[23] Ruthenberg, *Agricultural Development*, p. 51.
[24] For a discussion of the policy of indirect rule as applied in Tanzania see below, pages 111–113.
[25] Tanga Province, Provincial Office, "List of Suggested Functions of Native Authorities," 14 December 1951, Ref. no. 788/2/91, National Archives (302/A2/42).
[26] Handeni District, Tribal Council (Ufungilo) By-Laws, 1/1/56, National Archives (304/A2/49), translated from the Swahili.

support for their own opposition to the colonial regime. This opposition, born of the allegiance of the nationalist politician with the peasant, was especially felt by colonial officers who were attempting to bring about change in the rural areas.

The emphasis on special development schemes, the systematic use of compulsion, and the emergence of organized political opposition to British efforts to promote rural change—these were the legacy of rural development efforts that the independent African government received when it took over the task of ruling and developing in December 1961.

Postindependence Efforts to Promote Rural Development:
Continuity and Change

Rural development efforts of the immediate postindependence period are marked more by continuity than change: In one sense this was to be expected; the preindependence plans and techniques were still much in force. Indeed, in most cases, the personnel responsible for development policy and implementation were the same. In 1962, one year after independence, 61.5 per cent of the senior and middle-level civil service positions were filled by foreign officers.[27] Even where top-level expatriate personnel had departed, their African counterparts entered the positions guided by their past experience and institutionalized colonial attitudes, which did not differ substantially from those of the British colonial administration.

This continuity was a surprise, however, to the top political leaders, who expected that the peasant farmers would enthusiastically respond to their demands for change. The nationalist elite that led the independence movement believed that the peasantry

[27] As late as June 1968, 74.8 per cent of the senior- and middle-grade civil servants were Tanzanian citizens—5,478 out of a total of 7,323 officers. One hundred per cent Africanization is planned by 1980. *Standard*, December 27, 1968. Also see *Background to the Budget 1968–69*, p. 35.

would be as motivated by the achievement of political independence as they were. The peasant's conservatism, which had earlier been tapped by the politicians to mobilize opposition to the British administration was now expected to respond to the new government's exhortations to change, but in fact, the life style of the village in the immediate postindependence period remained largely unmoved and unchanged, as it had in response to the German intrusion and to the British period of control.

The drive for Tanzanian independence was relatively calm and nonviolent. In fact the first major survey of the economy and its potential was made a full two years before the achievement of independence in December 1961, yet it fully accepted the fact of African self-government in the very near future.[28] Serving as a transition document, this World Bank Report lay down the guidelines of economic planning and development for the country at least for the first five years of independence. The central theme of the report is contained in the opening paragraph.

This report has been written at a challenging point in the history of Tanganyika. Since September 1960 there has been for the first time a majority of elected ministers. This change should make it clear to the people of Tanganyika, as never before, that their future is in their own hands. Development depends on greater and more effective effort by those who produce. That the people should come increasingly to realize the connection between their own efforts and the improvement of their conditions of life is the main hope for rapid and satisfactory development in Tanganyika.[29]

By calling for a "greater and more effective effort by those who produce," the World Bank Report called for more effort from the peasant farmers who make up the bulk of the population. The Report pointed out the importance of the peasant farmers in the nation's economy by noting that they produced at that time approximately 55 per cent of agricultural exports and about 65 per

[28] World Bank Report.   [29] *Ibid.,* p. 3.

cent of all marketed crops. For all crop production including subsistence production, the peasant farmer's share of production was about 80 per cent.[30]

Thus, from the very beginning, the peasant farmer was the central figure in Tanzania's independent efforts at economic development. The World Bank Report suggested two major procedures for initiating greater productivity on the part of the peasant farmer. These procedures were labeled the "transformation approach" and the "improvement approach." These two terms were to be freely used by those who debated the course of Tanzanian development efforts during the first decade of independence. In essence, the transformation idea embodied the special scheme approach to rural development employed so freely by the British. Improvement, on the other hand, meant increasing agricultural extension efforts aimed at encouraging and educating the peasant to greater productivity on his existing, largely subsistence, holdings.

In the immediate postindependence years, there was a flurry of special schemes aimed at transforming the peasant's agricultural practices. One of the most prominent examples of the schemes was the village settlement program. Initiated by President Nyerere in 1962, this program aimed at settling scattered, unsettled peoples into permanent village communities.[31] The concentration of peoples in new village communities would enable the government to provide the people with social services and to direct them into the practice of new agricultural techniques. The President's call initiated two kinds of settlement activity throughout the country. The pilot village settlements, organized by the central government's Village Settlement Agency, were the recipients of large capital investments. In addition, however, unofficial resettlement activity spontaneously sprang up throughout the country. Many of these projects received marginal assistance from the government.

[30] *Ibid.,* p. 16.
[31] United Republic of Tanzania, Ministry of Lands, Settlement and Water Development, *The Rural Settlement Commission; A Report on the Village Settlement Commission to 31st December, 1965* (Dar es Salaam, 1966).

By mid-1966 the enthusiasm for resettlement as the method for transforming the rural areas had subsided. The pilot projects had proved to be extremely expensive and had consumed valuable resources with relatively little return. In addition, the settlers themselves did not perform as the officials had expected. The transition from peasant cultivation to the necessary disciplined agricultural techniques of intensive, estate-type agriculture was a difficult one, and for many was impossible in one generation. The settlers began to view themselves, somewhat correctly, as special wards of the government. From this position, they expected and often got special treatment from the central government, including, in most of the pilot settlements, monthly subsistence allowances. In addition to the huge capital investment, the new Tanzanian government provided health services, schools, and thirty shillings per month—all this to settlers who were not increasing their productivity. Clearly, this situation could not continue, and in a major reassessment of rural development policy in April 1966, Second Vice President R. M. Kawawa declared:

In the future, it has been decided that, instead of establishing highly capitalized schemes and moving people to them emphasis shall be on modernizing existing traditional villages, by injecting capital in order to raise the standard of living of the villagers. It is envisaged that such improvement might take the form of provision of water supply, better layout of villages, improved farming and production methods, and reorganization of land holdings.[32]

[32] Ministry of Information and Tourism, Information Services Division, "Address by the Second Vice-President, Mr. R. M. Kawawa, at the Opening of the Rural Development Planning Seminar, at the University College, Dar es Salaam on Monday April 4, 1966" (press release), p. 4.

The Second Vice President acknowledged the role played by the members of the Syracuse University Village Settlement Research Team in the reassessment of village settlement policy that led up to the change in policy announced here. See, in particular, the following studies made by members of this research team. Anthony H. Rweyemamu, "Nation Building and the Planning Process in Tanzania" (dissertation, Syracuse University, 1965) and Nikos Georgulas, "Structure and Communication: A Study of the Tanganyika Settlement Agency" (dissertation, Syracuse University, 1967).

A second type of rural development project meriting brief comment is the village irrigation scheme. The village irrigation schemes were also in the genre of the transformation approach to Tanzanian development, yet they closely resembled the ideas in Second Vice President Kawawa's 1966 speech, which emphasized modernizing traditional villages.[33] Typically, these village irrigation projects were located in villages where the traditional peasant farmer had already practiced irrigation in some form. The intent was to increase the productivity of such areas by the application of modern engineering and agricultural techniques and the better organization of the irrigators. In fact, a number of such projects were already in existence. The principal problem faced in the operation of these schemes was clearly social, for although they were relatively small-scale projects, the project had to run with considerable efficiency if the returns from the investment were to be economic.

The Mombo Village Irrigation Scheme in Tanga Region appears to be fairly typical. The original idea anticipated a relatively small-scale and inexpensive project. As it was reassessed by various expatriate experts, the capital outlay grew until the total cost lies somewhere between $95,571 (Shs. 669,000) and $112,602 (Shs. 778,215).[34]

The participants in the scheme were former peasant farmers, most of whom found it impossible to submit to the extreme disci-

[33] World Bank Report stated that "Given the inadequacies of rainfall over much of Tanganyika, irrigation schemes may be looked on as 'transformation' operations of particular promise." The First Five-Year Plan provided for a capital outlay of £9,150,000 over the 1964–1969 period for flood control and irrigation. A large proportion of this sum was to be used for the development of large-scale flood control and irrigation projects on river basin development, but a total of £5,000,000 was to be invested in village irrigation projects. See World Bank Report, p. 7, and United Republic of Tanganyika and Zanzibar, *Tanganyika Five-Year Plan for Economic and Social Development 1st July, 1964–30th June, 1969*, Vol. I, *General Analysis* (Dar es Salaam, 1964), pp. 47–49.

[34] Tanga Province, Regional Water Engineer, Estimate and Bill of Quantities for Mombo Irrigation Scheme, 11/6/66, and WD & ID, "Mombo Irrigation Scheme," a type-written report, 1967.

pline in work and timing that irrigation agriculture demanded. Thus the yields per acre in the first year of cultivation were not close to the expected yields, even though the farmers had to deal with only one crop at a time; this was especially discouraging because the scheme called for two crops in the ground at the same time in the future.[35] The Mombo scheme, based on sound development planning, was frustrated, too, by the intractability of the peasant farmer.

A third example of the special scheme approach to rural development is the cattle-coconut scheme, found primarily in Tanga District of Tanga Region. The intent of this project, originally successfully implemented in Ceylon and adopted at the end of World War II by the Ministry of Agriculture at its experimental station in Tanga, was to integrate dairy cattle with existing coconut groves. The introduction of dairy cattle in the area where the care and raising of cattle for any purpose were relatively unknown was seen to have a twofold benefit. The cattle would provide a second line of production through their milk and, just as important, their grazing would clear the coconut groves of weeds while their manure would fertilize the trees. Hopefully, grazing the cows among the coconut trees would also reduce the traditional and very destructive method of clearing the areas under the trees by burning.

The Ministry of Agriculture provided pipes for the water supply, fencing wire, and cattle dips for the schemes. The local district council provided pumps and cement for construction work. The cattle-coconut schemes represented a sophisticated and idealistic attempt to provide the transition from traditional agricultural organization and techniques to more progressive and productive efforts in the rural sector. The tone of this attempt is provided by an excerpt from a memo written by the originators of the project, two expatriate agricultural officers in Tanga.

[35] Based on conversations with the irrigation agronomist in charge of the development at Mombo, on interviews with officials in Dar es Salaam and, on intensive interviews with 35 of the 80 farmers in April 1967.

A gradual change over from tradition is always more acceptable than a complete break. With "cattle and coconuts" the gradual change of phaseology applies, thus simplifying the task of extension. However, Government officials have in the past been known for imposing regulations and having powers to enforce them. This has changed and it has been this backlog of mistrust which has had to be broken down before friendly confidence can begin to tackle the immediate problems. At first the people felt that this was just new tactics by Government to obtain taxes, it has been only slowly that they have realized that the change in approach is genuine.[36]

In 1962, the year in which this optimistic report was written, the number of cattle-coconut schemes in Tanga District almost tripled, from twelve to thirty-five.[37]

A further indication of the officers' enthusiasm is the fact that the regional agricultural officer, in a highly unusual tactic, wrote directly to President Nyerere requesting certain types of assistance for the projects. Referring to the President's recent visit in the district, he quoted the President as saying that he "foresaw the whole future of Agriculture and Animal Husbandry on the Coastal Strip" lying in the success of the cattle-coconut schemes.[38]

In June 1965 the value of the astounding growth and the viability of the cattle-coconut schemes were first questioned. Significantly, the doubt was expressed by a new regional agricultural officer, one of the first Tanzanians to hold this level post. In a report to his superior, the new RAO wrote:

The Co-ordinating Committee on c/c schemes here is compelled to put before you the facts confronting these schemes, because we feel

[36] Republic of Tanganyika, Ministry of Agriculture, Tanga Region, A. H. B. Childs and C. G. Groom, "Cattle and Coconuts—An Exercise in Agricultural Extension," Memo, 1962.

[37] Tanga Regional Agriculture Office, Correspondence to His Excellency, Dr. J. K. Nyerere, 14 February 1963 from Childs, Regional Agricultural Officer, Tanga Region, "Coconut-Cattle Schemes—His Excellency, the President's Visit."

[38] *Ibid.*

that unless we act quickly chances of their economic success in foreseeable future are very slight. . . .

In the past no . . . basic study was carried out and it is felt that several pronouncements of success in the past were merely based on arbitrary optimism, underestimating a great number of problems to be faced, and as such misinforming many people.[39]

The investigation conducted by the RAO revealed, among other things, the fact—fatal for a communal project demanding communal labor—that in some of the schemes the cattle were owned by only a few of the members of the scheme. Some people owned no coconuts, and others owned neither. The impact of this elementary fact upon communal work and involvement in the schemes was disastrous. The following statistics on the Maranzara cattle-coconut scheme in 1967 [40] will indicate the extent of the problem.

Number of members	120
Number of members owning coconuts only	60
Number of members owning cows only	10
Number of members owning neither	50

By September 1967 the number of schemes had dwindled to fifteen, and in the view of the officers in charge even these fifteen were marginal.[41]

In many ways the cattle-coconut schemes were a prototype of the special-scheme approach to rural development in Tanzania. The brainchild of expatriate officers, the scheme was introduced without proper preliminary investigation. The success of the schemes depended upon a substantial change in behavior by the

[39] Ministry of Agriculture, Forests and Wildlife, Agriculture Division, Tanga Ref. No. P/Sch/cat/coc, 19 June 1965, From RAO to Area Commissioner, "Cattle/Coconut Schemes."

[40] Ministry of Agriculture and Cooperatives, Agriculture Division, Tanga Region, "Cattle/Coconut Schemes—1967 Survey."

[41] Ministry of Agriculture and Cooperatives, Agriculture Division, Tanga Region, Regional Agricultural Officer to Director of Agriculture, "Cattle and Coconut Schemes."

peasant, including a willingness on his part to consolidate land holdings to make cattle grazing on large improved communal pastures possible, the adoption not only of cattle husbandry virtually unknown and undesired by the people of Tanga District, but also of dairying which demanded more discipline and effort in the regular milking of the cows than in the mere herding of cattle for meat products. And, if these changes were not difficult enough to introduce, the cattle-coconut effort was to stress communal effort which, although the contributions and rewards to members of the scheme were not equal, stressed the common benefit. The discrepancy between contribution and reward and a lack of understanding of the principle involved played havoc with the attempt to promote the schemes as communal projects. The effort to introduce cattle-coconut schemes, in short, employed considerable amounts of valuable resources with little or no return. The cattle-coconut scheme is the epitome of a project initiated without a thorough knowledge and understanding of the environmental and cultural restraints upon patterns of behavior. Enthusiastic agricultural officers injected financial and material support into this inadequately understood terrain with predictable results.

The experience with the special-scheme approach to rural development in the immediate postindependence period was probably inevitable. The independent government continued to feed upon the ideas of the colonial officers, who had stressed special schemes. The special schemes received new impetus when, after independence, foreign aid programs began to support these projects heavily. Except for the foreign aid factor, the schemes were not so different in concept or success from the special projects of the British. They involved large capital investment and were dependent upon expatriate initiative, planning, and administration. Each project called for radical changes on the part of the African peasant.[42]

[42] Officials in the Agriculture Division, Ministry of Agriculture and Cooperatives called attention to the fact that the coastal peoples of Tanga District were not cattle people and had little interest in dealing with them.

Finally, it should be noted that for each of these examples of the special-scheme approach to rural development the returns under any criteria were small indeed. Although some officials directly involved with village settlement claim that its final contributions to rural development cannot yet be measured, there is general agreement—and most importantly among the leaders who matter [43]—that village settlement did not prove effective. It is perhaps too early to assess the final impact of the village irrigation schemes. Certainly development planners underestimated the human and social problems associated with the discipline needed to make small-scale irrigation economically viable. There is general agreement that in terms of increasing agriculture productivity the cattle-coconut schemes were not feasible.

The participants in these special schemes, however, viewed the schemes as a "success," although in every case the farmers quickly added that more of this or that government assistance would bring about greater achievements.

Among the administrators of the projects, one seldom heard an exception to the bureaucratic rule that the project was in the process of becoming a success. The casual visitor or expert, so often taken to these projects to be shown that development was taking place in a particular district, found it difficult not to be impressed by the cleared fields, the new buildings, and the assembled participants. In the overall analysis of increased agricultural production, however, the transformation approach via special schemes contributed little. Even in those cases where there

---

A change requiring them to graze cattle on their coconut land was similar to the change required of the rice farmers when modern irrigation techniques were introduced and the number and regularity of their work hours were changed. Interview with Assistant Director, Agriculture Division, Dar es Salaam, July 11, 1967 and Assistant Director, Dar es Salaam, July 25, 1967.

[43] See Second Vice President Kawawa's speech quoted above. Also see President Nyerere's comments in his "Socialism and Rural Development," in *Freedom and Socialism,* p. 364.

had been a considerable increase in production, for example, in tobacco and wheat settlement schemes, it was debatable whether this increase would not have taken place anyway, with or without considerable government expenditure.[44]

In summary, the increase in agricultural productivity that did occur in the immediate postindependence period was due primarily to the increase in productivity of the individual farmer and not to the numerous transformation projects initiated during the period. While impossible to assess accurately, the productivity of the Tanzanian farmer and his standard of living does not appear to have changed substantially after independence. A survey of the economy in 1967 cited a 4.5 per cent increase in gross domestic product compared to a 6.7 per cent average annual growth rate for 1960–1966. The decline in growth in 1967 was attributed directly to the fact that the output of the agricultural sector for 1967 had increased by only 1.3 per cent because of poor weather conditions. Even the 1.3 per cent increase in total agricultural output masked an actual decline of one per cent in the agricultural output which was marketed because the self-consumed or subsistence output increased by 2 per cent. The harsh realities of these statistics are that the output of food and other agricultural products combined at 3.9 per cent per annum for 1960–1967 included an average increase in subsistence output of 2.1 per cent for the same period, which at best was just capable of keeping up with an estimated 2.5–3 per cent annual increase in population.[45] In bad years, such as 1967, sufficient food to feed the population was not produced. Thus, while the independent government enthusiastically dedicated itself to the task of development, and while there were a number of self-help projects throughout the countryside, the life of the peasant

---

[44] Based on discussions with the manager of Upper Ketete village settlement scheme in June 1967, with Marylyn Silberfein, member of the Syracuse University Village Settlement Project, in October 1967, and with Kenneth Baer in June 1968, and on my own observations.

[45] United Republic of Tanzania, *Background to the Budget: 1968–69* (Dar es Salaam, 1968), pp. 6–7, 103.

farmer was hardly affected in a material way by the change of government.

Such increases in agricultural production as did occur should be related to the extension efforts carried out by the Ministry of Agriculture and Cooperatives under the rubric of the "improvement" approach.[46] The Agriculture and Extension Divisions of the Ministry of Agriculture posted officers in each of the district headquarters, along with field assistants living in the villages, who advised on better techniques and seeds that would increase the yield of the individual farmer. Even so, a major study of rural development concluded in 1964 that

a comparison between the current situation and the situation as reflected in publications from the period of German colonial times gives the impression—admittedly difficult to substantiate—that very little has changed in methods of cultivation, plant-husbandry, use of fertilizers, erosion control, etc. Yields per acreage have apparently remained the same, in spite of the example of the estates and the advice and help practically forced upon the African farmers by agricultural officers. Where higher yields can be confirmed, they are usually the result of extraneous influences, such as better cotton seed or, in the case of manioc, higher quality plants.[47]

Thus, except for some notable successes, such as coffee production among the Chagga and the introduction of pyrethrum in Njombe District, agricultural improvement via extension efforts is difficult to evaluate in Tanzania.[48]

Postindependence political leaders envisioned a bright future for extension efforts; they assumed that the achievement of independence would rectify the mood of the rural population, which had become increasingly hostile to colonial prodding to change agri-

[46] K. Johansen, "Agricultural Planning in Tanzania," in G. K. Helleiner (ed.), *Agricultural Planning in East Africa* (Nairobi, 1968), p. 12.

[47] Ruthenberg, *Agricultural Development*, p. 19.

[48] See *ibid.*, pp. 69–77. Certain of Ruthenberg's conclusions regarding the effectiveness of extension efforts, notably the cattle-coconut schemes, are directly contradicted by my own findings.

cultural practices. It was ironic that the very party leaders who had encouraged resistance to the British extension efforts were now urging the farmers to accept the advice of extension officers, some being the same Europeans to whom the party leaders had organized opposition in the preindependence period.[49] Now in power, the nationalists sought to reverse the forces of opposition that they had formerly ridden and to guide these forces to bring about the very changes they had resisted.

Although rural development was complicated by harsh natural conditions, the central point of resistance increasingly appeared to be the intractability of the peasant farmer; this did not cease with the change of government. The new leaders found that the peasant farmer was not notably more responsive to the admonishments of his own kind to produce more, to use new techniques, to work more, than he had been to those of the colonial officer. Gradually, it was recognized that the central reason for low production in the rural areas and general rural underdevelopment and poverty was not the colonial experience, not the whims of nature, not the will of God (*shauri la mungu*) but the unwillingness of the peasant farmer to alter his accustomed behavior. This seeming intransigence caused frustration on the part of government officials and planners alike. In fairness to the African farmer, however, his stubbornness in the face of demands for change was more accurately laid to the fact that his survival was so close to basic existence that there was simply little or no room for risk. Thus his survival and that of his family was best secured by sticking to the tried and true farming practices rather than trying new ideas as yet unproved in the stern environment of East Africa.

Furthermore, the government which was the source of these demands for changed agricultural practice was still for most peasants an external center of power with which they had little or no contact, and in which they certainly had no role to play. The "Government" for most of the population was the district office,

[49] See *ibid.*, p. 106 ff.

the *boma*. It represented both threat and promise—the threat of tax collection, of forced agricultural practices, and the threat *or* promise of the establishment of order. On the other hand, the *boma* held the promise of material assistance in time of need, particularly during times of famine. The *boma* had been especially helpful under the British administration. In some areas of Tanzania such assistance is frequently needed. In Handeni District, for example, rainfall statistics indicate that as long as the major food crop is corn, famine is inevitable on an average of once every five years.[50] Thus while the village communities were extremely isolated from centers of government power, the individual always had access to the government during times of need. In this context, the government was viewed as both stern taskmaster and potential savior.[51] A kind of paternalism had developed throughout the preindependence history of Tanganyika. Traditional chiefs were expected to have stores of food for times of hunger; the Germans to some extent adopted a similar policy with a stronger emphasis upon compulsory provision, and in the British colonial period one almost gets the impression that the officers enjoyed the fatherly role of benefactor to the "native."

The paternal ethic was difficult for the independent government to reverse. First of all, the cry of the independence movement had been, "When you are independent *your* government will do more for you." It had to do more with less, however, since the departure of the colonial administration withdrew both men and considerable financial support. It proved both politically and technically impossible to deliver the goods to the peasant, who had been led to believe that independence would bring an increase in material benefits.

[50] Handeni *District Book,* Microfilm, National Archives, Dar es Salaam and Syracuse University.
[51] See J. C. Cairns, *Bush and Boma* (London, 1959), for a revealing and often amusing account of the kinds of demands expressed at the district headquarters.

In the face of this paradox the independent government launched an additional development effort which aimed primarily not at increasing agricultural productivity but at countering the paternalistic relationship between citizen and government. The "Peoples Plan" aimed at bringing about the participation of all the citizens in the nation-building process. In this respect this effort was successful. Almost every village came up with its self-help project; school buildings, community centers, and dispensaries, along with countless TANU office buildings, sprang up through these efforts. This phase of the development effort was extremely valuable in creating a sense of urgency and involvement in the minds of Tanzania's millions. But these efforts were in many cases transitory at best, aimed at satisfying the officials that this or that community was in fact joining the effort. Valuable as examples of nation-building spirit, the projects often did not coincide with actual needs and resources—thus one found dispensaries without medical personnel, hospitals without beds, and schools without teachers. The transformation of the peasant's agricultural practices and the instilling of a sense of self-reliance to replace the paternalism of years of colonial domination would take longer to accomplish.

In addition to the stubborn resistance—often, it should be stressed, well founded—of the peasant to agricultural change and the persistence of the paternalistic relationship between the peasant and the government, a third thread of continuity emerged tying the policies and actions of the independent government to the colonial past. This was the inclination to resort to compulsion to bring about the changes deemed necessary for rural development. In fact, less than three months after independence, some government spokesmen had already accepted the threat of force as a means of bringing about rural change and development. The shift to a greater reliance on compulsion, which I will argue in Chapter IV had by 1968 become an integral part of Tanzania's developmental environment, has been expressed in two ways. The first instance in which force or the threat of force had been used by the government was the forced planting of certain crops to prevent famine; the second, the use of compulsory labor on community projects. Both varieties of compulsion had their origins in the preindependence era and, in the case of the community work projects, date to the precolonial period.

The compulsory planting of required acreages of certain crops, usually drought-resistant, is the better documented of these attempts, as illustrated by a survey of both pre- and postindependence documents in Handeni and Tanga districts. A 1932 entry in the Handeni District Book declared, for example, that "all natives must cultivate cassava and sweet potatoes in addition to other foodstuffs. [The] reason for this order being the necessity for rootcrops, which are unassailable by locusts, in view of the danger of further infestations by locusts and possible famine." [52] In 1934 the order was elaborated upon in the following fashion: "Every adult male in the District must plant at least 200 cuttings of cassava within one month of 1st February 1934. Every male adult omitting to obey this order has committed an offense and is liable to punishment." [53] The district officer then commented:

The spreading of cassava growing in sufficient quantities to ensure a sufficient reserve of root crops to tide over periods of food shortage due to drought or locusts must necessarily be a gradual business. As serious droughts are certain to occur in this District at least every five years it behooves the District Officer to watch for any slackening in the maintenance of crops of cassava as when maize is again plentiful the Wazigua are certain to be prone to neglect it and previous difficulties will once more occur.[54]

The extent to which these planting directives might go is indicated in a letter from the Tanga District commissioner, which outlined the dimensions of the farms required in a crop campaign in that district in 1947. Item 2 in that letter announced:

[52] Handeni *District Book,* "Formal Orders Made by All the Native Authorities of Handeni during 1932."
[53] *Ibid.* [54] *Ibid.*

The Native Authorities were circulated regarding the dimension of the shambas to be cultivated. They are:
1. Married couples without regular employment—85 yards x 85 yards.
2. Bachelors without regular employment—70 yards x 70 yards.
3. Married couples in regular employment—50 yards x 50 yards.
4. Bachelors in regular employment—40 yards x 40 yards.[55]

In 1951 the Provincial Headquarters, Tanga, published a list of suggested functions of the Native Authorities. Among the suggestions was the following: "Require any person to cultivate land to such extent and with such crops as will secure an adequate supply of food for the support of such person and of those dependent upon him." [56]

The Handeni Famine Relief files report that "the order of one acre of cassava per taxpayer is being strongly enforced during the famine of 1952–53," and the *Local Government Memo—1954* declared:

Whenever in the area of the jurisdiction of any native authority there is or is likely to be such shortage of food that, in the opinion of the native authority, a famine exists or is likely to ensue, he may, subject to the general or special directions of the native authority, if any, to whom he is subordinate, issue orders within the local limits of his jurisdiction

(a) requiring any able-bodied male native to work on any public works, irrigation works, . . .
(b) requiring any native to cultivate land within the local limits of his authority to such reasonable extent as the native authority may direct.[57]

---

[55] Tanga, "Crop Campaign," 45/200/III, To Venerable Archdeacon Stephens, U.M.C.A., Kiwanda, P. O. Muheza from District Commissioner, Tanga, 4 March 1947.

[56] Tanga Province, "List of Suggested Functions of Native Authorities," Tanga 14 December 1951, Ref. No. 788/2/91, National Archives, Dar es Salaam (304/A2/42).

[57] *Local Government Memo—1954*, p. 26.

The later files of both districts also revealed the efforts to force the people of the areas to plant. The records of the district commissioner, Handeni, are indicative of the official attitude toward compulsory planting. In 1957 the outgoing district commissioner noted: *"Sorghum/Cassava Order:* Inspection of shambas is complete . . . prosecutions initiated . . . I consider this order essential to Handeni, and that while the going remains good pressure should continue to be exerted. It has undoubtedly saved the Center from a very bad year 1957, and, it is generally beginning quite definitely to catch on." [58]

The interim district commissioner was not so sure the compulsory planting was catching on, for in his memorandum to his successor, known as "handing over notes," less than a year later, he wrote, "Assuming good long rains and good progress with sorghum planting you might even consider repeating the compulsory 'one acre cassava or two of sorghum' order." [59]

One of the earliest moves by the independent government regarding the powers of the newly created district councils was to enable them to pass bylaws requiring people to plant. A circular of October 1962 noted that since some people were not adequately involved in farming, the central government had decided that the district councils should have bylaws by which these people would be forced to farm.[60]

As of March 11, 1967, only twenty out of a total of fifty-eight district councils had bylaws requiring one acre of a cash crop and one acre of a food crop. Eight of these had accepted the bylaw in 1964 and six in 1965. The model bylaw provided by the central government and generally accepted by the councils provided:

[58] Handeni, "Handing over Notes," From District Commissioner, Handeni, To the Provincial Commissioner, Tanga, 13 July 1957, National Archives (304/P4/42).
[59] Handeni, "Handing Over Notes, Foster/Reed Handeni District, February 1958," *ibid.*
[60] Ministry of Local Government, No. 46/62, 13 October 1962, "Amendment to Local Government Ordinances," LG Circular 12/01.

"Any person who contravenes or fails to comply with the provisions of these bylaws shall be guilty of an offense and shall be liable on conviction to a fine not exceeding five hundred shillings or to imprisonment for a term not exceeding six months or to both such fine and imprisonment." [61]

Nevertheless there was constant reference in the records of the councils to this or that resolution aimed at getting the people to plant specified crops or acreages. Other such resolutions aimed at getting the farmers into the field. One, for example, proclaimed that during the planting season everyone should be in the fields from 10:00 A.M. till 2:00 P.M.[62] Although it is difficult to unravel the many resolutions passed by the councils relating to planting, it appeared that a particular resolution might be passed several times by the council with no or only slight modification. In many cases such resolutions and bylaws served more to encourage the councilors and the citizens to plant than to enforce them. Nevertheless the threat of force was a very clear element in this effort to stimulate greater production in the rural areas. A Local Government circular of August 1967 indicated that more systematic and possibly more effective application of force to ensure compliance to these bylaws might be forthcoming. The circular was entitled "Enforcement of Bylaws," and announced: "The Ministry of Home Affairs has now agreed that the enforcement of Local Authority Bylaws is the concern of the police just as much as is the enforcement of any other part of the written law of the Republic, and that the police will take an active part in enforcing them." [63]

While the attempt to get individual farmers to plant is the major thrust of the force/compulsion approach to rural development, a second but related effort was an attempt to elicit a group farming

[61] Ministry of Regional Administration, Ref. No. LG 51/05, 11 March 1967, LG Circular 6/67, "Kanuni za Kilimo."
[62] Observed in Tanga District 1968.
[63] Ministry of Local Government and Rural Development, Ref. No. LG 85002, 2 August 1967, LG Circular 21 of 1967.

effort, known as block farming. While the initial efforts in this regard had no ideological content, the more recent efforts have such connotations and, in fact, this approach might be termed as midway between the stress solely on individual efforts and the ujamaa village concept.

In 1967–1968 the block farm constituted the major agricultural goal in Handeni District. The technique was not, however, novel in Handeni or Tanzania. Although the phrase, "block farm," was not employed, the first reference to the principle in the Handeni records occurred in 1954. The district commissioner, Handeni, wrote regarding cassava that the Handeni Native Council had passed a new rule concerning cassava planting that should be of great benefit to the district. The rule directed all cultivators to plant in a place chosen by their elders and directed the headman to protect these plantings adequately against vermin:

> Cultivators will now plant communally in village groups, although each taxpayer will be responsible for the planting of his own acres and it will remain his own property. Responsibility for vermin protection will be that of the village headman who will either build walls or organize a system of guards, this will be simplified, as wherever possible the plots will be planted as near to the village as practicable.

The district commissioner concluded that "the administration is giving its full support to this campaign and it is hoped, providing good rains are had, that the District will have acreage of cassava approaching 16,000 by April next year." [64]

The district commissioner's description of the Native Authority's new rule embodied the essential features of the block farm program which was promoted in Handeni in 1967 by agricultural officers out of the *boma* office. After a group of farmers cleared the land communally, it was surveyed and planted with one crop.

---

[64] Handeni, Famine Relief, 6/A.3/8, District Commissioner Handeni to Provincial Commissioner Tanga 7 October 1954, "Food Situation Report, Handeni District, September, 1954," National Archives, Dar es Salaam.

Each farmer tended his own plot and received the return from it. The only other communal activities might involve protecting the crops from wild animals or tending the plot of a farmer who was sick.[65]

There were also communal farms undertaken jointly by the members of a group. The most prominent examples were those farmed by women's groups and the TANU Youth League. Here the work was carried out communally, and the return was to the group, not to the individual.

Of the two districts studied here, the block farm was more important in Handeni. Although the block farm principle has been pushed with more or less enthusiasm in Handeni since 1954, by 1967 there was no evidence of the 16,000 acres of cassava or cultivated land which the district commissioner had envisaged in 1955. During 1965 and 1966 the stress in Handeni was on block cotton farms. The area commissioner initiated the effort, and he promised tractor assistance as a means of encouraging villagers to clear their blocks. The District Development and Planning Committee resolved that block cotton farms should be started in all ten divisions of Handeni.[66]

In 1967–1968 the major development effort in Handeni was on block cassava farms. The District Development and Planning Committee decided, at the area commissioner's direction, that each ward in the district should have at least one block farm.[67] Although the primary crop was cassava, cotton and sorghum were also included. The area commissioner was determined that Handeni was to be self-sufficient in food, and the one sure way to do this was to force the planting of cassava, which was both drought and pest resistant. Through the use of the party bureaucracy, the

[65] Based on discussions with the district agricultural officer, Handeni, 5 January 1968.
[66] Handeni District Development and Planning Committee, Minutes 13 October 1965 and *ibid.*, 20 September 1966.
[67] Handeni District Development and Planning Committee, Minutes 5 July 1967.

council, the government bureaucracy, and the police, the villagers in Handeni were subjected to probably the most persistent pressure to plant that the area had ever experienced.

This pressure made it difficult for the villagers to follow government directives one day and to go on one's way undisturbed the next, as they had in the past. Contingents of the national police with equipment that allowed them to move freely and rapidly throughout the countryside did "take people away." The area commissioner used his forty-eight-hour detention power and the police to jail the more outspoken opponents.[68] In this atmosphere considerable acreage was cleared and planted.

Opposition to participation in the block farms on the part of the Handeni peasant was fairly widespread but inarticulate. The amount of effort required of the individual in order to avoid conflict with the police was relatively little, and most people exercised the minimum compliance. Among the more touching protests to the block farms was an anonymous letter to all civil servants, cell leaders, and agricultural field assistants in one ward in Handeni District:

Consider the District Council of Handeni and the problems of its citizens, and stress them in their farming, but do not trouble them at their time of planting. First, you never remember the problem of

[68] The area commissioner could legally hold a person in detention for up to forty-eight hours without charges being brought. Such arrest has taken place at the order of the area commissioner or regional commissioner, and, while unpublicized, has been used in certain cases in an attempt to get people to carry out their developmental tasks. See Ministry of Local Government, Ref. No. PA 15/021, 10 March 1964; Local Government Circular 17/64, "The Administration and Control of Lock-ups." Item 5 (ii) "When any person has been arrested by order of a Regional or Area Commissioner under section 2 or 3 of Act 49 of 1963, he may be detained in a lock-up without a warrant being issued. He *must* be taken before a *District* Magistrate as soon as practicable. If within 48 hours he has not been brought before a *district* Magistrate, then he *must* be released." Emphasis is in the original. The effect here was to allow a forty-eight hour detention without legal redress.

hunger and if you do, chase those who have no job and no maize farms.

It is 3½ miles to the farm of 3 acres, one acre being for the wife. Try to consider at what time shall we cultivate maize? The wife has three children, only two of whom can walk. Now when will she walk to the farm? Isn't this development plan causing hunger? It is said that . . . there have been two people taken away, who are youths.

Agricultural Field Assistant take care of your job. It is not just for you to go all round in the villages chasing people in their farms where they obtain their livelihood, and sending them to the roads arranging them as rail lines. I have more to say but we are citizens of Handeni. We are very sorry, therefore Agricultural Field Assistant ——, Agricultural Field Assistant ——, and the VEO and cell leaders, you take unjust action. If you are tired of your job you better retire. It is unjust to force people to farm, farming is done willingly. As in relieving oneself, one is never forced, it would be a wonder if a person had to be told to go to the WC [toilet].

Send this letter anywhere in Handeni. I am sorry the paper is small and insufficient I have much more to say.[69]

A few weeks later the area commissioner addressed the District Council, obviously with the opposition to his agricultural policies in mind. He accused the councilors of calling him a dictator, but reminded them that it was because of his efforts that the people of Handeni would not be hungry that year.[70]

In the enforcing of the block farm policy, as in the enforcing of planting ordinances, the district technical assistants were coopted into the contradictory position of having to perform a policing as well as an advisory role; for example, a district officer in Handeni, when asked of his advisory role, answered that his work was supposed to be advisory, "but in fact, we have to use force."[71] The particular situation in Handeni led to a circular

[69] Letter dated February 5, 1968, no signature, but a fictitious post office box in Dar es Salaam was offered. The letter was forwarded to the district office but no action was taken.

[70] A paraphrase of the area commissioner's address to the Handeni District Council meeting, 29 February 1968.

[71] Interview, January 5, 1968, Handeni.

from the Ministry of Agriculture in May 1968 bearing the title "Agricultural By-Law: Handeni District Council." In the circular the Principal Secretary lectured all regional agricultural officers:

There were times in the past when officers in the then Department of Agriculture had to perform "police" duties particularly in the enforcement of rules and regulations which were enacted by the Local Authorities (now district councils).

It is the Agricultural Division's policy that such a conservative system is neither re-introduced nor perpetuated because it is against the ethics of proper Extension.

The Ministry's principal civil servant then concluded, "I am therefore against the appointment of Agricultural Staff as 'authorized Officers' for the purpose of enforcing District Council's by-laws and would be grateful if you would inform all concerned accordingly and initiate action to rescind the order." [72]

While there were block farms in Tanga District, they were not the most prominent feature of the developmental effort during the period in which this research was carried out, partly because there was little available land. Communal farms were a part of the varied approach to rural development followed in Tanga; these communal farms were very similar in organization to the communal self-help projects that will now be considered.

There is general consensus that in traditional African society the communal work projects or tribal turnouts were effective. While some such form of communal work was probably a practice in Tanga and Handeni, little evidence has been found that describes this practice. The ethnographic survey covering Handeni notes only that "a Zigula [Zigua] leader or chief received labour from his subjects who helped cultivate his fields. Some also appear to have received tribute in livestock, slaves and foodstuffs from

---

[72] Letter from Principal Secretary, Ministry of Agriculture, to All Regional Agricultural Officers, 16 May 1968, Ref. No. P/SCH/HA. Since the Ministry of Agriculture had the largest manpower in the districts the enforcement of this directive would have profound effects upon the efforts of district political leaders to police agricultural regulations.

other villages." [73] Evidence of the use of such procedures by the colonial administrations is much more readily available, however. The organization of compulsory communal work projects by colonial officials erased whatever voluntary character the communal efforts traditionally may have had.

The German administration issued a series of Labor Laws in 1907 that among other things regulated compulsory labor and normally permitted it only for public works. The laws also provided that in no case might forced labor be free; instead, it must be remunerated at the normal wage rates.[74]

The British examined early in their administration the German use of compulsory labor on the roads. A report from the district officer, Tanga, to the Provincial commissioner in 1926 reported that

after consultation with the elders of the various tribes living in Tanga District, no native custom exists whereby any native can be required by tribal authorities to work without pay either in the maintenance of roads in his neighbourhood, or in any other kind of work. 2. The construction and maintenance of roads was discouraged in the past, being regarded as a menace to tribal safety. 3. On the arrival of the Germans, however, a custom of unpaid road maintenance was instituted by them; this has been in force ever since, and is regarded by the natives as established custom. 4. This German established custom was carefully discussed with the elders and jumbes representing the various tribes, and all were most emphatic that, since this custom was a great benefit to all, it should be continued.[75]

A similar situation existed in Handeni District. The assistant district officer in charge reported in July 1926 that it was the

[73] T. O. Beidelman, *The Matrilineal Peoples of Eastern Tanzania;* Ethnographic Survey of Africa, East Central Africa, Part XVI (London, 1967), p. 68.
[74] Eberlie, "The German Achievement in East Africa," p. 205.
[75] Tanga District, "From District Officer Tanga to the Provincial Commissioner, Tanga," 19 July, 1926, Ref. No. 178/402, National Archives, Dar es Salaam (304/A2/42).

custom to use forced labor on the roads in Handeni. "Each village has a certain portion of which it is responsible for." [76]

Thus compulsory labor projects were an integral part of both German and British colonial administration. Curiously, the records of communal projects indicated much more detail to the form and organization in Handeni than is the case in Tanga District. It is likely that this fact is related to the much higher social and economic differentiation in Tanga than in Handeni. Therefore, the roads, schools, and hospitals in Tanga District were built either by the government for the town or by the numerous outlying estates that were entirely self-sufficient in social services. The relatively lower level of social, economic, and physical development in Handeni meant that anything to be done was done by the government, or by missionaries.

In 1955 the Zigua Tribal Council (*Ufungilo*) passed resolutions dealing with communal work. In 1956 the district commissioner in Handeni requested the provincial commissioner to provide model rules that would require the following:

(a) All able-bodied men excepting those named in para below may be called upon by their N.A. [Native Authority] to give up to thirty days free labour per year on essential public works which the N.A. will be carrying out for the benefit of their people.

(b) Persons in permanent and regular employment such as Chiefs, teachers, personal servants, etc. to be exempted from this compulsory service.

(c) Penalties.

The district commissioner announced in conclusion that the "Handeni Native Authority has decided to pass Rules to this effect." [77]

[76] Tanga Province, "To the Honorable the Chief Secretary, Dar es Salaam, From Provincial Commissioner, Tanga, 7th August 1926," National Archives (304/A2/42).

[77] Handeni, "District Commissioner, Handeni to Provincial Commissioner, Tanga 27 March 1956," Ref. No. L5/1/C/12/2, National Archives (304/A2/49).

The minutes of the Tribal Council Meeting a few months later described the district commissioner's efforts to convince the members of the council of the value of communal work:

> The District Commissioner explained to the members that most of the people do not like working without payment. All these years people have been working slowly, slowly by traditional methods. On the safaris of the D.C. he has tried to advise people to change from their traditional ways. In our country [of the D.C.] it is not a good thing for people to say that working without pay is not a good custom of civilized people. After discussions they agreed.[78]

The council then passed the resolution calling for thirty days of communal work and resolved that those who do not comply would pay one shilling a day for each day he did not participate.[79]

Two months later the question of communal labor again came up in the discussions of the Ufungilo. The secretary described the problem as he saw it:

> Most people have objected several times about working communally. These [*wasi wa mbuli*] heads of committees should organize and advise people to clear up this bad hatred by struggling hard. Most of the people put the blame on TANU. The Union, as I understand it, does not intend to frustrate the progress of citizens but instead encourages it. This position comes from the people who do not understand TANU.[80]

With independence in 1961 the new government set about to use the communal self-help technique to stimulate development. Schools, hospitals, community centers and TANU office buildings were built through communal efforts, and also wells dug and roads repaired. A great deal was accomplished through these communal

[78] Handeni, Ufungilo (Zigua Tribal Council), Minutes 30 July, 4 August 1956, National Archives (304/A2/12).
[79] *Ibid.*
[80] Handeni, Ufungilo (Zigua Tribal Council), Minutes 15–19 October 1956, National Archives (304/A2/12).

self-help projects during the early enthusiasm of independence. Gradually efforts were made to institutionalize these techniques. Again in the two districts studied here, the evidence of this effort is greater in Handeni.

The member of the National Assembly from Handeni discussed communal farming in an address before the DDPC in May 1966.

Chiwili is a traditional word of Kizigua and Kinguu [languages of the Zigua and the Nguu]. It means farming together. It is not a political term, but is an economic term. If one man fails to finish his shamba, his neighbors will organize a day when they can collect and help him. The owner of the shamba makes pombe [beer] and food for them so that they are able to eat and drink on the day of the *chiwili*.

I have considered the tradition of *chiwili* and I think that it should be put as a bylaw in this district. This should be as a call for cooperation in the villages. It should be a call for cooperation in farming and animal husbandry. A person who does not like to cooperate is to be found guilty and is liable to punishment. This plan should start from the ten house cell with the cell leader being the head.[81]

There was considerable discussion of the member's suggestion; and it was agreed that *chiwili* was a tradition in Handeni. The problem the members of the DDPC saw was how to decide and implement a just punishment. It was noted that the traditional punishment was to boycott the lazy man by not going to his business or, especially, to his social affairs. The district executive officer noted that such a bylaw could not be passed, but that it could be enforced by traditional methods as long as it did not go beyond the law. The committee finally passed a mild resolution that advised the citizens that they should practice the tradition of *chiwili* as their forefathers had. This form of communal farming was to be organized by the village development committees.[82]

[81] Handeni District Development and Planning Committee, Minutes 25 May 1966.
[82] *Ibid.*

As in the case of *chiwili* in Handeni District, communal self-help projects after independence never involved force under the legal statutes of the nation. In fact, however, undoubtedly there have been undocumented cases of the use of force or the threat thereof to ensure participation in communal projects which benefit the community. The use of the state's coercive power to ensure participation in farming projects where the benefit derived to the individual participants has already been noted. In the case of community self-help projects, somewhat ironically in view of the similarity of one's labor contribution to a tax, there has been no legal or quasilegal manner, beyond the area commissioner's power to detain for forty-eight hours, in which the police power could be openly used to obtain participation in a self-help project. As the district executive officer pointed out in the discussion of enforcement of the concept of *chiwili,* traditional means could be used for enforcement as long as they did not go beyond the law. In summary, an element of compulsion was present in the communal self-help projects that have characterized developmental efforts in independent Tanzania. In view of the colonial and precolonial experience with communal projects, this was to be expected. Furthermore, the threat of force for nonparticipation and the actual use of force signified in a dramatic manner the development of state power in the villages of Tanzania. Tanzanian citizens did not respond enthusiastically to the growing demands of self-government in a way sufficient to fulfill the glowing promise of independence. The slow pace of rural change, together with the increasing use of force, pushed the national leadership in Dar es Salaam to reexamine the assumptions upon which they had based the nation's development policy. Clearly, material and financial resources and expert help were not enough to revolutionize the countryside. Expatriate experts and technical officers were there, but alone they were unable to substantially increase the output of the peasant. The barriers to Tanzanian rural development were increasingly conceived to be primarily human, embedded in centuries of practice and habit. Radical measures to activate peasant initiative were necessary.

Developments in international politics, including the Zanzibar revolution in 1964, injected a more radical tone in Tanzanian national politics. As the Republic became entangled in the pressures of East-West world politics, officials began to doubt the value of the great reliance they had placed on external aid in national development plans. How could government pursue a neutral and idealistically independent line in international politics if the development of Tanzania was heavily dependent upon foreign aid? Increasingly, the principle of independence and self-reliance rather than political expediency dictated policy decisions. The most prominent example of principle over immediate material gain was Tanzania's breaking of diplomatic relations with the United Kingdom when the British government refused to take strong action to counter Rhodesia's unilateral declaration of independence in 1965. This symbolic protest against the birth of another white-minority-ruled nation in Africa was especially costly to Tanzania since it meant breaking relations with the nation which had been the major contributor to the former colony's development and resulted in the postponing of plans to provide a $21 million interest-free loan.[83] Subsequently, when the government did accept external aid, it increasingly rejected all policy commitments and steered a scrupulously neutral course in receiving aid from all sources, Eastern and Western.[84]

Internally, the army mutiny of January 1964 suggested an underlying dissatisfaction of key elements in the country and the fragility of governing institutions. The elections of September 1965, while accurately assessed as demonstrating democracy at work in a single-party state, also showed, through the defeat of two ministers, six junior ministers, and more than three-fourths

[83] *New York Times,* December 16 and 19, 1965.
[84] See President Nyerere's statement, "After the Arusha Declaration," in *Freedom and Socialism,* pp. 385–409.

of the incumbent members of the legislature, an underlying dissatisfaction in the countryside with the performance of the TANU government.[85]

Gleaned from the experience of the first five years of independence, the Arusha Declaration marked the turning point in Tanzania's independent history. From this point efforts to promote rural development became the central purpose in Tanzania's development efforts, shaping all other policies.

[85] For excellent assessments of both developments, see Bienen, *Tanzania*, chs. 11 and 12. For the elections in particular, see Maguire, *Toward 'Uhuru' in Tanzania*, p. 373.

CHAPTER IV

The Developmental Environment

Efforts to promote rural development in Handeni and Tanga cannot be assessed without considering the environments within which the political systems were functioning. Two dimensions of the developmental environment will be considered here—the physical and cultural.

The Physical Environment

The physical conditions that confront efforts to promote development in Tanzania can only be described as harsh. For the reader who is familiar with rural development in developed nations in the West or even with that in much of Southeast Asia, this point cannot be overemphasized.

One of the principal problems confronting peasant and government official alike is the lack of adequate water. Not only is there usually not enough water for man, beast, or crops, but of even greater importance, such water as *may* be available cannot be accurately predicted. Thus the farmer and the government planner are at the mercy alternately of unseasonable flood and drought. Average yearly rainfall data for Tanga District, covering the period from 1908 until 1949, are available. These data may be compared to an average yearly rainfall figure for Handeni District in 1960 and for the 1968 average rainfall for Knox County, Tennessee, which has average rainfall for a temperate climate.

Table 1 indicates the similarity between gross rainfall in Tanga District and the rainfall in the temperate climate of Knox County, Tennessee; both locations compare favorably with Handeni District, which receives roughly ten inches less rainfall per year than does Tanga. While the steady decline in yearly rainfall in Tanga District is ominous [1] the irregularity of rainfall in these areas is even more significant.

Table 1. Comparative yearly rainfall

Tanga	Handeni	Knox County, Tenn.
1908–14—61.49 inches	1960—34.15 inches	1968—45.85 inches
1931–37—54.62		
1936–45—53.52		
1946–49—44.30		

Sources: Rainfall data were drawn from (a) Tanga *District Book,* Tanga District Headquarters, Tanga, where the 1908–1914 figures were taken from the *Admiralty Handbook on German East Africa* published by the Germans in 1916 and (b) Handeni *District Book.*

Figures showing the irregularity of the rainfall pattern for Tanga District are offered in Table 2 for the month of May and are contrasted with the figures for the same month in Knox County, Tennessee. The farmer in Knox County can expect a fairly regular amount of rainfall, while the farmer in Tanga District clearly cannot. Thus the data indicate that in 1931 almost one-half of the year's rainfall in Tanga District fell in the month of May. While comparative data are not available for Handeni, the irregularity of rainfall facing the peasant is accentuated there by the fact that the district receives roughly ten to twenty inches less rainfall per year than does Tanga District.

[1] The decline of rainfall in the area was called to my attention by a botanist at the Sisal Research Station outside Tanga. A possible explanation of this decline in the Tanga District was the clearing of acre after acre of forest for the planting of sisal plantations.

Table 2. Rainfall for month of May, 1922–1935, showing irregularity of rainfall in Tanga District

Year	Tanga	Knox County	Year	Tanga	Knox County
1922	23.39 inches	3.82 inches	1929	4.24 inches	7.66 inches
1923	4.03	4.53	1930	2.64	4.21
1924	5.12	4.06	1931	22.2	3.71
1925	2.1	2.40	1932	16.1	1.59
1926	9.01	3.03	1933	3.6	4.45
1927	9.7	2.92	1934	17.4	4.41
1928	15.85	6.17	1935	7.3	4.46

Sources: Tanga *District Book.* Data for Knox County were provided through the courtesy of the U.S. Weather Bureau.

An excerpt from the Handeni *District Book* suggested what these statistics mean for rural development efforts. Written in 1959, under the title Maize,[2] the analysis is as follows:

According to local knowledge maize is only a comparatively recent introduction to Uzigua and Nguu. . . . It was only during the German rule when maize began to take the place of sorghum as the main staple foodstuff.

From this period until the Government inspired "grow more maize campaign" started just after the conclusion of the Second World War, maize acreage was probably static at about two acres per cultivator, the harvest of which, as a rule, was for family consumption [and] would suffice to carry them over to the next harvest.

Mr. Lesle-Moore . . . started the maize campaign, which due to the opening of markets and comparatively high prices paid, soon became the Wazigua's main cash crop. The previous cash crop of cotton dropped in production from tons 812 in 1948 to 18 tons in 1953, while maize export figures rose from nil to 3,000 tons over the same period. The immediate consequence of this big increase in maize growing was, strangely enough, a succession of food shortages and in some years, near famine conditions. *A study of Handeni's rainfall*

[2] Maize in the African context is the same as our own food staple, corn.

records would have indicated that a complete maize economy for this District would be disastrous.[3]

The report estimated that "on a maize growing economy one year in three will be a food shortage year, and one year in five will be a famine year."[4] Thus a successful effort to promote rural change in Handeni District brought food shortage and famine in its wake.[5] In addition to its impact upon agricultural production, the periods of heavy rainfall play havoc with communications and transportation. Not only is economic activity brought to a standstill in many parts of the country, but the officials involved in governing and promoting development are also unable to function in the localities during these periods.

The soil itself, by most standards, is infertile. This is true in both Tanga and Handeni and in most of Tanzania. And this limited fertility is extremely susceptible to destruction by the elements, the principal threat being from heavy rainfall. In addition, relatively little is known about the impact of modern agricultural techniques upon the tropical soils in the areas studied. The major resources of the area may be, as the national leadership professes, land and people, but the fertility of the land is a resource that is very easily destroyed, and its destructibility along with the irregular rainfall, may stymie the best-planned development projects.[6]

Another dimension of the physical environment is the relative abundance of land for the total population. In most of Tanzania, this is more a negative, than a positive factor in rural development.

[3] Handeni *District Book:* emphasis is this writer's.

[4] *Ibid.*

[5] For similar misjudgments of local conditions in Mali and Kenya, see John C. de Wilde *et al., Experiences with Agricultural Development in Tropical Africa* (Baltimore, 1967), I, 28 ff.

[6] For treatment of the delicacy of tropical soils in terms of its impact upon the society as a whole, see Pierre Gourou, *The Tropical World: Its Social and Economic Conditions and Its Future Status,* 4th ed. (London, 1966), trans. by S. H. Beaver and E. D. Laborde; and Colin Clark and M. R. Haswell, *The Economics of Subsistence Agriculture,* 2d ed. (London, 1966).

Time after time in independent Tanzania, officials have pointed out the need for Tanzanians to settle in villages and to live and work together, but the low population makes it easy for the farmers to continue moving about every few years when the fertility of the soil is exhausted. Handeni District, with a population density of 25.9 persons per square mile in 1967, is more typical than Tanga District's 135.9 persons per square mile. The Tanga density understates the actual density since a large proportion of the acreage of the district is covered with sisal fields that force the inhabitants into relatively dense settlement patterns. The population density for mainland Tanzania in 1967 was 34.8 persons per square mile.[7]

In Tanga District obviously a major problem in the eyes of the people and officials is the relative scarcity of land. As early as 1947 the district agricultural officer of Tanga wrote that "the land shortage for food planting on the Kwale peninsula (Tanga District) is acute owing to extensive coconut planting, and he considers that in other areas a similar state of affairs is approaching so that control to preserve adequate land around villages for food crops is essential." [8]

Because of the scarcity of land in Tanga District, most people lived in fairly permanent and densely populated villages. In contrast, the people of Handeni were more likely to live in temporary and very small villages that were widely scattered throughout the countryside. The houses in Handeni were generally constructed of mud and small trees and were relatively cheaply replaced when the inhabitants moved to another location. There were very few structures of concrete or other more permanent materials in the Handeni villages and there was a notable lack of permanent crops such as coconuts, oranges, or even bananas which would tie the farmer to a particular locale for an extended period of time. Settlement conditions in Tanga District were notable in contrast. These settle-

[7] Density figures are from *Preliminary Results*.
[8] Provincial Agricultural Office, Lushoto, 20 February 1947; Ref. No. 70/385, National Archives 304/A2/42.

ment patterns affected the two district political systems in different ways. The permanency of settlements together with the relatively dense settlement patterns in Tanga facilitated communication between *boma* and village, and this ease of communication made possible a governmental access to the people that was impossible in Handeni. Conversely, the Tanga people had a potential access to the district political system that was impossible in Handeni.

This brief description suggests that Tanga had a physical environment more hospitable to human existence than Handeni. Tanga was also more modernized than was Handeni. While precise comparative data are not available, it may be noted that in terms of a cash economy, infrastructure, and urbanization, Tanga was much more advanced than Handeni.[9] In spite of these differences, these districts had many cultural similarities at the village level that were important for understanding rural development efforts. These similarities may be more important in explaining locality response to development efforts than physical considerations are.

The Cultural Environment

While this research did not concentrate on the political cultures of Handeni and Tanga districts, the investigation of local response to rural development efforts revealed certain clusters of attitudes or beliefs that are major determinants of the locality's response. The traits that had a particular impact upon these government efforts were witchcraft, a paternalistic ethic, and what I have called the compulsion syndrome. While these cultural features were pervasive in the societies studied, they are treated here only as they affected the political systems' efforts to promote change.

[9] One index of the different levels of development in the two districts is the number of regular employees per district. In 1966, Handeni had a total of 1,054 regular employees while Tanga had a total of 31,888. See United Republic of Tanzania, Central Statistical Bureau, *Employment and Earnings 1966* (Dar es Salaam, 1966), p. 35.

Witchcraft

Traditional beliefs and superstitions may be difficult to research in any society, especially if the members of that society have the slightest suspicion that those beliefs may not be "modern" or may be frowned upon by the investigator. While witchcraft was difficult to appraise in the societies studied, it clearly influenced the behavior of the people in the rural areas. In fact, some individuals used witchcraft in a positive attempt to achieve political ends in the village political systems. Individuals used witchcraft to influence the course of events; and in at least one instance a village political system used it to resist the intrusion of the district political system.[10]

---

[10] The term witchcraft is used in this discussion in preference to the more technical distinction between witchcraft and sorcery offered in the excellent introduction by Middleton and Winter in their edited volume, *Witchcraft and Sorcery in East Africa* (London, 1963), p. 12. Middleton and Winter remark that "a person is not a sorcerer in the same sense in which a person is a witch. Witchcraft . . . is part of an individual's being, a part of his innermost self, while sorcery is merely a technique which a person utilizes. Thus in some societies it is even thought that a person's witchcraft can operate at times without his being consciously aware of the fact that it is doing so. This can never be the case with sorcery; recourse to it must always be on a deliberate, conscious, voluntary basis." They elaborate: "By definition, it is impossible for an anthropologist to observe the practice of witchcraft. Acts of sorcery, although theoretically observable, are rarely seen due to the secrecy which surrounds them. Furthermore, it is very probable that in many societies such acts, although widely believed to be common, may in fact rarely, perhaps never be performed. Thus the study of wizardry [the combination of witchcraft and sorcery, in the authors' definition] is almost exclusively the study of the beliefs which people have about the capabilities and activities of others and the actions which they take to avoid attacks or to counter them when they believe they have occurred." *Ibid.,* p. 3.

For examples of the use of witchcraft for political ends in Tanzania, see T. O. Beidelman, "Witchcraft in Ukaguru," in Middleton and Winter, *Witchcraft,* pp. 76 ff. The political function of witchcraft in a West African society is discussed in Paul Bohannan, "Extra-Processual Events in Tiv Political Institutions," *American Anthropologist,* LX (February 1958), 1–

The historian O. F. Raum has noted that accusations of witchcraft played a role in the politics of traditional East African life during the German period.

The intimate connection between political power and control of magic was known to few Europeans at the time. The accusation of witchcraft was, however, an essential part of African political dynamics. Chiefs had few direct means of imposing their will. Only exceptionally did a chief sell a subject into slavery. Fines, beatings, and imprisonment had to be sparingly used for fear of a mass exodus from his realm. The chief's power was also circumscribed by the known constitutional checks exercised by his kindred, age mates, and clan leaders. The chief, however, was not powerless. He could appeal to the argument of witchcraft. It consisted in accusing persons whose possessions the chief coveted, or rivals to his popularity, or such as disobeyed him or presumed upon a chiefly prerogative, of having imbued themselves with nefarious magic. This was done by insinuations. The person concerned, surmising whence they emanated, might try to appease the chief with presents, or make a confession (which led to confiscation of his property) or take to flight. If he hesitated he would be pointed out in the inevitable witch-finding process conducted by a diviner acting on secret orders from the chief. Such accusation would lead the public to demand his execution. The witch-finding technique had the consensus of the people; many of them might have been antagonized by a direct attack.[11]

The influence of witchcraft, in the areas studied here, especially as it affects development efforts, was more frequently cited in the public records of Handeni District. One of the earliest references to witchcraft in Handeni is made by the colonial official Sir Charles Dundas. Discussing the falling population in Zigualand during the early years of colonial rule, he suggested that the sacrifice of newly

---

12. Also for an excellent account of the pervasiveness and power of witchcraft in the village, see the anthropological novel, Elenore Smith Bowen's *Return to Laughter* (Garden City, N.Y., 1964).

[11] Raum, *"German East Africa,"* p. 182.

THE DEVELOPMENTAL ENVIRONMENT 87

born children was a measure taken by parents to counter other misfortunes.

Depopulation could result from epidemics, famines or wars, but in my belief the cause in Seguha [Zigualand] had been infanticide. In that case tragedy probably followed upon tragedy. For the scourge of the fly [tsetse] would most likely be ascribed the infants of ill-fortune; the practice of infanticide would become more general, reducing yet further the population with consequent aggravation of the evil, for the cure of which parents sacrificed their offspring.[12]

The Tanga *Provincial Book* also called attention to infanticide in Handeni in an examination of the same phenomenon in Pare District.

The Wasigua nigh exterminated themselves in this way until the Germans hanged so many that they gave up the custom, the existence of which they now heartily regret. The scarcity of youths and girls of marriageable age is noticeable in Uzigua and testifies to the number of infants that were formerly put to death.[13]

The Handeni *District Book* recorded the widespread influence of witchcraft and its impact in 1956:

Witchcraft is widely practiced amongst the Wazigua and Wanguu. The main cause probably springs from these people's desire to remain independent of each other and to place themselves in complete isolation from their neighbours. Each family has its own preserves of land, is its own Great Commoner and jealously guards those rights. Witchcraft is therefore resorted to to surround these individual interests with a magical protection which must of necessity be stronger than any other and so such ingredients as parts of the human body are added to concoctions to render them efficacious.

The wholesale use of witchcraft has come to light recently with the almost universal demand in this district for the services of the Kabwere White magic cult.[14]

[12] Charles C. F. Dundas, *African Crossroads* (London, 1955), p. 101.
[13] Tanga Provincial Book, "Infanticide in Pare."
[14] Handeni *District Book,* entry for 2 July 1956.

A former colonial officer who served in Handeni during 1952–1954 attests to

several instances where junior government officials, such as teachers or game guards, became ill and in some cases died as a result, it was said, of witchcraft. Generally, it seemed to stem from feelings of envy as a result of their comparative greater wealth or from accusations that they used their power to have adulterous affairs with local women.[15]

The last recorded evidence of the impact of witchcraft on the district's development is in an address made by the Handeni area commissioner to the district council in August 1964. He said that "citizens are hindered from progress because of witch doctors and liquor drinking [*uganga na pombe*]." [16]

The references to witchcraft noted here are but surface indications of a phenomenon that was pervasive at the village level in both Handeni and Tanga districts. My research revealed enough for me to conclude beyond doubt that witchcraft played an important role in both the politics of rural development and the relationship between the political systems studied.

The best example of the use of witchcraft to resist efforts to promote rural development came to light in Sindeni Ward. Ward officials told me that the people there did not want to live in larger, permanent settlements because of their fear of witchcraft which, in their view, would be increased by the proximity of other people and by the fact that the villagers would be unable to follow their usual practice of simply moving their village to another area when witchcraft or any other calamity threatened. Also in Sindeni, during the time of this research, wives of two agricultural field assistants were being treated for having been bewitched. The rumor was that some villagers had bewitched them because their husbands were associated in the minds of the people with a district effort to

[15] Correspondence, David Brokensha to the writer, May 21, 1969.
[16] Handeni District Council, Minutes 20 August 1964, National Archives, Dar es Salaam (304/15/8A/29).

THE DEVELOPMENTAL ENVIRONMENT   89

organize communal or block farms about which the people were very unhappy. In this particular area popular feeling was so great that one field assistant, the most local extension of the district agricultural officer's staff, spoke of his fear that the local people would burn his house because of their displeasure with the district government's efforts.[17]

Probably the most profound impact of witchcraft upon development efforts in Handeni was the fear of living close to other people, which was noted in the District Book and which was constantly called to my attention.[18] The spirit of distrust that was at the base of this fear was also present in Tanga District.[19] In this atmosphere, a farmer feared to leave chickens in the care of neighbors living only fifty yards away while he was hospitalized and children were afraid to eat food prepared in neighbor's homes. The importance of this distrust can hardly be overestimated in a nation where the national development efforts had a special emphasis upon cooperative efforts.

[17] Handeni, Sindeni Ward, February 15–17, 1968.

[18] A newspaper item called attention to this fear in another district. The area commissioner was quoted as saying "that villagers . . . had scattered through a fear of witchcraft and the belief that when people lived together, they bewitched each other." *Standard,* October 21, 1968.

[19] For a survey of the prevalence of this fear of witchcraft among the Digo along the East African coast, see Luther P. Gerlach, "Nutrition in Its Sociocultural Matrix: Food Getting and Using along the East African Coast," in David Brokensha (ed.), *Ecology and Economic Development in Tropical Africa* (Berkeley, 1965), pp. 255 ff. Gerlach considers the influence of the fear of witchcraft on economic development by noting, "The Digo commonly respond to the economic success of a fellow Digo by calling upon him to finance various kinds of ceremonials or rituals in which food and other goods are distributed. Digo wives characteristically become ill—possessed, at it were, by spirits which demand expensive curing rituals and such gifts as jewelry and clothes. The Digo who clearly refuse to share their wealth are frequently accused of being witches who become prosperous not by hard work but by cheating and stealing from their neighbors, often using black magic. At the very least they are denied financial and other aid if they need it." *Ibid.,* p. 255.

The Paternalistic Ethic

A well-documented trait of developing areas is the individual's inability to conceive that his own efforts can affect a change in his environment.[20] In Tanga and Handeni this trait had been reinforced by the belief that "government" could and should do everything. The term "paternalism" is perhaps overworked and certainly has numerous and contradictory connotations; nevertheless, in the villages analyzed the people believed that any and all problems can and ultimately must be solved by the "government." This cluster of attitudes is the basis of President Nyerere's program aimed at instilling a sense of self-reliance (*kujitegemea*).

This passive reliance upon government or external forces to solve every problem has a long history in Tanzania. In a society as subject to the cruel whims of nature as is Tanzania, it is obviously sensible to assume that one is not and cannot be master of one's fate. This factor also contributes to the importance of witchcraft as a means of determining one's destiny or at least explaining it. Nevertheless it is difficult not to conclude that the various governments to which the villages have been subjected have encouraged this attitude by their actions.

The *Handbook of Tanganyika,* gives an account of the British colonial decision to shift the traditional tribute in kind paid to traditional authorities to a cash payment or tax paid to the Native Authorities established under the system of indirect rule. The *Handbook* then concluded:

It was not realized at the time that in the case of many tribes, tribute in kind had been paid in the shape of food, as a form of self-help, for storage and for distribution by Chief or Headman in case of need. Commutation of tribute thus shifted the onus from the individual Chief or Headman to the native treasury for relieving distress and

[20] See the related concept of empathy in Daniel Lerner, *The Passing of Traditional Society* (New York, 1958), pp. 47–52.

THE DEVELOPMENTAL ENVIRONMENT

in particular for alleviation of famine resulting from crop failure.[21]

One of the early architects of British colonial policy in Tanganyika, when describing what subsistence agriculture meant in Tanganyika, inadvertently stated the development described in the *Handbook.* Sir Philip Mitchell wrote of subsistence agriculture, "It means exactly what it says. A man cultivates or he does not subsist; he reaps a crop or he starves—or did, for the long dangerous generations *before there were colonial governments to bring relief.*[22]

W. Arthur Lewis attributes the existence of the paternalistic ethic in West Africa to overcentralization of government. He writes: "The African villager has now come to take it for granted that the central government will provide water, schools, hospital service, roads and even electricity free, or at highly subsidized rates. The government is then caught between unlimited demands for public service and very limited willingness to pay for what they cost." [23] Of the two districts studied, the paternalistic ethic was more prominent in Handeni primarily because famine had been a constant threat here.

An excerpt from a letter from the Handeni district commissioner to the president of the Red Cross Society in Tanga in 1953 indicated the extreme to which the British colonial government sometimes went in response to the needs of the local people:

The Medical Officer also recommended that as many people as possible be given regularly cups of hot sweet tea. . . .

If you can find it possible to help us, I shall be delighted to show any of your representatives around the famine areas, and they will be free to inspect the ways in which the money is spent.

Needless to say, if any of your representatives chose to spend some

[21] Moffett, *Handbook,* p. 101.
[22] Philip Mitchell, *African Afterthoughts* (London, 1954), p. 136. Emphasis is this writer's.
[23] W. Arthur Lewis, *Politics in West Africa* (Toronto, 1965), p. 54.

time here in organizing relief, that would be most popular, especially with the local people.[24]

This commissioner's position was not typical of the attitude of the colonial officer to the needs of the Zigua during times of famine. As is discussed below, the colonial officers made a concentrated effort to get the people of Handeni to prepare for famine by planting enough of the proper crops so as to be able to cope with the inevitable adverse weather conditions. The fact is, however, that the villagers were aware that if famine occurred their needs would be met at the district *boma*. All indications are that their convictions were accurate. Thus, in spite of the efforts of the government to get the people to prepare for years of famine, they were not successful. Part of the reason for this failure was the existence of the aura of paternalism that colonialism cultivated. The government of Tanzania is today engaged in a concentrated effort to destroy this attitude.

While self-reliance as espoused in the Arusha Declaration became a national goal in 1967, the attack upon the paternalistic ethic had been in progress since independence in 1961. I had the distinct impression that African officials were more hard-boiled in attempting to eradicate this attitude than were their colonial predecessors. To return to the example of Handeni, in 1962, shortly after independence, a delegation approached the district commissioner to request famine relief. They met a district officer instead and were told that

hunger is caused by the District Council not working together with the central government on the problem of hunger. The D.O. insisted that they should not be given food freely just because the Zigua traditional habit is to help their elders at any time, when food is sufficient and when in famine. He disapproved the request.[25]

[24] Handeni, Famine Relief, Agriculture, 6/1/8/III, "To the President Red Cross Society, Tanga, 28 February 1953 from District Commissioner."
[25] Handeni District Council (Ufungilo), Minutes 5 February, 1962, National Archives, Dar es Salaam (304/L5/8A/29).

Later in the same year, the now redesignated area commissioner addressed the District Council on the question of famine. The area commissioner "told the Council to leave and forget about the famine Agenda because people only wanted free food stuffs for which the council had already spent [Shs.] 100,000/–. This is due to the fact that they remain without farms. You go and tell them to farm." [26]

In 1967 a Tanga regional officer, on tour of an area suffering from insufficient food, responded to an assembled village's request for assistance by saying, "Yes, government officers will help you. We'll help bury you after you die of laziness." He then pointed out the lack of any evidence on the part of the village for achieving self-reliance.[27]

Tangible evidence of the paternalistic ethic was not so prominent in Tanga District as it was in Handeni. This was true for two reasons. First, the physical environment made life and existence much easier in Tanga than in Handeni. Water was more abundant and there were many stands of coconut trees. The coconut tree is a ready source of food, including fats, and little effort is involved beyond the initial planting of the seedling. In addition, in the areas of Tanga studied here, the sea provided an easy source of protein.[28] The second reason was that the economy in Tanga was more developed than in Handeni. There was a sizable cash economy that enabled citizens to avoid dependence for their survival upon a single crop.

However, the paternalistic ethic was not absent from the villages

[26] *Ibid.*, 18 June 1962.
[27] This account given me by the officer involved.
[28] This writer's impression of the relatively sufficient food and diet is substantiated by Luther Gerlach's findings among the same Digo people further north in Kenya. He notes, for example, that "while the Digo food production system was not as good as Sulymani [Gerlach's informant] would have it, it certainly was better than many government officials believed," and that "the government of Kenya believed that the Digo food economy was much poorer than was actually the case." Gerlach, "Nutrition," p. 245.

of Tanga. In a general meeting in one village in Tanga, the people said that the government had to repair the decaying walls of the village well. This same group complained that one of their greatest problems was the lack of hospitals. To this, the divisional executive officer replied that there were hospitals in the area, one of which was only three miles away. The villagers' reaction to this revelation was: "Yes, but how do we get to them?" [29] This frame of mind typical of the villagers is more than a sense of personal inability to shape one's destiny. It is instead a special sense of how to shape this destiny for individual and community. It is, in brief, through the "government."

The present campaign to instill the principle of self-reliance recognized the need to destroy this ethic before rural development can take root. The prominence of "self-reliance" terminology in village discussions indicated that at least verbally the villagers were accepting the message, although these discussions were in most cases in the presence of government or party officials.

The Compulsion Syndrome

The paternalistic ethic is closely tied to the compulsion syndrome, the third dimension of the cultural environment that became evident during the course of this research. As discussed in Chapter III, compulsory enforcement has been present in Tanzania's rural development efforts since the first colonial government's attempt to direct the villagers' behavior. One scholar has attributed the root cause of the first major rebellion under colonial rule to the efforts of the German administration to force communal farming of cotton on neighborhood units.[30] As I have noted, the use of force was not unknown or unapproved in the British colonial experience, and compulsion as a development technique is fairly

[29] Migombani, 26 March 1968.
[30] See the excellent account in John Iliffe, "The Effects of the Maji Maji Rebellion of 1905–1906 on German Occupation Policy in East Africa," in Prosser Gifford and William Roger Louis (eds.), *Britain and Germany in Africa* (New Haven, 1967), pp. 560 ff.

clear in colonial policy. Indeed, the existence of some degree of compulsion is an accepted fact in any political system and is so acknowledged here. My central concern, however, is the extent to which force is accepted, by officials and by the people, as a legitimate technique for the promotion of rural development in independent Tanzania.

From the early days of independence, there were numerous statements in public records indicating that some officials were willing to use force if necessary to bring about the changes they sought. There is little doubt, however, that a resort to force was increasingly accepted as a legitimate development technique during the first five years after independence. This increasing acceptance is likely tied to the officials' increasing frustration with their inability to bring about the desired changes by reason alone.[31] It may also, however, be a reflection of the fact that the people themselves expected force to be used and accepted such tactics as legitimate. In any case, less than three months after the achievement of independence, the potential use of force to bring about rural development had already been accepted at the regional levels of the government. The minutes of a meeting of the regional commissioner, the administrative Secretary, and all district commissioners of Tanga Region held on March 6, 1962, reported the conclusion: "The work of arousing the enthusiasm of the people for village development schemes must be shouldered jointly by political leaders and Government officers in the field. The Regional Commissioner felt that if the people failed to respond to persuasion and exhortation it might be necessary to resort to coercion." [32]

[31] Consider the theoretical analysis of this trend in Aristide R. Zolberg, "The Structure of Political Conflict in the New States of Tropical Africa," *The American Political Science Review*, LXII (March 1968), 70–88.

[32] Tanga Regional Development Committee, "Note of a Meeting held in the Regional Commissioner's Office, Tanga at 9 A.M. on 6 March 1962, between the Regional Commissioner, Tanga Region, the Administrative Secretary and all District Commissioners of the Region," National Archives 304/p4/2.

One month later at the first meeting of the Regional Development Committee, this policy was given sanction by a representative from Dar es Salaam: "The District Commissioner, Tanga (rural), said that he, and doubtless other District Commissioners, would be glad of guidance as to how far Government would be content to rely upon persuasion only to achieve production targets, and how far it would go in backing the use of stronger methods." The regional commissioner then asked the representative of the central government for guidance as to the government's policy on this point. The representative replied that "Government was quite prepared to use methods stronger than persuasion if persuasion failed. Local Authorities would be expected or even required to pass by-laws which might be necessary to enforce increased agricultural production and these by-laws would be enforced by the Local Authorities themselves." [33]

The officials involved in promoting rural development have mixed feelings about the use of force rather than persuasion. Nevertheless, an atmosphere which may be called the "compulsion syndrome" was a pervasive feature of the relationships between government and the people in the areas studied here. I see no necessary conflict between the use of compulsion in development efforts and the encouragement of democratic ideals. Gunnar Myrdal has dealt with the tendency to confuse the absence of compulsion with democracy and modernization in his monumental study of Asia.[34] He notes that

our investigation has convinced us that the success of planning for development requires a readiness to place obligations on people in *all* social strata to a much greater extent than is now done in any of the South Asian countries. It requires, in addition, rigorous enforcement of obligations, in which compulsion plays a strategic role.

[33] Tanga, Regional Development Committee, Minutes of First Regional Development Committee, Tanga, April 6, 1962, National Archives 304/p4/2.

[34] Gunnar Myrdal, *Asian Drama: An Inquiry into the Poverty of Nations,* Vol. I, II, III (New York, 1968).

This value premise runs parallel to, and is partly identical with, the quest for national consolidation . . . and, in particular, effective government. It would not in principle conflict with the ideal of political democracy, which only concerns the manner in which policies are decided upon.[35]

The statements of President Nyerere himself are indicative of the conflict at highest councils in the nation over the role of force in securing the changes desired. In a major position paper on ujamaa villages President Nyerere discussed the issue of compulsion, saying that persuasion, not force, was the way to move the society to accept and participate in ujamaa villages. The President went on to accept the possibility that compulsion might in some cases be necessary.[36] He wrote: "It may be possible—and sometimes necessary—to insist on all farmers in a given area growing a certain acreage of a particular crop until they realize that this brings them a more secure living, and then do not have to be forced to cultivate it." [37]

Nyerere thus set in motion a year-long debate with himself over the proper role of compulsion in his government's rural development efforts. A few weeks later he discussed the organization of ujamaa villages before the National Conference of TANU: "We must not try to rush this development; what matters is not the speed but the direction in which we move. We must encourage and help people, not try to force them." [38]

Three months later, in January 1968, the President spoke to a conference of officials of the Ministry of Local Government and Rural Development about the revolution in which they were involved. He declared that

it was generally thought that the main function of the Ministry was to govern people . . . to maintain law and order. The justification of law and order was development not just sitting and yawning idly.

[35] *Ibid.*, I, 67.   [36] Nyerere, *Freedom and Socialism*, p. 356.
[37] *Ibid.* Also see John Lonsdale, "The Tanzanian Experiment," *African Affairs,* LXVII (October 1968), 330–344.
[38] After the Arusha Declaration," in *Freedom and Socialism*, p. 407.

During the colonial days it was alright, because it was part of keeping the peace of the world, but to bring about an economic revolution people's bodies and heads must be shaken first. . . .

Then, the *Standard* reported, President Nyerere, "looking at the Minister for Local Government and Rural Development," said: " 'So Bwana, let us have some bylaws to check this laziness. We are poor and we have to do something to get rid of this poverty.' " [39]

A few weeks later in speaking of the ujamaa villages at the University College, Dar es Salaam, the President said, "The essence of these villages was that people had to be allowed to make their own decisions and their own mistakes and 'only if we accept this are we really accepting the philosophy of Socialism and Rural Development.' " In further elaboration of the role of the leader, Nyerere said that "a good leader would explain, teach and inspire. In an Ujamaa village he would do more as he would lead by doing. He would be in the front of the people showing them what could be done, guiding them and encouraging them. He would be with them." He added, "You do not lead people by yapping at their heels like a dog herding cattle. . . ." And in conclusion, the *Standard* reported,

President Nyerere said that the real object of development in Africa was the people and it was important they developed their minds in an atmosphere of freedom, which was absolutely fundamental.

What was important was to break the cocoons of ignorance but not to whip them and pretend that to be development. Force could not be used to develop the mind of the people.[40]

While there is absolutely no question about Nyerere's commitment to human freedom, it is evident that the hard practicalities of rural change have raised questions in his mind as to the limits of persuasion and reason. The debate obviously moved toward an interim conclusion in the President's own mind almost one year later in a major position paper which drew upon the theme of his

[39] *Standard,* January 3, 1968. [40] *Ibid.,* January 22, 1968.

closing comments at University College quoted above. Nyerere said:

If the purpose of development is the greater freedom and well being of the people, it cannot result from force. For the proverb tells the truth in this matter: you can drive a donkey to water, but you cannot make it drink. By orders, or even by slavery, you can build pyramids and magnificent roads, you can achieve *expanded acreages of cultivation,* and increases in the quantity of goods produced in your factories. All these things, and many more, can be achieved through the use of force; but none of them result in the development of people. Force, and deceitful promises can in fact, only achieve short-term material goals. They cannot bring strength to a nation or a community, and they cannot provide a basis for the freedom of the people, or security for any individual or group or persons.[41]

Nyerere then noted two factors that were essential in developing the people. The first was leadership through education and the second was democracy in decision making. He stressed that

leadership does not mean shouting at people; it does not mean abusing individuals or groups of people you disagree with; even less does it mean ordering people to do this or that. Leadership means talking and discussing with the people, explaining and persuading. It means making constructive suggestions, and working with the people to show by actions what it is that you are urging them to do.[42]

Beyond stating the need for open and free discussion, he did not examine the nature of the democratic decision-making process. Instead, he turned immediately to the question of how to carry out the decision democratically arrived at. He expanded on the theme "discipline must follow decision":

The greater freedom which comes from working together, and achieving things by co-operation which none of us could achieve alone, is only possible if there is disciplined acceptance of joint decisions. . . .

[41] Julius K. Nyerere, "Freedom and Development," *Standard,* October 18, 1968; emphasis is mine.
[42] *Ibid.*

Once a community has democratically decided upon a particular self-help scheme, everyone must co-operate in carrying out that decision, or pay the penalty which the village agrees upon. . . . The acceptance of community discipline is only a problem in Tanzania when our people do not understand the implications of the changes which we have already effected in our lives. In traditional society we had discipline —often very severe. It was accepted by everyone, and everyone co-operated in imposing it. Our problem now comes not from the discipline itself, but from a lack of understanding about the machinery which is necessary for discipline in a modern state, and from a failure to realize that different kinds of discipline are needed in the organizations of a modern society.

The President concluded his argument by asserting, that "we must have both freedom and discipline. For freedom without discipline is anarchy: discipline without freedom is tyranny." [43]

There is no doubt that middle level officials and some at the highest levels have all along been more willing than the President to resort to force to promote change. For example, the regional commissioner of Tanga in a speech to the Handeni District Council in March 1967 declared: "The time of persuading citizens to work for their own benefit is finished. It's necessary from now to enforce them to work hard. The government will take severe steps with those who are not willing to work in the jobs that they have been instructed to do." [44] There is evidence of difference between the view articulated by President Nyerere and those by other officials in the nation on the question of force and rural change. There has certainly been a gap between the policy articulated at the center and its implementation in the field.

There is considerable evidence suggesting that the use of force is not only expected but is viewed as legitimate by those toward whom the rural development efforts are directed. Two sources sup-

[43] *Ibid.*
[44] Handeni District Council, Minutes 22 March 1967, Appendix A, "Speech of Regional Commissioner."

porting this view are the records of the deliberations of the district councils and the responses in village surveys to questions of how best to organize self-help projects.

The record of deliberation on the techniques of securing rural development was most clear in Handeni. In July 1962, a few months after independence, the Handeni District Council passed a resolution to the effect that "any person not participating in development projects should be punished by six strokes." [45] In June 1965, according to the minutes of the meeting, a member of the Handeni District Council expressed the opinion "that voluntary jobs [self-help] were compulsory from colonial times and people used to do them, but not now. He asked members to agree to support voluntary jobs by force. They passed it." [46] And in 1967 the Handeni District Council discussed the implementation of the Arusha Declaration and agreed with the suggestions of the district executive officer that the people should farm more. The councilors were also of the opinion that the people should be punished "even by strokes in public." [47]

Public record of the acceptance of force as a legitimate technique of promoting change was less evident in Tanga District. The use of bylaws to ensure the planting of certain acreage of staple crops was accepted in Tanga, as in Handeni, and compulsory participation in self-help projects was understood. There was, however, less discussion in the district council of these techniques.

The village-level response to force was similar in both districts. Time after time in responding to the question, "What is the best way to organize a self-help project here?" the ultimate answer would be to use force.[48] This is not to suggest that the villagers

[45] Handeni District Council, Minutes 2 July 1962, National Archives (304/L5/8A/29).
[46] Handeni District Council, Minutes 23 June 1965, *ibid*.
[47] Handeni District Council, Minutes 17 February 1967.
[48] The grass-roots research upon which this finding in part depends was conducted in one division in both Tanga and Handeni District for more intensive investigation of the general problem of rural development. Sub-

approve of the use of force. It is to suggest that the use of force by the officials to secure peasant participation was expected and, it would seem, accepted by these same peasants as a legitimate technique. Ironically, it would appear that the villagers may have accepted compulsion as a legitimate developmental technique more readily than did their leaders.

During one village meeting, the divisional executive officer called the women to task because they had not started a communal chicken project that was to be carried out by the women with an initial donation from the area commissioner. After lecturing the women for several minutes and asking individuals to recite points from the Arusha Declaration, the divisional officer asked, "What is necessary to get you to work in development projects? Do we have to bring the *Kiboko* [infamous rhinoceros hide whip used by the Germans]?" The response from the assembled women of the village was, "Bring it, bring it." [49]

In 1969, President Nyerere announced a fundamental and potentially revolutionary decision giving greater authority to the village communities to punish those inhabitants who did not participate in community self-help projects. The directive considered traditional communal efforts in Tanzania:

almost everywhere every able-bodied person took part. If for any reason, a member of the community was absent from the joint task then he or she faced some penalty which would compensate the community for his or her failure to join in the work.

Sometimes they were fined and had to contribute a goat, sheep or chicken, or some other form of refreshment, which was then used for the benefit of the people who were working. Sometimes the defaulters

---

sequently, one ward was chosen in each of the divisions and, finally, sample villages were chosen in each ward for village level research. The villages ranged from a traditional village consisting of eighteen households, to a Youth League communal farm, to a large village situated as a satellite to a sisal estate.

[49] Paraphrased from meeting, April 28, 1968.

were barred from using the thing that was being constructed, or found that when they needed help it was not available.

The President continued:

Since independence we have encouraged self-help projects of all kinds, but we have refused to allow local communities to impose any sanctions on those few individuals who, without good reason refused to take part. The Government has now decided to change this. Under certain conditions certain kinds of sanctions imposed by the local community will be allowed. . . . Village development committees will . . . in future be allowed to impose other traditional sanctions on those who do not take part in a self-help activity which the village development committee has itself declared to be a self-help project.[50]

Nyerere thus chose to come to grips with the question of the application of force to bring about rural change by the technique—unusual in any society—of decentralizing the responsibility for applying coercion to the local communities themselves. In effect, the President also shifted the question of the morality of the application of force in developmental efforts to the same villages which would benefit from the developmental effort in the first instance. Forced planting that is initiated and enforced by an external agency is quite different from that coercion originating from within the locality as is envisaged here by President Nyerere.

While the effects of this decision on rural development efforts in Tanzania are unclear at this time, two potential extremes may be suggested. First, should the local communities adopt the President's suggestions with energy, they may harass individuals in the villages, especially if the committee making decisions is not representative of the general consensus of the village.[51] The first reading

---

[50] Julius K. Nyerere, "To Stop Shirkers: President's Measures," *Standard*, October 18, 1968.

[51] There was some uncertainty as to the composition of the institution that would be making developmental decisions and specifying the nature of local punishment in the localities. President Nyerere referred to the village development committees; however, the *formal* village development

of the bill to provide ward development committees with this authority in the National Assembly elicited considerable questioning from the members as to its implications. Specifically, they questioned whether this bill would institute "forced labor" in the countryside. The Minister for Rural Development defended the bill by noting:

> The Ward Development Committees Bill, 1969, was not aimed at introducing forced labour but at protecting the majority decision against those few people who did not want to take part in developing projects. . . . Mr. Kisumo told the House that this was the essence of democracy—where the few would not be allowed to oppose the majority. He said at present some leaders were experiencing difficulty in enforcing work on self-help projects.[52]

At the opposite extreme, President Nyerere's proposal implicitly assumes that the local committees will consider and decide to participate in self-help projects that contribute to national objectives. It is possible, and likely in some localities, that the local community will simply choose not to participate in nation-building projects at all.

The latter extreme assumes that there will be virtually no external involvement in village affairs. Such will almost certainly not be the case. The most likely development will be a compromise between these two hypothetical extremes that will blend nation, regional and district involvement in and direction of village affairs but that will encourage greater responsibility for administering the collective will of the local community by the local community.

---

committees were being replaced by *ward* development committees (see p. 154). The bill introduced into the National Assembly in January 1969 that would make the President's directive law was referred to as the Ward Development Committees Bill, 1969. See *Standard*, December 24, 1968, and January 9, 1969, *passim*. If the bill were approved, "every committee will have the power to make orders requiring all adult citizens resident within the ward to participate in the implementation of any development scheme." *Standard*, December 24, 1968.

[52] *Standard*, January 9, 1969.

THE DEVELOPMENTAL ENVIRONMENT

The synthesis between the extremes of forced change on the one hand and change by persuasion on the other, with greater decentralization of both decision-making and enforcement authority, seems to set the stage for the second decade of Tanzanian development efforts. The higher echelons of national leadership have clearly opted for the technique of persuasion over compulsion on both moral and practical grounds. In presenting the Second Five-Year Plan to the national TANU conference in May 1969, President Nyerere clearly announced this decision when he declared, "We make a big mistake if we try to force people to produce certain amounts or even to cultivate certain acreages of cash crops." He concluded, "Persuasion may appear slower than force, but it is more effective." [53]

Thus President Nyerere has come to grips with the problem of force versus persuasion in development policy. The second decade of Tanzanian development must also confront the twin cultural restraints upon the process of modernization, witchcraft and paternalism. Tanzania's leaders have launched an impressive attack on both these themes during the 1960's. The physical conditions in Tanzania are so formidable that rural modernization demands a particularly successful assault upon these cultural restraints if national goals are to be achieved.

[53] *Tanzania Second Five-Year Plan,* p. xvi.

CHAPTER V

The District *Boma:* National Outpost

The efforts of the Tanzanian government to institute change in the rural communities involves the penetration of thousands of villages, the most isolated and most traditional political systems in Tanzania. The attempt to penetrate these villages is not the first, by any means, and the current effort is inescapably bound up in the efforts that have preceded it.

The great variety of kinds of villages in Tanga and Handeni makes description of the typical village very difficult. The most common village consists of from fifteen to twenty huts, with the most manifest theme of community being kinship. Other villages, including those studied here, may have been formed around a mission station, an Asian general store, or an adjacent sisal plantation.[1]

For most of the diverse peoples of Tanzania, the colonial rulers were the first to attempt to interject some external bureaucratic apparatus into the village. There were exceptions, however; for example, the Sambaa, the Chagga, the Nyamwezi, the Sukuma, the Ha, Haya, Zinza and the Nyakyusa had institutional arrangements resembling a state system based primarily upon tribal identity.[2]

[1] A more complete discussion of the village is taken up in Chapter VI.
[2] See Edgar V. Winans, *Shambala: The Constitution of a Traditional State* (Berkeley, 1962), and R. G. Abrahams, *The Political Organization of Unyamwezi* (Cambridge, 1967).

Although it is difficult to determine the precise nature of the precolonial systems in Tanga and Handeni, district books provide a general sketch of village political systems. In Tanga, prior to the intrusion of the Arabs from the twelfth century, the coastal peoples appear to have had a very small-scale political organization consisting primarily of a council of village elders that had little or no impact outside the village itself.[3]

In Handeni, however, the political system of the Zigua tribe was quite different. A British colonial officer, writing a general commentary in 1947 on the Zigua, noted that

> for purposes of defense the Zigua by 1850 had travelled one stage further than their neighbors in the evolution of a system of local control. From the original patrician state, they had developed a clan system and even on occasions, in time of great danger had achieved a temporary federation of clans. . . . Whatever may have been the cause of his existence, in the clan-leader one can see some semblance of a personality worthy to be called ruler as opposed to the paterfamilies of the coast or of Bondei. The clan head had his council of elders by which he stood or fell; to alienate their sympathies for him would have spelt ruin for him. Likewise when a federation of clans was achieved, all action was in the hands of a major council of clan leaders, each supported by his advisers. The most important federations were formed when the power of the Sultan of Zanzibar was first felt. The Zigua clan heads did not welcome the posting of Arab garrisons on the coast and regarded this move as a direct and immediate menace to their own sovereignty. In 1882 the forces of a Zigua federation under Bwana Heri defeated an army sent against them by the Sultan and—given time—with the Sultan proposing serious reprisals, the Wazigua might have achieved complete and final union under one chief.[4]

[3] Tanga *District Book,* and H. M. T. Kayamba, "Notes on the Wadigo," *Tanganyika Notes and Records,* XXIII (1947), 80 ff.
[4] Tanga Region, "Tribal Government," *The Provincial Book.*

Colonial Intrusions

The Arabs, who were sending an army against the Zigua in the late nineteenth century, had been in contact with the east African coast for centuries and had some control on the coast at least from the early nineteenth century.[5] And the Arabs were the first external power to leave a clear mark on the political systems of present-day Tanzania. Since their intent was trade with the coast and the interior, they secured control over access routes to the interior by establishing Arab settlements along the coast and by setting up caravan routes up the Pangani River into Handeni and then to Mount Kilimanjaro. The Arab relationship with the village political systems was utilitarian, usually involving alliances with local leaders to allow for passage of caravans. Where there was no such leader, or when he was not cooperative, the Arabs established their own man, known as the *akida* or *liwali,* supported where necessary by an armed garrison. The *akida* was usually an Arab or a Muslim-educated Swahili [6] who served as the intermediary between the colonial administration and such local political organization as existed. He had the responsibility for maintaining law and order, for the assessment and collection of taxes, and for the organization of compulsory labor when required.

The German colonial venture into East Africa confronted this extremely thin overlay of Arab colonization along the trade routes

[5] Kenneth Ingham, *A History of East Africa* (New York, 1962), p. 61.

[6] Swahili is used here in the sense defined by Coupland. "The Swahili is 'a mixture of mixtures,' arising . . . from the impingement of Asiatic immigrants on the Bantu who lived on the coastland or were brought down to it from the interior as slaves. Every degree of Afro-Asiatic combination and wide diversity of physique and culture are to be found in their ranks; but they possess—and have disseminated far inland—a common tongue, a Bantu language freely modified by Arabs and betraying also in its vocabulary the influence of Asiatic and European invasion." R. Coupland, *East Africa and Its Invaders* (New York, 1965), p. 28.

and in the coastal towns. After displacing Arab rule, the German colonists formed the country into twenty-one districts that split the area of Tanganyika into geographical areas which extended beyond the village on something other than a tribal basis.[7] All but two of the districts were placed under the charge of a district commissioner. The district commissioner was responsible to the governor of the colony for the maintenance of law and order in his district as well as the collection of taxes. The Germans, through the office of the district commissioner, adopted the system introduced by the Arabs of delegating the carrying out of these functions at the village level to the *akida*. On the coast where political organization wider than the village was nonexistent, the Germans adopted the Arabs' *akida* system virtually intact. Inland, where there was some tribal political organization on wider than the village level, the title of *akida* was often applied to the chief. Thus the *akida* could be either a local authority, deputized to carry out the orders of the German district commissioner, or an alien with the same task. In some of the inland areas the man holding the office of *akida* was actually referred to by the people as "the sultan." [8]

The *akida* was assisted in the villages by individuals appointed by him and known as headmen or *jumbes* who were responsible for law and order and the collection of taxes in their areas of jurisdiction. Though the German colonial adventure in Tanzania was to last for only twenty-two years, the district-level organization that the Germans introduced is still today the basic unit of political and administrative organization in the rural areas of Tanzania. Another important contribution of this period was the Germans' impact on the importance of tribal identity in determining political behavior. When they arrived, they found tribalism weak, but "by

[7] Moffett, *Handbook*, p. 78.
[8] For this general discussion see Moffett, *Handbook*, pp. 78 ff; R. F. Eberlie, "The German Achievement," pp. 181–214, and United Kingdom, Colonial Office, *Development of African Local Government–1951* (Dar es Salaam, 1952). The immediate point is based on my own discussions in Handeni District.

entering into regular relations with an African chief the Germans gave recognition to his position," and thus, "helped to stabilize the tribal set-up." [9]

The British appear to have found little difficulty in adopting the local administrative districts created by the Germans, and they used the *akida* in early efforts to make contact with the villages.[10]

From the beginning of British rule, colonial officers were interested in reviving tribal society and government. Faced with the large size of the districts and the underdeveloped state of communications, the British colonial administration established sub-district units known as divisions, which were based primarily on the geographical area of a precolonial tribal chiefdom. Prompted by the policy of indirect rule in Nigeria, colonial officers wrote the Native Authority Ordinances of 1921 and 1923 that promoted indigenous authorities by requiring any chief, headman, or council of elders recognized by the governor to maintain order and prevent crime.

Sir Donald Cameron, appointed governor of the colony in 1924, intensified the effort to revive indigenous institutions. An official report stated:

By 1925, the confidence of the people had been secured by just administration and the advent of a new Governor, who had seen the effectiveness of local administration through the chiefs in Nigeria, gave the opportunity for a transformation in principle and practice. . . . Their [Native Authority Ordinances] application involved ascertaining who were the traditional leaders of the people whether chiefs of large areas or small, or headmen of village communities; recognizing their authority, both executive and judicial; conferring on them new functions which made them the forerunners of the rapidly developing local government institutions of today; and providing them with

[9] See: O. F. Baum, "German East Africa: Changes in African Life under German Administration 1892–1914," in Vincent Harlow *et al., History of East Africa* (Oxford, 1965), II, 170.
[10] Ingham, "Tanganyika," pp. 550 ff. and Margaret L. Bates, "Tanganyika: Changes in African Life 1918–1945," in Harlow, pp. 625–641.

the financial resources from which not only the costs of tribal administration but those of nascent social services could be met.[11]

At first the concept of indirect rule aimed at eventually providing a democratic system of local government based on some form of representation. Proponents of indirect rule stressed that traditional forms of government had democratic features, and they expected that these democratic tendencies would flourish with the encouragement of the colonial authorities. Various types of councils, both formal and informal, did develop. The government's report on local government in 1954 indicates the heterogeneity of these institutions.

> Broadly speaking, the same components are to be found in most districts. There are first the chief or chiefs who are the native authorities sometimes accompanied by their sub-chiefs, and parallel with them in the coastal districts, the appointed executives. Here it should again be emphasized that the office of chief normally contains strong democratic elements: he does not succeed solely by hereditary right, but also by consent of the people. The second component is that of representatives of the village headmen, a body of Africans who in some parts are hereditary or are direct executive appointments by the chief, and on others are selected by, or with the assent, of the village community. Thirdly come the representatives of the people, usually chosen by the divisional council, covering a chiefdom or comparable unit, or by the commoners in some cases, part or all of the commoners are directly elected in the divisions. Finally, there are useful men—junior Government officials, traders, priests and teachers, for example—and occasionally women selected from subordinate councils or co-opted by the council, or nominated by the chief or the District Commissioner.[12]

While indirect rule was successful in varying degrees, it is no great surprise that Tanga District was one of the least successful in the implementation of indirect rule, since no real leadership

[11] *Local Government Memorandum*, p. 3.
[12] *Local Government Memoranda*, p. 6. Also see Moffett, *Handbook*, pp. 101 ff.

existed above the village level. In the three coastal divisions of Tanga, it was necessary for government to appoint chiefs and to administer directly.[13]

By independence in 1961 there existed more than fifty rural local authorities covering the same areas as the administrative districts. These authorities functioned through a type of council for the district. All but six of these councils were established under the Native Authority Ordinance of 1927. Although not formally representative, in fact, these councils did allow considerable representation of local views in the affairs of the district. Along with these quasirepresentative councils, there existed, at independence, a smaller number of local councils established under the Local Government Ordinance of 1953. These included eleven town councils and six rural district councils. These councils were fully representative with the authority to make decisions for the area within a general framework provided by the ordinance. The full development of such rural councils in all districts was hindered because the African leadership was unwilling to accept the condition of some degree of non-African representation by nomination.[14] By 1960 events at the national level had overtaken the development of local government institutions. Independence would be achieved before the further development of institutions of local governance.

The District *Boma*

For the majority of Tanzanians, the center of government and politics is the district *boma*.[15] And for government officials in Dar

[13] Tanga Region, *Provincial Book*. Also see Philip Mitchell, *African Afterthoughts* (London, 1954), pp. 133 ff.
[14] See Stanley Dryden, *Local Administration in Tanzania* (Nairobi, 1968), pp. 98 ff.
[15] *Boma* is the Swahili word for fort or fortresslike structure. It was used by the British to refer to the usually fortlike construction of the district headquarters. Today, the term *boma* is still the common term for the district offices and will be so used throughout this study.

es Salaam, access to the countryside is through the sixty district offices.

The single most important official in the *boma* is the area commissioner. The independent government redesignated the office of district commissioner to be the area commissioner, probably in order to emphasize the Africanization of the post. Districts were renamed areas, but the term district is in common usage to refer to the geographical area, to the district council, and administrative headquarters. However, Africans do not use the term district commissioner.

The area commissioner is a political appointee. Because the new independent leadership was well aware of the difficulty in linking the periphery with the center, the leadership decided to attempt to politicize the entire structure by making leadership in the independence movement a requirement for the office of area commissioner.[16] Of forty area commissioners appointed in 1962, thirty-five came from leadership positions in TANU, most at the district level.[17] Because each commissioner was an appointee of the center and was not a native of the district where he was serving, his loyalty was to Dar es Salaam. Another facet of this politicization was that the area commissioner was simultaneously to hold the office of secretary of the district TANU organization. (See Charts 1 and 2, which show the organization of party and government and suggest the degree of overlap between the two from the region to the village level.) Because he occupied these two positions in the district political system, his informal influence was formidable, subject only to other centers of political power that might exist in the district.

[16] See discussions in Henry Bienen, *Tanzania: Party Transformation and Economic Development* (Princeton, N.J., 1967), pp. 119 ff, William Tordoff, *Government and Politics in Tanzania* (Nairobi, 1967), pp. 99 ff, and Stanley Dryden, *Local Administration in Tanzania* (Nairobi, 1968), pp. 24 ff.

[17] Bienen, *Tanzania,* p. 138.

Chart 1. Political organization: From region to district.

Government positions	Party positions

REGION
(17 in nation)

Regional Commissioner *   = †   Regional Secretary *
                                Regional Chairman
Regional Administrative Secretary
                                Regional Executive Secretary

Regional Development Committee ‡
(Chaired by Regional Commissioner, members including technical officers in region and party officials.)

Regional Executive Committee
(Chaired by Regional Chairman with Regional Commissioner, members of Regional Working Committee, all District Chairmen, and District Secretaries. Other members noted in text.)

DISTRICT
(60 in country)

Area Commissioner   =   Area Secretary
                                 District Chairman

Area Administrative Secretary
District Executive Officer
                                 District Executive Secretary

District Council
(Chaired by District Chairman of TANU, composed of councilors from each ward, of some nominated members. Two districts—Mbozi and Mufindi—do not have councils.)

District Executive Committee
(Chaired by District Chairman of TANU, with Area Commissioner, 10 members elected by

Chart 1. Political organization (*continued*)

Government positions	Party positions
	annual TANU conference. Other members noted in text.)
District Development and Planning Committee Chaired by the Area Commissioner, with District Chairman of TANU, District Executive Officer, members of the finance committee of the district council, and the technical officers posted in the district.)	
	District Working Committee (Chaired by District Chairman of TANU, with Area Commissioner and four persons appointed by the chairman as members.)

Note: This chart attempts to organize in a simple manner a very complex organization. As there is considerable variation throughout the districts studied and the nation as a whole, the chart should be used as a general guide to the subnational political organization in Tanzania.

* Positions are listed in an order that *generally* reflects the standing in the hierarchy although, as explained in the text, this varies from one locale to another.

† When two positions are linked by an equal (=) sign the two positions are occupied simultaneously by the same individual.

‡ The institutions centered on the chart represent distinct fusions of party and government. Institutions distinctly inclined toward government or party are so positioned in this chart.

In Handeni District there was virtually no other center of influence or power, since the other institutions were relatively weak at the district-wide level. For any activity at the district level, the area commissioner was the key figure. In Tanga District, however, the relative influence of the area commissioner was less, as there were more centers of power with which he had to compete—the regional commissioner and the regional offices of the various ministries.

There are seventeen regions in Tanzania. Each of the regions has a regional headquarters, which is similar in composition to the district headquarters except that it is one level removed from the center of national power in Dar es Salaam rather than two steps away as is the case of the districts. Both districts studied here, Handeni and Tanga, were located in Tanga Region. The Tanga district headquarters were therefore in the same town as were the Tanga regional headquarters. This was not a unique situation since seventeen other district headquarters were also located in the regional headquarters towns. As is suggested here, the presence of the regional officers, both government and party, did affect the political process in the district.

In addition to regional officials in Tanga, the area commissioner had to share his power with more highly developed groups in that district, including workers' groups and tribal groups. Although the area commissioner was a powerful figure, his political influence was very much a product of these other centers of power. For example, during 1966 and 1967 the area commissioner of Tanga District complained that technical officers of the various ministries failed to attend meetings of the District Development and Planning Committee, of which they were members and which was chaired by him.[18]

There were other members of the area commissioner's office who tempered the role. In both Tanga and Handeni, the righthand man of the area commissioner was the area secretary, a civil service appointee from the Department of Regional Administration.[19] Ideally, the area secretary handled the administrative problems of the *boma* while the area commissioner was free to deal with more substantial issues. In the immediate post-independence years there

[18] Local Government Circular No. 20, February 28, 1963. Tanga District, Minutes of the District Development and Planning Committee 28 May 1966. See also *ibid.,* 12 July 1967 and 11 September 1967.

[19] Although the Ministry had been subjected to numerous reorganizations since independence, the Department of Regional Administration was in the Ministry of Regional Administration and Rural Development as of August 31, 1968. Other departments in this ministry were Rural Development, Local Government, Social Welfare, and Culture. *Standard,* August 31, 1968.

was considerable distrust between the civil servants and the area commissioners, especially if the Tanzanian civil servant had served in the colonial administration. In Handeni, one old-line civil servant serving as area secretary complained that he could not work with "these politicians" and subsequently retired.[20]

The district commissioner of police in the cases studied here, and particularly in Handeni, worked very closely with the area commissioner, although he might also be considered a technical officer (see below). The one and only source of legitimate coercive power was the police Field Force Unit from the district headquarters.

Invariably there was an "assistant to the area commissioner" in the *boma,* who was in fact the district head of the security police, the Central Intelligence Division (CID) of the Ministry of Home Affairs. While there was little concrete information about his role, it was general knowledge that the CID dealt with certain types of criminal activity and had a role in maintaining the security of the nation. There were rumors of a network of informers who worked with the CID officer and who reported on those who "talked against the government." In Handeni, the CID officer played an important role; in Tanga, a much less important role.

A final group in the area commissioner's office is the entourage known as messengers. Instituted by the British administration, the messengers did the odd jobs in the office—running errands, sweeping the floors, and performing the ritual of preparing the morning and afternoon tea. After independence, messengers had the same duties, but they might be even more important than they were in colonial days. Observation of the messengers at work revealed that they were important mediators between the area commissioner and the area secretary and the public at large. They served as gatekeepers controlling access to the area commissioner.[21]

[20] Based on my conversations with the officer involved.
[21] For a discussion of the concept of gatekeeper exemplified so vividly by the messenger, see Easton, *A Systems Analysis,* pp. 87 ff.

In his political role, the area commissioner wielded great power in his ability to help individual citizens. In a society where material benefits and opportunity for advancement were limited and where the career alternatives to involvement in the government were virtually nil, his influence was tremendously important. His letter was the passport to government jobs and some educational opportunities.

The other facet of his political role was his coercive power. His most important legal power was the right to hold someone in detention for up to forty-eight hours without charges. Either he or the regional commissioner could order this arrest, and, while unpublicized, it has been used in certain cases in an attempt to get people to carry out their development tasks properly.[22] While the area commissioner wielded considerable power in the district political system relative to every other source of power, his ability to effect change through the use of this power was limited indeed.

The political power of the area commissioner depended upon a mix of his distribution of personal favors, his selective use of very limited coercive powers, and his political persuasion. Of these three, his ability to direct change in the district was dependent primarily upon the last. This political persuasion, central to the effort to promote rural development, is the principal concern of this analysis.

During colonial days, the role of the district commissioner was primarily administrative, and at independence the area commis-

---

[22] Ministry of Local Government, Ref. No. PA 15/021, 10 March 1964; LG Circular 17/64, "The Administration and Control of Lock-ups," Item 5 (ii): "When any person has been arrested by order of a Regional or Area Commissioner under section 2 or 3 of Act 49 of 1963, he may be detained in a lock-up without a warrant being issued. He *must* be taken before a *District* Magistrate as soon as practicable. If within 48 hours he has not been brought before a *District* Magistrate, then he *must* be released." This power was used in Handeni District in December 1967 in an attempt to get settlers on a village settlement to weed their sisal fields. Emphasis is in the original.

sioner inherited all the administrative duties of his predecessor. While he was responsible for law and order and supervising government activity in his district, in recent years there has been an increasing emphasis on his responsibility to stimulate rural development.

As he became more responsible for development, his political and administrative roles have tended to merge. From this merging, a third role, that of policy making, has developed. It would be underestimating the independence of individual British colonial officers in the field to suggest that the colonial district commissioner did not formulate policy for his district.[23] The district commissioners obviously did so, as the district records show. It is likely, however, that the merger of the political and administrative roles for the purpose of rapid change led to more district-level policy making by the area commissioner than was practiced by his predecessor. Much of this policy was never revealed in national plans and probably not noted at the central offices in Dar es Salaam. The personal whims of the area commissioner, however, could shape quite clearly the direction of development efforts in the district. Often the policy that emerged was in conflict with the advice of the technical officers assigned to the district; of this more will be noted later.

District Officers: Technicians

The district commissioner's "team" was the name given to the district representatives of central government ministries under the British colonial government. However, the word "team" suggests a spirit of collaboration between the district officers and the area commissioner that is not always the case today. The core of the team for any district includes the district agriculture officer, the

[23] See, for example, the excellent study by J. Gus Liebenow, *Colonial Rule and Political Development in Tanzania: The Case of the Makonde* (Evanston, 1971).

education officer, the rural development officer, the cooperative officer, and the health officer, and each has a staff of varying sizes in his office.

Ideally, the area commissioner would consult with these men, plan the development of the district, and then work through them to bring about the desired development. In fact, this was only partially the case. Often the officers were very briefly posted in a district; before they could become acquainted with the programs of the area, they were transferred to another post. In a discussion with one district officer, I soon discovered that I knew more about the district than he did. This officer had served in the district for only two months, and he would be leaving for another assignment the following week. Unfortunately some officers spent most of their time in the relative comfort of the *boma* office and were out of touch with the rural areas.

The most important technical posts were those of agriculture and community development, and it would appear that these were often the most adequately staffed. Both of these offices were very much involved in the political processes of the district. The emphasis upon rural development placed these two officers in a key position vis-à-vis the political system. While their role was theoretically an advisory one, today they have become political activists in Tanga and Handeni districts. One district officer, when asked of his advisory role, answered that his work was supposed to be advisory "but in fact, we have to use force." [24] Another officer remarked that he organized meetings for discussing why the villagers should participate in block farms, but he added that after the meetings he had to use force. When I asked him to explain what he meant by force, he said that some of the opponents to the scheme were "taken away." The district agriculture and rural development officers, then, were very closely associated with the office of the area commissioner and the threat of coercion that he can use to stimulate change in the district.

[24] Interview, January 5, 1968.

The area commissioner did not seem to coordinate his efforts very effectively with the offices of the other technical officers. He scheduled political seminars that interfered with their technical responsibilities, and he tended to initiate programs without consulting them for technical advice.

District Council

The institution that most formally represented the various village communities in the district political system was the district council. Even in the context of Tanzania's short period of independence, the district council in its present form was a relatively new institution. The concept of a representative council through which the views of the people could be voiced was certainly not unknown during the precolonial period, as President Nyerere has often emphasized. He noted, for example, in his essay "The African and Democracy," that "the traditional African society, whether it had a chief or not and many . . . did not, was a society of equals and it conducted its business through discussion." Nyerere then called attention to one scholar's contention that the elders sit under a tree and "talk until they agree." [25] The British seized upon the tradition of representative councils and attempted through the policy of indirect rule to institute broadly representative, if not popularly elected, councils in Tanganyika.

The major innovation that they sought—and it was a major one —was to expand the area and the number of peoples under a particular council.[26] This expansion, in reality a nation-building process, took place during the 1950's. In the early part of that decade, the British particularly encouraged advisory councils for the Native Authorities, the colonial government's principal agents under

[25] Julius K. Nyerere, *Freedom and Unity: A Selection of Writings and Speeches 1952–1965* (Dar es Salaam, 1966), p. 103.
[26] See A. L. Le Maitre, "Memorandum on the Setting up of District Councils," December 1957, National Archives (304/C7/4).

THE DISTRICT *BOMA* 123

its policy of indirect rule.²⁷ The British district commissioner of Tanga District noted in their regard:

The primary object of Advisory Councils to the Native Authorities is to give every one an opportunity of having their say in local Government either personally or through their representatives. It is the intention of Government that local Government should not be only the work of the Native Authorities and the employees of the Native Treasury, but that local Government should be a communal effort in which the Native Authority is the leader and the executive head.²⁸

Late in 1950 the colonial administration initiated the formation of popularly elected district councils. Due to the emerging national movement and its opposition to the district councils in the form that the colonial administration proposed, there was little progress in their formation.²⁹

As created in 1962, the district councils were expected to become centers for democratic representation of localities' views at the district level and to provide the institutional base from which local government would grow.³⁰ As constituted, the authority of the council was broad, always subject, however, to the final approval of the central government minister under whose portfolio the affairs of local government might fall. The council could issue bylaws covering everything from the hours during which alcoholic beverages might be consumed in the district to the number of acres each family must have planted in cassava and the standards that

²⁷ For a discussion of this development in West Africa, see Martin Kilson, "Grass-roots Politics in Africa: Local Government in Sierra Leone," *Political Studies*, XII (February 1964), 47–66.

²⁸ Tanga District, From the District Commissioner, 23 December 1952, Ref. 1124/304: National Archives 304/45/1124.

²⁹ Under the tutelage of the colonial administration, the councils were to have reserved seats for the major racial minorities. The nationalist leaders opposed the councils because of this discrimination against the African majorities. See Dryden, *Local Administration*, p. 128.

³⁰ Ministry of Local Government, "Local Government Report 1963" (Dar es Salaam, mimeographed, 1963).

must be upheld in the district markets. It was authorized to provide a wide range of social services and could, at the time this research was conducted, lay and provide for the collection of local taxes to pay for these services.[31] Subsequently, however, the district council's power to lay and collect taxes was drastically curtailed by the central government decision to deny their power to collect both the head tax, or local rate, and the tax on agricultural products.[32]

TANU, the single political party in Tanzania, controls the nomination and election of district councilors to represent a ward, a geographical area in the district. The number of wards in a district was dependent upon both population and the geographical area covered. The nature of party control over the candidates for district council was similar to that over candidates for election to the national legislature.[33] A nomination was made by a petition of support signed by twenty-five registered voters, not necessarily party members. All such nominations were then presented to the annual conference of TANU for the ward concerned. This conference voted on the names, and the list of names together with the number of votes cast for each candidate was then submitted to the district executive committee of TANU, which selected two of the names for the election. The first time this electoral procedure was implemented, in October 1966, an investigation of a nonrandom sample of just over one-half of the districts found that the district executive committees intervened in approximately 4 per cent of the wards' nominations.[34] Usually, the district executive committee selected the two candidates who received the highest number of votes from the Branch Conference.

[31] Dryden, *Local Administration*, p. 128.   [32] *Standard,* June 20, 1969.
[33] See United Republic of Tanzania, *Report of the Presidential Commission on the Establishment of a Democratic One Party State* (Dar es Salaam, 1965).
[34] Simon Hardwick, "Local Government Elections in a One-Party State," *Journal of Administration Overseas,* VIII (April 1969), 129.

Ultimately, the choice of the district executive committee was subject to the approval of the TANU Central Committee.[35] In the same sample of councils for the 1966 elections the Central Committee intervened in the nominations of only 11 out of 736 wards, or in just over 1 per cent of the wards considered in the sample.[36] During the by-elections of 1968, the Central Committee exercised its veto power over roughly 8 per cent of the candidates nominated from the district level.[37] While the center could exercise control over the candidates who appear for local council seats, it used this power with considerable restraint. At any rate, the citizens of the ward were finally presented with a choice between two candidates who had the endorsement of the party; the voters elected one of these to represent their ward on the district council.[38]

In addition to the elected members of the councils, up to ten members might be nominated to each council by the President of the Republic, by authority he has had since 1966. These nominated members might be civil servants, members of the district executive committee of TANU, or other notables whom the Presi-

[35] Consider Bienen, *Tanzania,* p. 189.

[36] Hardwick, "Local Government Elections," p. 129.

[37] This calculation is unofficial and is based on figures drawn from *The Standard,* August 24, 1968, and subsequent issues. With 22 unopposed candidates, and with candidates for 48 other seats assuming at least two candidates chosen by the district executive committee for each seat, the total number of names considered by the central committee would be 118. Among these nominated candidates, 10 names were not approved by the central committee, constituting roughly 8 per cent of those candidates considered. *Standard,* August 28, 1968.

[38] See *Proposals of the Tanzania Government on Local Government Councils:* Government Paper No. 1–1966 (Dar es Salaam: The Government Printer, 1966), p. 3. Also see Hardwick, "Local Government Elections." Prior to the establishment of this arrangement for electing the councilors in 1966, they had been chosen by informal elections under the Local Government Election (Rural Areas) Act, no. 3 of 1962, were never held because of the delay and difficulty in rearranging general election polling districts to coincide with district council wards and the completion of a common register. See Tordoff, *Government and Politics,* pp. 113 ff.

dent, after consultation with district leaders, might see as beneficial to the council.[39] Handeni District, for unexplained reasons, had no nominated members on the council.[40] The more important technical officers from the central government and the district executive officer of the party did, however, sit in on the meetings from time to time.

The chairman of the district TANU organization automatically became the chairman of the district council. He was thus first a party official and second the chairman of the council. The most important influence on council affairs was exercised either by the chairman or by the civil servant who was directly responsible for the administrative affairs of the council, the district executive officer. The district executive officer (DEO) was appointed by the Local Government Service Commission, a national body, and was assisted in his duties by the treasurer of the council, who was also appointed by the Local Government Service Commission.[41] In the immediate office of the council were found the usual coterie of clerks and messengers, all of whom were local people who for various reasons had been given the favor of a government appointment.

The district executive officer was a key figure in the functioning of the district council. He could completely dictate the affairs of the council or he could operate as the executive assistant to the council chairman. In the two districts studied here, the two extremes were found. In Handeni District, the DEO virtually dictated

[39] See the discussion in Hardwick, "Local Government Elections," p. 131.

[40] In response to my questioning, the staff of the Handeni council responded that there were no nominated members, and the list of councilors bore no such names. In contrast, the Tanga list of councilors prominently displayed the nominated members under the heading, "Nominated Members." This relative imprecision of organization is an indication of the contrasting levels of institutionalization of the council in the two districts.

[41] Ministry of Local Government, LG Circular 15/1963, "The Local Government Service Commission Regulations."

the council's every move. If, for example, during council meetings, the discussion strayed to the concerns of the councilors, he promptly returned their attention to the agenda he had prepared. His mastery of the meeting was complete, and the councilors had little chance for debate upon what they had in mind.

In Tanga two DEO's were in office while this field work was conducted. Both appeared efficient as executive officers but did not dictate the proceedings of the meeting. In fact, one of them did not even attend the council's meeting. It was clear that the contrasting roles of the DEO's in the two districts was due in part to the differing levels of institutionalization achieved by the councils in the two districts. Institutionalization here refers to the process by which organizations and procedures acquire value and stability. The level of institutionalization can be determined by the adaptability, complexity, autonomy, and coherence of its organizations and procedures.[42] The last three of these conditions were markedly more apparent in the Tanga District council than in the Handeni council.

The relative influence of the DEO in the district council was also related to the political sophistication of the councilors and to the personality of the chairman of the council. In Handeni, the chairman definitely acquiesced to the leadership of the DEO. In Tanga, this was not the case, for the chairman was himself a very forceful man.

The day-to-day affairs of the council were directed by the civil servants or bureaucratic employees of the council headed by the DEO. While the chairman of the council was also available to participate in the business of the council, his participation tended to be with political problems rather than with the administration of the council's affairs. He was concerned, for example, with why

[42] Institutionalization is used here in the sense suggested by Samuel P. Huntington, *Political Order in Changing Societies* (New Haven, 1968), p. 12.

a ward was not participating in a nation-building project or with why a village was hostile to the advice of the agricultural assistant who worked there.

As under the British system of local government, the work of the council was, in theory, to be carried out by committees of the council. Again in the cases studied here, the district executive officer was primarily responsible in Handeni, while in Tanga District the executive officer and the chairman of the council shared the responsibility for the work of the council and the committee. The membership of the various committees that ostensibly carried on the council's work was determined by the DEO and the chairman in both districts. In Tanga, by council decision, the memberships of the committees then chose their chairmen who, in turn, constituted the most important finance committee.[43]

Theoretically, the district council was to meet at least four times a year. In both Tanga and Handeni, it did not meet this often and was subject to sudden and unexplained postponements. In session, the council was a very inefficient body and the councilors themselves were relatively uninformed about district affairs.

Certainly, the district council had not in practice developed into the representative institution of local government that its creators, both colonial and independent, envisaged. Its governing role has been steadily deteriorating since the council's inception in 1962. The erosion of tentative governmental responsibilities was due not only to the much-discussed paucity of experienced personnel in the council,[44] but also to the central government's steady absorption of the most important duties of the council. This increased centralization of governmental responsibilities was due only in part to the inefficiency and incompetence of the local councils. It was also a result of the virtually inevitable clash between the drive for integration and centrally determined development objectives and

[43] Tanga District Council, General Meeting, Minutes 29 September 1967.
[44] See Tordoff, *Government*, p. 116, and Dryden, *Local Administration*, pp. 113 ff.

the persistence of local desires for participation and representation in decisions that affected the localities. Norman Miller's study of local politics in Tabora District of Tanzania found the attitude of central government officials summed up quite well in the district executive officer's comment that "we try to discourage them from meeting." [45]

The representative role of the council has been further eroded from below by the profusion of development committees on the village, the ward, the division, and, finally, on the district levels.[46] These committees were composed of representatives of party and government and, while their primary purpose was promoting and directing development projects, they also were directly involved in performing other governmental and representative functions. The representative role of the district council has been further dissipated by the parallel institution of the District Development and Planning Committee, the district-level equivalent of the development committees at the subdistrict levels.

Thus the district council, which at first I viewed as the most important institution for representing the locality interest in the district and national political system, was functioning at the time this field work was completed in a rather attenuated fashion. The councilors were seen, and saw themselves, as media for communication of policy decisions to the countryside. Theoretically they could function as an important means for presenting to district officials the reactions of the rural areas to government policies, but in reality the party organization served this function much better. Thus the future of the district council in Tanzania was very much in doubt. The minister of finance, during the presentation of the budget speech for 1970, announced: "The precise functions of the District Councils during the next two years will be the sub-

[45] District Executive Officer, Tabora District, quoted in Norman N. Miller, "Village Leadership and Modernization in Tanzania: Rural Politics among the Nyamwezi People of Tabora Region" (Ph.D. dissertation, Department of Government, Indiana University, 1966), p. 186.

[46] For a discussion of these committees, see Chapter V and VI.

ject of careful examination. . . . Pending the outcome of such deliberations, Government has . . . decided that with effect from . . . 20th June, 1969, District Councils will cease to levy produce cess."[47]

In this same speech, the minister announced that as of January 1, 1970, district councils would no longer collect local head taxes.

A consideration of the history of the district council in Tanzania suggests that the present tenuous existence of the council may be a reflection of the artificial base of the district as a unit of representation and government in independent Tanzania. The effort of the central government to penetrate and activate the rural areas to the tasks of national development suggests that the district unit may have been an effective base for colonial rule and administration but that it is less effective as a unit for national self-government and development. The technical administrative officers may still reside in the colonial edifice of the district headquarters but the activation of energies for national development must take place in the countless political subsystems at the subdistrict level. The effort to involve the peasant in the process of development and governing has given renewed recognition to traditional institutions of local government and representation and has necessitated the

[47] *Standard*, June 20, 1969. The cess was a tax on produce collected through the marketing procedure. The Kenya Second Five Year Development Plan entailed the transferring of decision-making authority from the district councils to the central government. In appraising this change in the role of the district council, Colin Leys has suggested that the political conflict over local issues will not disappear, "just because the decisions now lie in different hands, but will be brought to bear on the central government . . . instead of on council officers and councillors. The councils acted as a buffer between the people and the central bureaucracy" (Leys, "Kenya's Second Development Plan: Political and Administrative Aspects," *East Africa Journal*, VII (March 1970), 10. Author's Note: In January 1972, President Nyerere announced the modification of the district councils into district development councils together with a further shift of authority to central government teams which were to operate with greater freedom at the district level but with more responsibility to the locality. *Standard*, January 28, 1972. The impact of this decision upon the district council as an institution and the political systems in general is unclear.

creation of new or restoration of old institutions at the more local levels of society.[48]

During the time this study was conducted, the district council was an institution very much in the control of the central political system. This control extended over its meetings, its finances, and its agendas. It is revealing to note that while the councilors accepted the essentially administrative role for the council, they conceived of a more active representative role for themselves. It is questionable whether the councils could have effectively engaged in making policy for the districts and in implementing it themselves. On the other hand, they have never tried to do so. Certainly the kernel of locality interest expressed by the councilors may explain why central agents controlled council activities so completely. It also explains, one might surmise, why the councils met so infrequently. Undoubtedly, national plans for development demanded central control. They also, however, demanded local acceptance and participation. The degree of central control exercised over the district councils almost certainly stifled any existing local initiative.

The Political Party: Instrument of Fusion

The ubiquitous thread of the district organization of TANU, the national political party, inextricably linked the district institutions. It was often impossible to determine where party organiza-

---

[48] The most prominent examples of these institutions of representation and government were village- and ward-level development committees that were being promoted at the more local levels of Tanzanian society; these will be considered in Chapter VI. In many cases these committees were essentially a formalization of councils that already existed and that could be referred to as traditional. Consider the following: Julius K. Nyerere, "Freedom and Development," *Standard*, October 18, 1968, Julius K. Nyerere, "To Stop Shirkers: President's Measures," *ibid.*, October 18, 1968, and Clyde R. Ingle, "Compulsion and Rural Development in Tanzania," A Paper Delivered at the Joint Annual Meeting of the African Studies Association (USA) and the Committee on African Studies, Montreal, Canada, October 15–18, 1969.

tion and activities ended and where those of the state began. This fusion of party and state was best symbolized in the person of the area commissioner, who was both the chief representative of the central government in the district and the secretary of the district party organization. This fusion of party and state was a result of the intentional decision to establish a single party system and to allow, indeed, encourage, civil servants to participate in party affairs.[49] While the political party is the principal institution integrating village and state in Tanzania, there was a discernible gap in the district party organization between village and nation. This gap was best shown through an analysis of two distinct segments in the district party organization—the party bureaucracy and the elected locals.

The Party Bureaucracy

The accountability of the district party bureaucracy was divided; officials were responsible, on the one hand, to the area commissioner in his role of secretary of the district party organization and, on the other, to the district chairman of TANU, who was elected by locals. The party bureaucracies varied in size, but all were headed by the district executive secretary, who was appointed by the national party bureaucracy. The responsibilities of the district executive secretary for the party were similar to those performed by the area secretary for the area commissioner's office and the district executive officer for the district council. He was primarily the party executive officer, responsible for the administrative matters of the district party organization. In most cases, and in those studied here, he was not a local man. He might be assisted in his immediate district party office by a centrally appointed treasurer. Below him in the district party bureaucracy were the branch secretaries. The branch was the major unit of party organi-

---

[49] See President Nyerere's article, "Democracy and the Party System" in Nyerere, *Freedom and Unity;* also see Lionel Cliffe (ed.), *One-Party Democracy* (Nairobi, 1967), p. 14.

zation prior to independence. Subsequently, the branch tended to become coterminous with the governmental and political units known as the wards or the divisions. In the merging of party and government after independence, the party branch was subsumed into either the ward or the division where the party organization was created along with and overlapping the government organization. There were exceptions, however; for example, TANU branches might exist in an industry or on an estate. In Handeni and Tanga, I often heard more references to the ward and divisional organizations of TANU than to the branch organizations. The branch secretary's primary function was to collect TANU dues for the branch and to look after matters of party organization. His major concern was to keep up and increase the membership of the party in the branch. Generally, once each month he reported to the district office.

In the district party bureaucracy the executive secretary was the key man. Having, in most cases, attended party seminars given by the TANU ideological arm, Kivukoni College, in Dar es Salaam, he was usually responsible for directing such seminars for party subordinates in the district. The full extent of his duties was likely to be dependent upon his personality and ability and the demands made upon him by the area commissioner and by the district chairman of TANU. Generally, as was the case in Handeni and Tanga, the office of the executive secretary of TANU was in the same building as the office of the chairman of the party. At the same time, however, the executive secretary was very much at the beck and call of the area commissioner.

Throughout the nation there was little distinction in the districts between the party bureaucracy and formal party leadership. The result was that from time to time the district executive secretary might play a leading role in the affairs of the district. For example, the executive secretary of Handeni played a very active role in the affairs of the Handeni District Council, of which he was a co-opted member. In one particular case, he was very much involved in swaying the elected council members to accept a decision of the party and government hierarchy that the elected members were plainly not predisposed to accept. In Tanga, on the other hand, the executive secretary of TANU stayed completely out of the meetings of the district council. The chairman of this particular council needed no assistance from anyone in running the affairs of the council, and certainly not the meetings of the council.

In 1968 high national party officials attempted to separate the roles of party bureaucrats and party elected leaders. Second Vice President Kawawa in an address to all district executive secretaries emphasized this distinction. It was reported that he "told them that their duties to TANU were great as they were the party's civil servants because it was not enough to run the party with only politicians, we have got to have people who will put our policies into action." Kawawa explained that "TANU offices should be better informed about the people's difficulties than Government offices because TANU was for the people and as such it must know their problems and also try to solve them." [50]

The party involvement in the affairs of the district system was so great that it is difficult to see how the distinction between party leaders and government leaders and between party civil servants and government civil servants can really be maintained.

The Elected Locals

Local representation in the district party organization emanated from the district annual conference of TANU. This conference was composed of two delegates elected by each branch in the district, all branch chairmen, all branch secretaries, and most of the other party and government officials from the district. Ordinarily there was also a branch annual conference that met once

[50] *Standard,* August 15, 1968. Also see P. Msekwa, "Party Civil Service," *Mbioni* (Monthly Journal of Kivukoni College), IV (November-December 1967), 70–73.

each year, and among its general duties was that of electing ten members to the district executive committee. This committee was "responsible for the carrying out of the decisions of the national Conference, the National Executive Committee and the Regional Conference as far as that District is concerned." [51] Ordinarily, the district executive committee met once every three months.

Henry Bienen has contended that the district executive committee was the most active and important of TANU committees outside the nation's capital,[52] because the central government simply did not have enough trained personnel to post officers in all of the district offices: "This is a crucial point for understanding TANU's role in Tanganyika: because of the weakness of the state apparatus, it has fallen to TANU organizations to handle many tasks which, in developed countries (including the Soviet Union), are considered government rather than party concerns." [53]

In addition to the ten elected members to the district executive committee, there were other locals, elected through other sources, who were, in this writer's view, more important than the elected members. They included the district chairman, elected for a two-year term by the district annual conference; the district executive secretary; delegates from affiliate organizations, which included the Union of Tanzania Women (UWT), the National Union of Tanganyika Workers (NUTA), and the Tanganyika African Parents' Association (TAPA); the members of the regional committee resident in the district; and four members of the district working committee appointed by the district chairman.[54]

In contrast to Bienen's view, in Tanga and Handeni the district executive committee was not the most important TANU committee outside the center. Rather, the district working committee was the most important district unit of the organization. The

[51] The Constitution of TANU, found in Tordoff, *Government*, p. 241.
[52] Bienen, *Tanzania*, p. 98.   [53] *Ibid.*
[54] The Constitution. For brief discussions of the affiliate organizations see Tordoff, *Government*, pp. 79–86.

TANU constitution stipulates that "up to four persons *appointed by the Chairman*" (emphasis is mine) shall join the chairman and the district executive secretary, and the area commissioner, in composing the district working committee, which "shall be the organ concerned with the supervision of the day to day administration of the affairs of the Party in the District." The constitution further stipulates that the working committee shall meet at least once every two weeks. In fact, the working committee usually meets much more often than that. By the very demands of its duties the working committee must be composed of people who live close to the *boma*, simply so that days do not pass before the committee can meet. Thus the committee was basically a *boma*-based group. It was likely to be primarily local in composition with at least the local party regulars and the elders represented. In effect, therefore, party decision and district policy were likely to be very much *boma* centered. Directives from Dar es Salaam were received, of course, but the interpretation and implementation came from the *boma*. While the orientation of district policy was the *boma*, the makeup of the working committee—five locals and two representatives of the central party organization—suggests that the local influence on district policy matters could be great. In the two cases studied here, the personality of the district chairman seemed to be a crucial factor determining the degree to which locals were prominent in directing district policy.

Undoubtedly the most influential local in the district political system was the chairman of the district party organization, who was also chairman of the district executive committee and chairman of the district council. The chairman's actual ability to direct the affairs of the government in the district depends on his power relationship vis-à-vis the power of his main political competitor, the area commissioner. It was very difficult to decipher the realities of the relationship between these two men, and in the two cases studied here the factors that determined the relationship seemed to be unique.

Obviously, the "boss" of Handeni District was the area commissioner. He consulted the chairman and took him on most important trips throughout the district, but as far as I could tell, the chairman had never in any way come into conflict with the decisions of the area commissioner. In Tanga, the chairman was a very impressive leader in his own right who appeared not to have to consult with the area commissioner before making his decisions. The very nature of the two districts was of considerable importance here. In Handeni, for example, if the chairman wanted transportation from one village to another he had to depend upon the means provided by the *boma*. In Tanga, on the other hand, there were numerous means of transportation available, including private automobiles. The chairman in Tanga was not totally dependent upon the whims of the district office under the direction of the area commissioner. In addition, the regional commissioner, the immediate superior to the area commissioner, was readily accessible to the chairman along with other regional officials. Handeni was always short of finances and totally dependent upon the assistance of the center; Tanga, on the other hand, while its financial condition was troubled by the slump in sisal prices, still had a sizable independent source of funds that allowed the district to be more independent from the center, and thus the center's officers.

One personal experience will illustrate the relationship between these two men in Tanga. When I asked the area secretary for permission to attend a committee meeting scheduled for the following day, he replied that since the area commissioner was out of town, there would be no meeting. Later in the day the district chairman of TANU suggested that I come to the meeting the next day. When I told him that the area commissioner's office had announced that the meeting would be postponed, he replied, "Nonsense!" picked up the telephone and ordered the meeting be held as planned. The meeting took place the next day, with all of us, including the area secretary, present. This type of authoritative decision from the district chairman would never have occurred in Handeni.

In summary, the district party chairman was the most important local party official, and the characteristics of the district system itself largely dictated the ability of the locality spokesman to exercise a greater or lesser degree of authority in the district completely independent of any personal characteristics.

District Development and Planning Committee

While the party is the thread that sews together the district political system, there has been a need for some formal institution through which the various elements of the party and government could coordinate their efforts to promote development. The institution that has emerged was originally known as the District Development Committee (DDC) and is now the District Development and Planning Committee; some observers call it the most important institution in the district.[55]

While formally established in 1963 as a committee in the committee system of the district council, the DDC was preceded by, if not patterned after, the informal British colonial institution, the "district team." The East African Royal Commission Report described the team concept as follows:

There are two main official agencies for improving rural living conditions, including better land use. These are the provincial and district teams and the local government bodies. It is now common practice [1955] in East Africa for the central governments to work through teams at provincial and district levels. The typical arrangement is for the district commissioner to be chairman of the district team and for

[55] See Tordoff, *Government,* pp. 118 ff; Dryden, *Local Administration,* pp. 47 ff, and Bienen, *Tanzania,* pp. 322 ff. For a view of the dubious worth of the DDC that coincides closely with my own, see R. G. Penner, "Financing Local Government in Tanzania," unpublished manuscript, July 1970. I am grateful to Professor Penner for providing me a copy of this extremely useful work prior to its publication as *Financing Local Government in Tanzania* (Nairobi, 1970). For a study of the similar institution in neighboring Malawi, see R. A. Miller, "District Development Committees in Malawi," *Journal of Administration Overseas,* IX (April 1970), 129–143.

all the district heads of departments to be members as well as representatives of the public of all races. Often members of local government bodies are also members of the team, and thus liaison is maintained between the two principal agencies for development.[56]

The district team concept persisted after independence. Informal committees emerged in an effort to bring some coordination and order to the self-help projects initiated after independence. The government order formalizing and integrating the committees in 1963 aimed at providing the institutional framework through which the development works initiated by the various governmental arms from local councils, to party, to various agencies of the central government, might receive some coordination and direction at the district level.[57]

The government hoped thereby to avoid duplication of effort and waste and at the same time to guide the developmental energies of the localities into realistic and productive channels. The order establishing the DDC noted:

> The position at present is that there are in each district two distinct bodies; i.e. the District Council and the District Development Committee, both engaged in the same work of development and both being advised in the preparation of development plans by the same department filled officers. This set-up has created a duplication of efforts and in many cases, has resulted in uncoordinated development in the districts and uneconomic expenditure of manpower and money.[58]

The membership of the DDC included the area commissioners, the members of the finance committee of the district council, all the departmental technical officers in the district, the chairman of TANU, who in most cases was also a member of the finance committee of the council, and the district executive officer. In Tanga, but not in Handeni at the time of writing, the DDP also included

[56] *East African Royal Commission Report 1953–1955* (Cmd. 9475), (London: H.M.S.O., 1955), p. 371.
[57] See Bienen, *Tanzania*, p. 322.
[58] Ministry of Local Government, LG Circular 20/63, 28 February 1963.

representatives from the subdistrict levels and the divisional executive officers.[59]

The area commissioner chaired the committee; his principal duty was to review and assess, with the technical officers' advice, the development plans of the village-level development committees throughout the district. The committee would then "coordinate and arrange priorities of all these proposals received and form a development master plan for the district." [60]

The order establishing the DDC concluded:

It will be necessary for the main District Development Committee to meet often, say once a month, in order to evaluate the work which is being carried out and to review generally the progress of the plans which are being executed. Except on policy matters the main District Development Committee will be the Executive Committee of the Council for all development work in the district.[61]

By 1967 the name of the DDC was changed to District Development and Planning Committee (DDPC). In Tanga and Handeni during the time of this study, the DDPC was no longer meeting each month; rather it met approximately four times a year. The meetings themselves were rambling affairs, and while few decisions were made in the meetings they appeared to serve a very important communication function not only between the government officers and the councilors who participated, but also between the officers themselves. Others have pointed out the lack of contact, formal and otherwise, that seemed to exist between the government civil servants even when they were posted in the same district and lived in the same small town.[62]

Interestingly enough in one of the two meetings of the DDPC that I attended in Handeni, the area commissioner and the district

[59] Tanga District Development and Planning Committee, Minutes 5 May 1967, Appendix A, "Address of the Chairman."
[60] *Ibid.* [61] *Ibid.*
[62] See Miller, "Village Leadership," and Georgulas, "Structure and Communication."

chairman never showed up at all. In their absence, the district executive officer of the district council took over the meeting and ran it with an iron hand. He was obviously very influential and, one began to suspect, more decisive in the affairs of the council than any other man in the district.[63]

During the meetings the councilors who were present did express their dissatisfaction with certain aspects of the district policy, including a complaint about inadequate marketing procedures of the cooperative society and a request that a new well be included in the district plan for a councilor's village. During the course of the meeting lasting from 10:00 A.M. till 4:30 P.M., the coop officer defended himself to no one's satisfaction, but it appeared that the well assignment would be changed.

The Tanga meeting of the DDPC was notably less oriented to development projects and more directed to the problems of governing. The area commissioner did not appear for this one either. The discussion centered around such items as what to do with the unemployed who kept roaming into Tanga city. Another prominent question was whether or not a section of forest preserve should be opened for the people. Here the forest officer was very much on the defensive, with the general sympathy of the members of the committee. They were all obviously a bit concerned, however, that politics might overrule their "technical" opinions. In the Tanga meeting when the question of planning new development projects for the next year was broached, the general spoken opinion was that all projects started the year before should be completed before any new ones were started.

While the DDPC had not succeeded in spurring development on the village level, it is probably accurate to conclude that it did have a useful communication function to perform in the district political system. This function was not insignificant, because it was obvious in the meetings which I attended that much of what was revealed

[63] For a similar view of the district executive officer see Penner, *Financing Local Government*, ch. 2.

was unknown by the participants. This was true for government officer and district councilor alike. The DDPC then had a positive contribution to make to the integration of the district political system at the *boma* level. How effective it may be in linking the *boma* to the villages is in question.

Summary

This assessment of the district political system shows the heavy influence of the central government. The representatives of the center include all the technical district officers, the area commissioner, who also was the appointed secretary of the district party organization and the top-level bureaucratic arm of the party in the district. In addition, while the district council was the foremost representative of the localities in the district system, it was a weak body, and even the executive officer and treasurer of the council were appointed from the center. In the districts studied, the district executive officer was a powerful man in the system, while the treasurer was not; this was particularly true in Handeni.[64]

The chairman of TANU was the principal representative of the localities in the district political system. The district executive committee of the party is local in origin and orientation, but the direction of the district political system was charted primarily by the area commissioner and the technical officers, and while the locals may grumble and advise, they usually had little impact on the decisions that affected the destiny of the district.

To establish that the primary influence in the district political system was central in origin and orientation is not, however, to say that the district system performed in accordance with the directives from Dar es Salaam. Because of the interrelationships between the various actors and institutions at the district level and below, a system of political action in the district was set up, that authorita-

[64] For collaboration on the power of the district executive officer, see Penner, *Financing Local Government,* ch. 2.

tively allocated values for the district independently from Dar es Salaam and that had a life of its own. However, the district system itself was very definitely limited in the extent to which it could impose district values at the subdistrict levels.

CHAPTER VI

From *Boma* to Village

In Tanzania the ultimate objective of the national political system is to reach into the villages and to activate the peasants for the development effort. The district headquarters is the farthest extension of national influence in the countryside, and the great majority of the population will be touched, if at all, only by agents of the district political system, who ideally may also be a part of the national political system. Most of this contact will come not through the *boma*-level activity, however, but through other political systems or protopolitical systems intermediate between *boma* and the individual. While the district is the most distinct of the political systems between the capital and the village, two other structures below the district are playing an increasingly important role in the development of Tanzania.

Division

The divisions in most cases had been based upon precolonial tribal chiefdoms, and the British had made them the base of native authorities and representative councils.[1] After independence the division retained its title but was reduced to a mere administrative unit in the district governmental system. The divisional councils were abolished, and village level councils, which existed solely on

[1] See Tordoff, *Government*, p. 9.

an informal basis, were to relate themselves directly to the popularly elected district council.

I studied the linkages between villages and the *boma* in one division in both Tanga and Handeni districts. In Tanga District, I conducted field work in Pongwe Division, which was both tribal and traditional in its geographical base and which during the early days

Chart 2. Political organization: From division to village

Government positions	Party positions

DIVISION
(Tribal in base, 350 in country)

Divisional Executive Officer *   = †   Divisional Secretary *
(This post was abolished in 1969 and replaced by post of *Divisional Executive Secretary* of party.)

                                           Divisional Chairman (often referred to as Branch chairman of party)

                                           Divisional Executive Secretary (often referred to as Branch Secretary)

Divisional Development Committee ‡
(Plans to organize were announced in 1967. Membership was to include Divisional Executive Officer, Divisional Chairman of TANU, district councilors from the division, and technical officers posted in the division.)

WARD
(Formerly only the constituency of the district councilor, the ward was being reconstituted in 1968 as formal unit of government next to village.)

Ward Executive Officer   = Ward Secretary
(formerly the Village Executive Officer)

                                           Ward Chairman

Ward Development Committee
(These were to replace and consolidate Village Development Committees starting in 1968. Members were to

Government positions	Party positions
include Ward Chairman, Ward Executive Officer, the district councilor and two cell leaders from each existing VDC in ward.)	
VILLAGE (These were not a formal unit after the reorganization of Village Development Committees into Ward Development Committee, 1968.)	
TEN-HOUSE CELL There was one cell leader for every ten-house grouping in the villages —both a government and party post.)	

Note: This chart attempts to organize in a simple manner a very complex organization. As there is considerable variation throughout the divisions studied and the nation as a whole, the chart should be used as a general guide to the subdistrict political organization in Tanzania.

* Positions are listed in an order that *generally* reflects the standing in the hierarchy although, as explained in the text, this varies from one locale to another.

† When two positions are linked by an equal ($=$) sign, the two positions are occupied simultaneously by the same individual.

‡ The institutions centered on the chart represent distinct fusions of party and government. Institutions distinctly inclined toward government or party are so positioned in this chart.

of British rule was known as Digo South. The population, primarily Digo, was 33,447 in 1967 with a total of 5,700 taxpayers.[2] With a total of 10,559 households in the division, it is possible to calculate that on the average 54 per cent of the households had at least one member paying the local tax in 1967. There were six subdivisions in Pongwe Division. These subdivisions, known as wards, were the constituencies of the district councilors. The division office of Pongwe was located at Pongwe minor settlement, about ten miles from Tanga on the Tanga-Korogwe road.

[2] Tanga, Provincial Commissioner, Tanga To District Officer, Tanga 12, January 1928, Ref. 9/31, National Archives (304/45/14B); *Preliminary Results;* and interviews with divisional executive officer, Pongwe, January 1968.

In Handeni District my field work was in Chanika Division. While traditionally one of nine chiefdoms in Handeni District, Chanika was known as a section of Handeni town. The total population of Chanika in 1967 was 31, 530, of whom 4,300 were taxpayers.[3] The percentage of households with at least one member paying local taxes was 64 per cent for the 6,753 households in the division. There were six wards in Chanika. The Chanika Division office was in Chanika-Handeni, contiguous to Handeni town, and was located forty-three miles from one extreme boundary of the division along the major highway linking Handeni to the rest of the country. Communication between villages in the division was at times virtually impossible, and while communication in Pongwe Division was difficult by Western standards, in comparison with that of Chanika, it was very good indeed.

Even though there were close ties between the district and division officers, there was still considerable independence of action at the division level. The district and the subdistrict organization in Tanzania had undergone rapid reformulation of structure and process—a characteristic of most developing systems. Thus any analysis of the division system is very much a description of what it was and what it was becoming.

The key actor in the division at the time this study was completed was the divisional executive officer. "Bwana Divisional," as he was known, had duties in the division similar to those of the area commissioner at the district level. The office was created in 1963, when the official position of chief was abolished by the repeal of the African Chiefs Ordinance, and it became necessary to appoint another official to take up the governing duties formerly performed by the chief in the division. The divisional, who exercised much the same powers formerly held by the chief, had the power to arrest for certain offenses, the power to require a person to appear before him, and the power to seize property that he be-

[3] *Preliminary Results* and interview with divisional executive officer, Chanika, February 27, 1968.

lieved to be stolen. The Magistrates Courts Act of 1963 made the divisional executive officer a justice of the peace and gave him limited judicial power. It did not authorize him to try cases.[4] In a number of publicized cases divisional executive officers have abused their power. As early as 1965 a government circular stated that divisionals were using their power incorrectly, particularly their arrest power.[5] President Nyerere himself, on the national radio, deplored a tragedy in which thirteen accused tax-defaulters died of suffocation in a divisional jail near Mwanza in 1968.[6]

A special committee of the district council appointed the divisional executive officers, subject to the approval of the regional commissioner, until mid-1968, when the Local Government Services Commission, a central civil service commission, took over that responsibility. This commission also appointed the district executive officer.

In the past, the nature of the divisional's appointment had made his political influence an important consideration in recruitment to this position. In the earlier years there was conflict between the divisionals and the party officials in some of the districts.[7] This problem declined in importance as the distinction between party and civil service was blurred. In addition, the divisionals came more and more to play a key role in TANU affairs in the divisions. In most cases they were appointed because of their party connections, and in 1967 the divisional executive officer was made the secretary of the TANU branch in the division.[8] Finally, in early 1969, the post of divisional executive officer was officially abolished

[4] Tordoff, *Government*, p. 116, Dryden, *Local Administration*, p. 118, and Ministry of Local Government, Ref. No. LG 12/01, 7 October 1964, LG Circular 39/64, "Responsibilities of Divisional Executive Officers to Arrest and Lock up People."

[5] Regional Administration, Ref. No. LB 14/025, 22 July 1965, LG Circular 37/1965.

[6] *Standard*, May 1, 1968.   [7] See Tordoff, *Government*, p. 116.

[8] Handeni District Council, Finance Committee, Minutes of the Combined Meeting of the Finance Committee and the Working Committee of TANU, 23 July 1967.

with the similar level position being titled divisional executive secretary.[9] The position then came totally under party control. The secretaries, who were to take up their positions when the Second Five-Year Development Plan came into operation on July 1, 1970, were to be assistants to the area commissioners. In the words of a national party official, the divisional executive secretaries were "to serve as guides to the people in the villages in nation-building" and "as a bridge between the people, the party, and the Government."[10] The secretary was not to have the power to detain people; instead this power was shifted to the ward executive officer, the next lower rung in the political and administrative hierarchy.

During 1968, the divisional executive officer was the chief administrative officer and the chief appointed political party officer in the division. He was assisted in his administrative duties by a number of village executive officers, usually one for each ward in the division. These men, consequently renamed ward executive officers in the reorganization of early 1969, were the chief administrative officers in the wards and were officially appointed by the district council leadership because of their political influence.[11] As a case in point, the finance committee of the Tanga District Council notes in its minutes of June 1967 the hiring of a village executive officer at the "advice of the Regional Commissioner who, in his travels found a vacancy for a VEO. He advised the District Executive Officer to hire this man who before had been carrying on the work of TANU in the area."[12]

While wearing both government and party hats in 1968, the

[9] *Standard,* January 11, 1969.   [10] *Ibid.*
[11] The appointment of divisional executive secretaries was to be in three phases. One hundred and two would take their posts on July 1, 1969, another group in June 1970, and, finally, the remaining posts, to total 350, would take up their positions in June 1971. *Standard,* January 11, 1969. It is unknown to what extent the former divisional executive officers simply shifted to the new post and to what extent new personnel were added. Furthermore, since my field research was terminated before this reorganization took place, the impact upon the divisions considered here is unknown.
[12] Tanga District Council, Finance Committee, Minutes, 6 June 1967.

divisional executive officer was assisted by the branch secretary of the party who performed functions in the division similar to those performed by the district executive secretary in the district. The branch secretary, a salaried official, functioned as a subordinate to the divisional executive officer and was in effect the executive officer of the party organization in the division. Thus the fusion of party and government at the divisional level had become complete, in fact, before the reorganization of 1969. While definitive conclusions are impossible, this reorganization appears to have replaced these two positions at the divisional level with one official, the divisional executive secretary, operating directly under the direction of the area commissioner rather than through any intervening influences of the district council. In the two divisions studied here the branch executive secretaries at the division level were concerned primarily with collecting TANU dues. In contrast to their high status in preindependence days when the branch secretary was the ranking party official in the division, their leadership role in 1968 was not great.

One other officer operates at the core of the division political system, the division chairman of the party, who is elected by the division annual conference. The annual conference was composed of the incumbent chairman, the branch secretary, all members of the annual district conference in the division, all ten-house cell leaders, all district councilors in the division, and one representative each from the Women's Section, the TANU Youth League, and the Elders Section.[13] In the divisions under consideration, the chairman of the party played a definitely secondary role to the divisional executive officer.

Plans were announced in 1967 for the reestablishment of a division-level committee to represent the various wards and villages in the division.[14] A division-level committee had existed be-

[13] *The TANU Constitution,* Article IV.
[14] Tanga District, Development and Planning Committee, Minutes, 11 September 1967.

fore and shortly after independence, and the new committee, to be called the division development committee, would receive development plans and requests from the ward development committee, which was to replace the earlier and more numerous village development committees. By providing consideration of development plans and problems at the division level before submission to the district development committee, the government hoped to better coordinate the efforts of government and party for the development of the division.[15]

The division development committee membership was heavily party oriented—the divisional executive officer, the district councilors, the chairman of TANU from the division, the secretary of TANU, one other member from the TANU organization, one civil servant from every ministry in the division, and three members to be nominated by the committee itself.[16] As of July 1968 the division development committee was not yet functioning in Chanika or Pongwe. One reason for this delay was that the reconstitution of the village development committees into ward development committees had not yet been completed.

Again and again villagers expressed in interviews and discussions the feeling that the divisional executive officer loomed large in their perceptions of government and access to it. The division office buildings themselves indicated the tone of the political process in the divisions. In Chanika the division office was located in the back of the primary court building, an open-air structure with two rooms in the rear. "Bwana Divisional" was a former schoolteacher who had been the driver for the district TANU secretary during preindependence days. He was continuously traveling throughout the division, and his agents in the countryside, the village executive officers, were constantly in touch with him. For the village executive officer this usually meant a trip to Handeni to visit the office once a week, depending upon the urgency of business and the conditions of travel. District officers

[15] *Ibid.*   [16] *Ibid.*

who had business in the division were supposed to check in with the divisional executive officer. If a visitor went into the division for any purpose, the divisional was to be informed. In Chanika, the divisional worked closely with the chairman and the branch secretary. When I tried to secure permission to work in the division, the divisional refused to take the decision of approval upon himself. He insisted that we should meet with the chairman and the secretary. Raising his crossed fingers, he said, "We are like one."

In Pongwe, the branch TANU office housed the offices of the divisional executive officer, the branch secretary, and the branch chairman. Also in this spacious building were the offices of community development workers and one classroom of the local primary school. The divisional executive officer of Pongwe was of the local tribe, the Digo, and the son of a former chief. While the divisionals from both Pongwe and Chanika were capable men, the former was much more independent in his operations than was his counterpart from Chanika. The local chairman and the party secretary in Pongwe were very much in the background.

In 1968 then, divisional executive officers were the key links between the villages and the district political systems, in particular in so far as the coercive arm of the state and the access to government action was concerned. For party activity in the division, the divisional was the central figure. Although some developmental activity was pursued by the various ministries in the divisions outside the influence and direction of the divisional and the party, the plan for the division development committee aimed at coordinating this and all activity under the direction of the divisional executive officer. In fact, most activity in the divisions was already under his direction, and there was pressure from the district office in Tanga for the divisional executive officer to play a more decisive coordinating role. In October 1967 the Tanga Finance Committee of the district council passed a resolution aimed primarily at the agricultural field assistants that declared that "the Divisional Executive Officer is the head of the Division and should know the works of his clerks, field assistants, medical assistants and all employees of all ministries of the government in the division." [17]

While formally working directly under the district executive officer, the divisional executive officer, wearing both the government hat and party hat, was responsible to both the district council bureaucracy and the party bureaucracy at the district headquarters. While no conflict between these divided loyalties was revealed here, the potential for such conflict was removed by the 1969 reorganization plan that made the divisional a party representative directly responsible to the area commissioner.

In fact even in 1968 all affairs—local government, central government, and party—were funneled through the divisional executive officer if they had relevance to the division. Thus while at the district level there was some differentiation of leadership structures, at the division level there was virtually no such differentiation. In fact the 1969 reorganization of the division level structures seems to have provided for further consolidation in form, which in fact already existed.

Subsequently, the next lower rung in the administrative and political hierarchy was to be given more specialized duties. This investigation and subsequent events gave me the impression that the efforts to reach the villages have resulted in a decentralization of duties with a subsequent reformulation of roles at the levels of the hierarchy intermediate between village and district.

Ward

During 1968 the ward was being reconstituted throughout Tanzania as the most local unit of government next to the village

[17] Tanga District Council, Finance Committee, Minutes, 16–18 October 1967.

itself. Prior to this time it had been only the constituency from which the district councilor was elected. Now, however, the ward was to serve as a focal point for a consolidation and reorganization of the village development committees, which had played such a prominent role in the early years of the nation-building effort in Tanzania. At that time, each village or a group of villages was encouraged to organize a village development committee. The composition of the VDC varied, though generally the party representative from each ten-house cell, the cell leader, was a member of the committee along with all the representatives of the various ministries in the area. While the degree of organization and activity of the committees varied, being virtually nonexistent in the areas studied here, it has been estimated that at one time there were as many as 7,000 of these committees throughout the countryside.[18]

The VDC was to meet, discuss the problems of the village, and plan the development effort for the year. This plan was to be submitted to the DDC for consideration, alteration, approval, and, in many cases, some funding. In similar fashion, the DDC was to submit the district plan, which included the more feasible of the village plans, to the regional development committee.

An assessment of the effectiveness of the VDC's in operation depends upon the criteria of success. Undoubtedly they were the focal points of initiative and motivation for many self-help projects in the nation. In most cases, however, the VDC's did not have enough technical competence to determine the most practical development projects.

In addition to its purely developmental role, the VDC also functioned as a local representative council. Most often this was an informal role performed without central government prompting. It has been suggested that the government intended that the

[18] René Lemarchand, "Village by Village Nation Building in Tanzania," *Africa Report X* (February 1965), 11–15; Tordoff, *Government,* pp. 119 ff, and Dryden, *Local Administration,* pp. 44 ff.

VDC's should be a combination of village council, elders council, development committee, and party committee.[19]

By early 1968 the reorganization of the VDC's was under way.[20] Members of the new ward development committee would include the ward TANU chairman, the secretaries (probably one) of TANU, the district councilor, two cell leaders from each existing VDC in the ward, and ministry representatives in the area.[21] The work of the WDC, as described in the minutes of the Tanga District Development and Planning Committee included: 1) the organization of farming, 2) nation building works, 3) developing the villages, 4) development of schools and adult education, 5) security and the flow of strangers in the villages, 6) culture, 7) cottage industries, and 8) participation in the instructions being given the WDC's.[22]

One village executive officer, working directly under the divisional executive officer, would be the secretary of the WDC. The WDC would be chaired by the ward chairman of TANU. The VEO would also be the secretary of TANU in the ward. Thus the link between government and party was similar from district, to division, and now, to the ward.

At the time this work was carried out it was unclear what the future role of the village development committee was to be. The situation was further complicated in October 1968 when President Nyerere placed new responsibilities upon what he termed village development committees. In a major policy paper, "Freedom and Development," the President called for discipline in the

---

[19] See Bienen, *Tanzania,* pp. 349 ff.

[20] The plan was announced in Tanga District in September 1967, and in June 1967 in Handeni. Tanga District, Development and Planning Committee, Minutes, 11 September 1967, Appendix A; and Handeni District Council, Finance Committee, Minutes of the Combined Meeting of the Finance Committee and the Working Committee of TANU, 23 June 1967.

[21] Tanga District Development and Planning Committee, Minutes, 11 September 1967, Appendix A.

[22] *Ibid.*

participation in local self-help projects; a discipline to be imposed by local communities.[23] A supplementary directive written by the President specified that village development committees would in the future "be allowed to impose other traditional sanctions on those who do not take part in a self-help activity which the village development committee has itself declared to be a self-help project." [24] In the cases studied here, formally organized village development committees were almost nonexistent.[25] Informal councils of elders did exist in some of the villages and did function intermittently. In addition, in most of the special project villages there existed special committees that did, in effect, "govern" the affairs of the village or project. Furthermore, the policy of building ujamaa villages prescribed the creation of committees that would govern democratically the affairs of the village.[26] It may be assumed then that when President Nyerere used the term "village development committees" in the directive referred to here, he had in mind the organizing and governing committees of the development projects throughout the country and the formally organized ward development committees which were emerging during early 1968. Although the reorganization was not complete in 1968, it was the latter that would constitute the formal link in the governmental structure instead of the numerous, ill-organized and poorly functioning VDC's which had existed previously.

[23] Julius K. Nyerere, "Freedom and Development," *Standard*, October 18, 1968.

[24] Julius K. Nyerere, "President's Measures to Stop Shirkers," *Standard*, October 18, 1968.

[25] In one village in Tanga District, a villager during a general meeting inadvertently responded to my question, "What is the work of the village development committee here?" by asserting, "We've never seen one here." The ward chairman and district councilor hastily assured me that the VDC did exist. However, the point was clear. Interview, March 26, 1968. In 1965 the Handeni District veterinary officer "complained that he had experienced some difficulty because the VDC's had not been meeting as they were supposed to." Handeni District Development and Planning Committee, Minutes, 23 December 1965.

[26] Nyerere, "Socialism and Rural Development."

Though the work of the WDC was to be similar to that originally intended for the village development committees, in actuality there was considerable confusion in the two wards where this research was pursued as to just what the WDC was to be doing.

In Tanga District, I studied the ward-level political system in Marungu ward, one of the six wards in Pongwe Division. Marungu is about fifteen miles from Tanga on the Tanga-Pangani road. It includes four villages, Marungu (adult population 781), Marungu Amani (adult population 490), Geza (adult population 336), and Migombani, whose population was unknown but which appeared to be between that of Marungu and Marungu Amani.[27] Of these four villages, three are primarily unitribal in composition; the fourth, Marungu, is a mixture of peoples who have migrated to Tanga District to work on the adjacent sisal estate.

Before the institution of its new ward development committee, Marungu ward had only one village development committee, which actually represented all four villages through the presence of cell leaders from every ten houses in each of the villages.

In April 1968 the divisional executive officer of Pongwe called for a meeting at Marungu in order to organize the new ward committee and to choose the two cell leaders who were to be among its members. The fifty cell leaders from the four villages attended, and the chairman of TANU for Marungu, the village executive officer and the district councilor led the meeting. After the meeting was called to order, the divisional delivered a lecture on local government. He told the cell leaders:

Before independence the government started at the top and went down. It went, from the Queen, to the Government, to the Provincial Commissioner, to the District Commissioner, and then to the chiefs, to the sub-chiefs, to the headmen and then to the village elders. Now

[27] Discussions with village executive officer, 16 April 1968.

FROM *BOMA* TO VILLAGE

the government starts at the bottom and goes up. We decide first in the village and ward and then send it to the District, then to the Region, then to the National Assembly and then to the President.[28]

The divisional then turned to the responsibilities of the ward development committee. He emphasized the responsibility of the WDC to see that people were working and reminded the meeting that there was a district bylaw that stated that a man must farm. He said that the WDC could decide what to do and then carry out its decision, but he did not elaborate, so that it was left unclear in the meeting just what the WDC was expected to do.

The divisional referred to a standing conflict between the traditional leaders and the cell leaders in the ward. He noted that the elders felt that the cell leaders should come back to the villages and report what was decided in the meetings. If the elders approved, then it would be all right to proceed. If they did not approve, then they expected the policy to be changed. He declared that from now on the elders would have to come to the ward meeting if they wanted to be involved in the decisions of Marungu Ward. Even though the four villages which constitute Marungu Ward were at the most two miles from the TANU office where this meeting was taking place, the four villages, nevertheless, had a very distinct feeling of village identity. Some of the elders had obviously declined to participate or support the decisions reached by the Marungu VDC in the past. At this meeting, however, a good number of the cell leaders were themselves elders.

The meeting then turned to the task of nominating and electing two men from the group of fifty cell leaders assembled to be members of the ward development committee. The election itself was a meticulous affair presided over by the divisional. The care that he exercised in making sure that everyone understood the procedures

[28] A paraphrasing of the meeting at Marungu, TANU Office, April 28, 1968.

and in demonstrating that the election was absolutely fair was an impressive seminar in the teaching of self-government.[29]

The man who received the highest number of votes was the former chairman of TANU in the ward. His runner-up was a clerk with the adjacent sisal estate. They were to join the chairman of the Marungu Ward TANU organization (a very dignified elder), the VEO (a former branch secretary of TANU), the district councilor, and the co-opted technical officers in the ward as members of the ward development committee.

In Handeni District, I observed ward-level politics in Sindeni Ward of Chanika Division. Sindeni, in contrast to Marungu Ward, is spread over a vast area of relatively unpopulated bush land. The communications center, if not the geographical center of the ward, is at Sindeni, which was on the Handeni-Korogwe road about seventeen miles from Handeni. In 1928 a district commissioner described Sindeni in a fashion that is relatively accurate forty years later. He wrote:

Sindeni on the Handeni-Korogwe main trunk road is 19 miles [from Handeni] and no description. There is an excellent well at Sindeni, water being plentiful but slightly brackish. The village of Sindeni is infested with spirrilum tick and it is inadvisable to pitch a camp too near the village. Cotton sales are held here in the season and there is one small *duka* [general store]. This village is much used by labour passing to and from Korogwe.[30]

Prior to the reorganization of the ward level government, Sindeni Ward contained three village development committees in the villages of Kwamkono (which is approximately seven miles south-

---

[29] My research assistant and I were drawn into the mechanics of this election. As we were the only men there who were assumed to be objective, we were involved in reading the names from the ballots and in writing the names of those nominees on the ballots for the approximately 20 per cent of the participants who were illiterate. The actual counting of the ballots was done before the open meeting by my research assistant.

[30] Tanga Provincial Book, "Road Reports and Itineraries, From Handeni to Mgambo via Sindeni—1928."

east of Sindeni), Kwambilu (which is about ten miles from Sindeni), and Sindeni. All of these are small settlements. The Zigua, the predominant ethnic group in Handeni, have an aversion to permanent settlement in villages containing more than one clan. Thus there are hundreds of small-scale villages spread throughout the area that consist of no more than fifteen to twenty households. The actual population of Sindeni Ward is unknown. The total number of taxpayers for the ward was 1,027 in 1968. If the district executive officer's estimate that roughly 20 per cent of the eligibles pay their taxes is correct, then the number of adult males in Sindeni would be around 5,000.[31] At this time the number of taxpayers in Sindeni was 307, in Kwamkono 234, and Kwambilu 486.

Even under these difficult geographical circumstances there did exist a semblance of political structure for Sindeni Ward. The TANU chairman of Sindeni lived about four miles by foot from the *duka;* the councilor lived about three miles away, and the home of the village executive officer was nearby. The VEO was almost continually traveling in his attempts to collect taxes and TANU subscriptions [32] throughout the ward. The councilor had no significant role to play in the ward system, while the chairman and VEO worked closely together. In addition to these formal officers, however, one of the sons of the Asian *duka* owner played a very important role in ward affairs. Through the owner of the *duka* the political leaders of the ward had access to resources and, probably most important, a truck that provided transportation. The *duka* itself served as the post office for the whole area. The *duka*'s post

[31] Interview, Handeni, February 28, 1968.

[32] TANU subscriptions, or dues, were six shillings per year, usually paid by the month. While statistics were unavailable for Handeni, in August 1968, the dues-paying membership of TANU in Tanga District was 5,415. *Standard,* August 28, 1968. If this membership is compared to the number of households in Tanga District, only 9 per cent of these households would have a member who was a dues-paying member of the party. Household data is taken from *Preliminary Results,* p. 23. There is a notable dearth of information on grassroots, *dues-paying* membership in TANU. See Bienen, *Tanzania.*

office box in Handeni, seventeen miles away, was the number used by all the notables of the area. If one wanted to communicate with the VEO or the chairman, one sent a letter to this post office box or left a message at the *duka*.

Because of the inaccessibility and the distances involved, communication between the villages of the ward was very difficult. Ward leaders usually would communicate only with Sindeni village and with two informal subdivisions of the ward, Kwamkono and Kwambilu, where there did exist political structures through which the VEO and the chairman could function. In Kwamkoni, the site of a mission hospital and a primary school, the political figures were a local official who was known as the "mayor," a chairman of the TANU Youth League, and a village development committee. In Kwambilu a TANU Youth League communal sisal farm served as a kind of center of political activity for the area. Most of the people involved in this development project were above average in political motivation. The chairman of the scheme was the ward chairman's chief contact in that area.

The village development committees in Sindeni, Kwamkono, and Kwambilu had not been reorganized into a ward development committee. In fact, it appeared that no one understood how this reorganization was to take place. On February 16, 1968, the joint meeting of the three VDC's took place under a mango tree at Sindeni. The VEO responsible for the ward announced that "the heads" had decided that Sindeni, Kwamkono, and Kwambilu would be one and that the center of the ward's activities would be at Sindeni. The district councilor read the council resolution bringing this about, but no one mentioned the organization of a *ward* development committee to replace the three village development committees they already had. An undercurrent of grumbling from those assembled, especially from the fairly numerous Kwamkono group, became apparent when they discovered that since Sindeni had no TANU office building, the citizens of the ward would have to build one there. Kwamkono and Kwambilu citizens already had their

TANU office buildings, and now they were expected to assist in the building of a TANU building for the ward at Sindeni. The most vocal opposition came from some of the Kwamkono elders, who declared that they would "like the Sindeni citizens to build, since we built." [33]

After much bickering, the VEO and the chairman denounced the elders from Kwamkono for "poisoning the mind of the youth" by discouraging the building of the office at Sindeni. In the Zigua language they also lambasted the dissenters for causing such a fuss in front of a guest—this researcher.[34] An incident during this debate revealed the nature of authority in this area. A young man entered the debate at one point with the zealous demand, "We must build the TANU office building!" This demand brought an indignant retort of *"Bwana Mdogo, Keti!"* from one of the elders present. The precise translation of this command is, "Little man, sit down!"; and the younger gentleman sat.

Finally, the VEO and the chairman announced that a consensus had been reached on the TANU office in Sindeni and they proceeded to discuss the site for the building. A committee selected from those present inspected the proposed site, which was just across the road, while the man who had claim to the plot expressed his unwillingness to give up this claim for the TANU office. The meeting finally convinced him that he should and passed a resolution asking the district council, the community development division, and TANU office in Handeni for assistance in building the office.

Among other matters considered in this meeting was the question of whether there should be a TANU Youth League organization at Sindeni. The village executive officer had obviously received orders to the effect that there should be. There was little enthu-

---

[33] From notes taken at the meeting on February 16, 1968.

[34] This incident is indicative of the influence the researcher may have on the situation he is investigating. In most cases, he is likely to be completely unaware of the nature and degree of his influence.

siasm among the youth present. In fact, the sentiment can be summed up in one youth's question: "Do we get paid?" The promise of membership cards and uniforms did not seem to compensate for the fact that they would not get paid.

The subject of taxes took up much of the village executive officer's time at the meeting. He complained that the people were not paying their taxes;[35] he reminded the cell leaders of their responsibilities as leaders and declared that he was holding them responsible for the paying of taxes in their ten-house cells. Then he proceeded to call upon the most neglectful and have them announce to the meeting how many of their people had paid their taxes for the month.

Of tremendous significance here was the fact that the cell leader, the most important arm of TANU in the villages, was being used as a tax collector. When I asked the district executive officer about the impact of this practice upon the government's efforts to promote development, he insisted that the people did not resent this. "Rather," he said, "they welcome it, since they view the cell leader as their savior." "By acting as the intermediary between the villagers and the government, the cell leader is able to keep the Field Force away." The Field Force was the mobile police unit stationed at the district headquarters which, through the use of Landrovers, was able to move fairly readily throughout the district.[36]

The meeting took up the question of a marriage-divorce-dowry dispute that had been too much for Kwamkono to settle on its own. The VEO and the chairman had spent several hours previously listening to the ins and outs of the dispute in Kwamkono and now it was being elevated to the ward level for discussion. The five-hour meeting adjourned around four o'clock with no decision being reached.

Throughout this meeting the composition of and the justification of the new ward development committee was not at issue, and it

[35] From notes taken at the meeting on February 16, 1968.
[36] Discussions, Handeni, district executive officer.

appears that no one really understood what was involved in the reorganization. In July 1968 the TANU office at Sindeni had not moved beyond the discussion stage and, in fact, there was a reluctance even to talk about it. In short, the ward-level political system in Sindeni was most intermittent in its activities. Is primary function, which it performed inactively and ineffectively, was to communicate division-level and district-level decisions to the villages. The fundamental task of the VEO and the ward-level government structure was to collect local taxes—a difficult task subsequently dropped by central government decision on January 1, 1970. In their efforts to extract taxes, ward-level officials—the central figure being the VEO—worked through the village-level authorities, and, the VEO freely threatened to call for coercion from the district *boma.*

Of the individuals who were involved in the ward system, the ward chairman of TANU, an elder and former headman, appeared to command considerable respect throughout the ward. The VEO, a relatively young man, was the son of the former district chairman of TANU for Handeni District. Although a Zigua from Chanika Division, he was not from the ward in which he served. The Asian *duka* owner, mentioned earlier, was extremely influential as an adviser, as a source of communications and resources in the ward, and, finally, as an actor in the system itself. It was he, for example, who took the request of the people of the ward for typhoid injections *directly* to the area commissioner, who, in turn, granted the request. In discussing the Asians, ward officials said, "They are just like the Zigua" (*sawa sawa Wazigua*). The district councilor, seldom seen around the *duka,* was relatively uninfluential in local ward affairs. A fifth man playing an important part in the ward system was the agricultural field officer. Stationed at Sindeni, he was responsible for the Ministry of Agriculture's programs in the whole of Chanika Division. He was of importance in Sindeni Ward because his home and headquarters were there, and he worked closely with the chairman and the VEO. His network of five agricultural field assistants throughout the area was also useful to the chairman and the VEO. Of all the government ministries active in the area, Agriculture was the most crucial, since the agricultural field officer was involved in weighing and buying the farmer's produce and from time to time had a truck or Landrover at his disposal.

Sindeni Ward in Handeni District differed most from Marungu Ward in Tanga District in its harsh geographical conditions. In the thinly settled area of Sindeni mere communication was difficult; to govern and to collect taxes was next to impossible. Ultimately, the people could merely retreat from the penetration of external political systems. The ward-level political system, though relatively undifferentiated and intermittent in function in Sindeni, did have links with the village political systems. It had difficulty, however, directing the energies and resources of the villages to the externally determined ends.

Marungu Ward, in contrast, was thickly settled. The ward political system had constant contact with the village systems of which it was composed. It was questionable, however, whether the Marungu Ward actually was any more effective in turning the energies of the people of the villages to the developmental and related tasks sought by the external political systems. The persisting unit in both Marungu and Sindeni was the village political system, and when comparing the village systems in these two wards, it became obvious that village isolation from the external world was more than geographic in nature.

Village

The seven villages upon which this analysis of village political systems is based range in scale and complexity from Maranzara in Sindeni Ward, Handeni District, to Marungu in Marungu Ward, Tanga District, and include a variety of villages between these two extremes.

Maranzara, a typical village of the Zigua people, the predominant ethnic group in the area, consisted of eighteen households located about three miles from Sindeni. There was no commercial activity of any sort, and the people were engaged in subsistence agriculture and had only intermittent contact with the money economy.

Marungu, in contrast, was composed of a mixture of tribal groups and was relatively large, with an adult population of 781. The people of Marungu were employed on a nearby sisal estate, and while most were involved in the money economy, they were invariably engaged in some individual agricultural activity. There were numerous modest commercial activities in the village ranging from the coffee/tea houses to comparatively sophisticated *dukas* equipped with kerosene refrigerators and usually owned by Asians.

While most people in Handeni District lived in villages similar to Maranzara, there were other types of villages in the area. Sindeni village, for example, consisted of a *duka* and a few service centers—a road worker's camp, a cooperative warehouse, a dispensary open two days a week, a small hotel, and a weekly market area. The reason for settlement at this particular point was the presence of a permanent water supply and the junction of major district roads. Although most of the villagers in this thinly settled area lived at least one mile from the *duka* itself, a few civil servants had established their residence near the *duka*.

The village of Kwamkono had grown up around a mission station and hospital. Motor vehicles had access to Kwamkono only in the dry season. In contrast to most villages in Sindeni, there were residents from tribes other than the Zigua in Kwamkono. Kwamkono was atypical, too, in that there were numerous small-scale commercial enterprises and a community center that had been built by self-help and opened by President Nyerere. The commercial shops were dependent primarily upon the relatives of patients coming to the mission hospital, hospital employees, and a nucleus of local civil servants.

In Marungu Ward, the villages considered in addition to Marungu were Marungu Amani and Migombani. The people of Marungu Amani did not work on the nearby sisal estate, but were farmers whose main source of cash income was derived from copra processed from the many coconut trees in the area. There were a few small commercial shops in the village and two development projects, a cattle-coconut scheme, and a community chicken farm. Approximately one mile from Marungu Amani lies Migombani. The two villages were similar in many ways. Both were inhabited by the Digo people who engaged primarily in subsistence farming for their livelihood.

The final village considered in this survey is Kwamsala in Sindeni Ward. A communal sisal farm village initiated by the TANU Youth League, Kwamsala was relatively small, had no *dukas* or other commercial activity. Having been built by former laborers from sisal estates in the area, it was of mixed tribal base and was distinctive in its degree of politicization; for example, villagers sang nation-building songs as they cleared the land.

Visits and conversations held in these seven communities attempted to determine the nature of the political system in the villages, the links these systems had with external political systems, and ultimately the effects that both systems had upon the developmental process. Despite the efforts of the central authorities to penetrate and shape the behavior of the villages, the most dominant fact of village affairs in all these villages was their relative autonomy and isolation. This was true, it may be surmised, for the great majority of Tanzanians, for whom the most salient structure in life was the village. This seemed to be almost as true for the villages of Marungu Ward, fifteen miles from the urban center of Tanga, the second largest city in the nation, as it was for the villages of Sindeni that were seventeen miles from Handeni, in a district generally conceded to be among the less developed in the nation, sometimes cut off from the rest of the country for several months a year.

The village is subordinate to a greater or lesser degree to the central and other intermediate political systems, but it is capable of responding to threats to its autonomy and may be able to resist or manipulate efforts of external political systems to control it. The extent of this ability can be regarded as a measure of the village's political development. It is thus conceivable that the village political system may in fact develop in response to the pressures that external systems place upon it. This development may be turned to the achievement of the goals the national political system has established for the nation; or this development may jeopardize national plans by allowing villagers to successfully resist national efforts to control their behavior and resources.[37]

Ten-House Cell

The most important structure in the political system of Tanzania's villages is the ten-house cell (*nyumba ya kumi kumi*).[38] The ten-house cell is a modern institution in local party organization. In August 1963 the National Executive Committee of TANU discussed the establishment of a cell system throughout the country and passed a resolution to strengthen the leadership of TANU.[39] This committee reaffirmed the resolution at its meeting in April 1964 and suggested that it should be put into effect immediately. In December 1964 the committee acknowledged that the cell or-

[37] For an elaboration of this thesis, see Colin Leys, *Politicians and Policies* (Nairobi, 1967). Also see Harumi Befu, "The Political Relation of the Village to the State," *World Politics,* XIX (July 1967), 612.

[38] For an exhaustive and excellent study of the cell system in one area of Tanzania, see Jean Fox O'Barr, "Ten-House Party Cells and Their Leaders: Micropolitics in Pare District, Tanzania" (Ph.D. dissertation, Department of Political Science, Northwestern University, 1970).

[39] This treatment of the background of the cell in Tanzania is heavily dependent upon Wilbert Klerruu, "Whys and Wherefores of the TANU Cell System," *Monthly Newsletter of Kivukoni College,* III (June 1966), 3–11. Dr. Klerruu was writing at the time as TANU publicity secretary. Also see Bienen, *Tanzania,* pp. 356–360, and Boniface Njohole, "The TANU Cell System," The University of East Africa, Political Science— Paper 6, Dissertation, Dar es Salaam, March 1967.

ganization had not yet taken place and resolved that "TANU Cells, each consisting of ten houses should be established and consolidated all over the country; and that all Regions and Districts must improvise membership registers which should be utilized effectively to facilitate the monthly returns of membership, from the Cell to the National Headquarters." [40]

Thus every ten houses would comprise one cell, and all TANU members in these ten houses would be members, from whom one would be chosen as cell leader (*ma-balozi*). In accordance with the single party system, the cell was conceived to be both an instrument of governance and party organization. A party spokesman, Dr. Wilbur Klerruu, noted that the cell system was intended to:

a. enable people to express their views and opinions to TANU and Government and to communicate the policies of TANU and Government to the people;

b. consolidate unity and extend leadership to the village level so that leaders can easily be accessible to the ordinary people;

c. obtain information regarding social and economic development in the villages and forward it to the branch organs of TANU; and

d. "ensure the security and survival of the Party, Government and the nation by seeing . . . that all laws and regulations are obeyed." [41]

The functions performed by the cell system have varied in time and place throughout the country. In some areas, particularly near borders with unfriendly or troubled neighboring countries, the cell system has served primarily as a security system, informing on all unusual people or happenings in the area.[42]

Observers of Tanzanian development efforts have emphasized

[40] Klerruu, "Whys and Wherefores," p. 4.
[41] Quoted in *ibid.*, p. 5. Paraphrased here.
[42] See Bienen, *Tanzania*, p. 358.

the role of the cells in the promoting of rural development projects. Henry Bienen reports that in early 1965 Second Vice President Kawawa outlined the work of the cells under three main headings: as communicating between the people, the party, and the government, as "coordinating the work of the cells with that of the development committees," and as promoting the security of the nation.[43]

The government's White Paper on Local Government Councils of 1966 [44] suggested that village development committees should be composed of all cell leaders in a ward. In the 1967 reorganization of local government structures there were to be two cell leaders on the most local of the development committees, the ward development committee. These two men were to be the formal link between the WDC and the villages or village.[45]

The Cell Leader

In 1968 the cell leader was the most prominent individual actor in the political systems of the villages I studied. His duties as stated by a party official were to:

(a) explain to the people the policies of TANU and the government.
(b) articulate people's views and opinions and communicate them to TANU and the government.
(c) be responsible for collection of party dues.

[43] *Ibid.*
[44] United Republic of Tanzania, Government Paper No. 1—1966, *Proposals of the Tanzania Government on Local Government Councils* (Dar es Salaam, 1966), 3.
[45] In 1968 there was considerable variation throughout Tanzania as to the extent to which the consolidation of VDC's into WDC's had been carried out. In Handeni and Tanga districts the reorganization had occurred. For areas where it had not occurred see the brief description for another region of Tanzania in C. Gregory Knight, "Field Work and Local Government: An Example from Tanzania," *African Studies Bulletin*, XII (December 1969), 270. Jean O'Barr also found that it had not yet occurred in Pare District. O'Barr, "Ten-House Party Cells," and discussions.

(d) persuade people who are not members to become members of TANU.
(e) play their role in safeguarding the peace and security of this country by seeing to it that laws and regulations are obeyed.
(f) urge people to pay their taxes properly.
(g) foster strong cooperation among the cell members.
(h) . . . take overall charge of the affairs of the party in the cell.
(i) . . . be the delegate of the cell to the branch annual conference.[46]

On the one hand the cell leader was expected to communicate government and party policies to the villages. On the other hand, the party, with the strong support of President Nyerere, expected him to articulate the villagers' views to TANU and the government. He performed the first of these functions remarkably well. Actions and decisions taken in national and district offices were, in the villages studied here, relayed with considerable efficiency to the villages. It is open to question, however, how effectively the cell leader delivered the views of the people to higher points in the hierarchy.

In fact, my findings suggest that if the message was critical of government policy or revealed poor response to official directives, it was likely that the information simply would not be communicated beyond the ward level. These messages, which were most important for the effective performance of national development goals, were the ones most unlikely to be communicated to national decision makers.

Government and party officials also expected the cell leader to consider collection of the head tax from his constituents as one of his prime responsibilities. However, the behavior of the cell leaders in the areas studied here indicated they did not see their primary role to be that of tax collector. Any doubt about the wisdom of government and party efforts to promote local development by appointing government and party's most local representative as the

[46] Klerruu, "Whys and Wherefores," p. 10.

chief tax collector was undoubtedly reinforced by a consideration of the relatively low level return for these efforts. The government decided to abolish this tax and thus this responsibility for the cell leader as of January 1, 1970.[47]

While this discussion has centered on what officials saw the role of the cell leader to be, it is perhaps more important to consider what the villagers thought of the cell leader and his work. Undoubtedly they realized that his work included the responsibilities outlined by the authorities, but in their eyes the first responsibility of the cell leader was to the cell and the village.

The chief function of the cell leader in the context of the village was the maintenance of order. Order as a concept here refers primarily to minimizing conflict involving disputes over dowries or other property. Seldom do these disputes expand into wider political systems. An example where the cell leader functioned judicially in a local dispute only to have the dispute escalate to higher authorities was revealed in the testimony in court of a case of a man who charged his former concubine with stealing. During the formal court hearing of the case, it was revealed that after a quarrel the lady in question "demanded payment for services rendered and the matter was sent to a *TANU cell leader* who ordered [the gentleman involved] to pay her 20 shillings." [48] As the gentleman did not pay the 20 shillings as ordered by the cell leader, the lady subsequently took matters into her own hands and the disagreement escalated to the formal court system as a charge of stealing.

In most cases the cell leader attempted to settle local disputes himself; if he was unsuccessful he would probably take the matter to a council of cell leaders. Here the convergence of roles and institutions becomes most complex. This council might be operating under the guise of the village development committee, as an informal council of elders or merely as a group of village leaders

[47] *Standard*, June 20, 1969.
[48] *Standard*, November 7, 1969; emphasis is this writer's.

discussing a village dispute.⁴⁹ All were found in the villages studied here. The designation of the type of institution did not appear to be determined by the nature of the problem within the village. Rather it would appear that the village council could take various forms and that no one particular form for dealing with disputes internal to the village had yet emerged.

The Cell Leader as Village Leader

The cell was a constituency within the village. Each cell elected a cell leader who represented his constituency in the affairs of the village and the ward. In some cases, the villages might be so small that only one cell leader represented the village in ward and district affairs, as in Maranzara with its eighteen households. In the larger villages many more cell leaders were chosen. In Marungu, for example, theoretically there could have been thirty-nine cell leaders.⁵⁰ In a large group such as this, it was inevitable that leadership both formal and informal should emerge.

In Kwamkono, Sindeni, where the cell leaders totaled approximately thirty, there emerged an informal leadership around two men—a cell leader, known by all as "the Mayor," and the chairman of the TANU Youth League. When the village executive officer, the TANU chairman, or anyone else needed to make contact with the authority of Kwamkono, he had to deal through the Mayor. This was a completely informal office at the village level both in national statutes and in village custom, but it functioned very effectively within the setting of Kwamkono.

---

⁴⁹ For evidence that the village development committees were composed largely of traditional leaders, the elders, in another part of Tanzania, see Norman N. Miller, "The Political Survival of Traditional Leadership," *Journal of Modern African Studies*, VI, no. 2 (1968), 194.

⁵⁰ This figure is based on the assumption of a minimum of two adults per household. Thus for an adult population of 781, there would be a possible maximum of 390 households. With one cell leader for every ten households, there could have been 39 cell leaders. The number is undoubtedly less than this possible maximum.

Scholars have made efforts to sort out the traditional and modern bases of village authority and leadership in the developing areas.[51] The question of who occupies the cell leader role in Tanzania is a perplexing one. Was he merely the elder of the ten houses, the best educated, or the most TANU-oriented man in the village? Any attempt to answer this question empirically is a trying one. As Henry Bienen has pointed out for the national level, the traditional leadership does not exclude party supporters, educated men, or men with a "modern" viewpoint. Norman Miller contends that at the district level, traditional leaders rank last, but that at the village level traditional leaders are "nearly as important as the party leaders." [52] In Tanga and Handeni districts this research suggests that the cell leaders were a mixture of traditional leaders, primarily elders, and more forward-looking leaders. The term "more forward-looking" is used here, because it is as precise as one can be. The characteristics of this group would include youth, party orientation, and leadership, in some cases, and a greater verbal commitment to the government and the goals of development.[53] The elder representation in Sindeni Ward, Handeni, was very strong. At meetings of the village development and ward development committees, not only were the elders in the majority, but they were also the leading spokesmen.

In Marungu, by contrast, the elders were less active in the meetings of the committee. There was some obvious conflict between the elders and some of the more forward-looking leaders. For example, a division-level official complained at a ward development committee meeting that the elders in the area often objected to

[51] For Tanzania, see Miller, "The Political Survival," Bienen, *Tanzania*, pp. 349–360, and Maguire, *Toward 'Uhuru.'*

[52] Norman N. Miller, "Village Leadership."

[53] These conclusions are based on my observations of village-level meetings of cell leaders in all the villages considered here, my observations of cell leaders' participation in the meetings of ward development committee meetings, and my discussions with the cell leaders and relevant party and government officials at all levels.

decisions made at these meetings, but they did not take the meetings seriously enough to always attend. He warned the assembled cell leaders that those who did not attend the meetings had no grounds for complaint. In the same area, a ward-level official complained that the elders had insisted, against his advice, that a public market for the ward be built in one of the smaller villages some distance from the multitribal village which served as a source of labor for the adjacent sisal estate. Now, he pointed out smugly, the market building was unused except for the occasional drying of copra, while local farmers took their produce to the larger village where the wage-earning residents bought even though there was no formal market in the village. Needless to say, there was no income for the local government treasury from the unused market in the smaller village.

Further indication that the Marungu Ward village political systems might be more cell-leader oriented than was the case in Sindeni Ward was the response to my question in the Sindeni village of Maranzara regarding how the individual would settle a dispute with a fellow villager and how he would settle a dispute with a person from another village.[54] The responses are presented in Table 3. While the conditions for the administration of such a question are never ideal in an African village, the results indicated a feeling in this particular village that the institution for settling disputes was the cell leader or the elders. In this ward, cell leader and elder, depending in part upon the size of the village, were likely to be the same person.[55]

[54] The question was: "If you had a dispute with a friend in your village, what would you do to solve this dispute?" (*Kama hupatani na rafiki yako toka kijijini pako, utafanyaje ili mpatane?*) and "If you had a dispute with someone from another village, what would you do to solve the dispute?" (*Kama hupatani na mtu kijiji cha jirani yako utafanyaje mpatane?*)

[55] The Maranzara responses raise an intriguing proposition that could not be pursued further. The circumstances of the administration of the questionnaire allowed the segregation of women from men. The women seemed overwhelmingly to suggest the cell leader as the institution through which the dispute might best be settled, rather than the elder. One might

Table 3. Methods of dispute settlement in a small village *

"How would you settle a dispute with friend in own village?"			"How would you settle a dispute with man from another village?"	
	Men (n-15)	Women (n-20)	Men (n-15)	Women (n-20)
Go to elders	5		7	1
Ask man to excuse	1		3	
Go to cell leader or slight variation	3	11	2	12
Go to elders and cell leaders	1			
Stop disagreement	1			
Go to elders to cell leaders to chairman to VEO	1			
Go to VEO	1			
Totals †	13	11	12	13

* Based on results of questionnaire administered to citizens of Maranzara, Sindeni Ward, February 23, 1968.

† Since all respondents did not answer these questions, the totals do not equal 100 per cent of n.

An experience in Kwamkono gives further credence to the proposition that the cell leader and elder tended to be the same. The village executive officer and the TANU ward chairman called a meeting of all cell leaders. While there should have been approximately thirty cell leaders for the area, in fact there were nine men,

---

propose that the women were more eager to break away from traditional authority than were the men. Such a proposition would first assume that the elder and cell leader were not the same individual. The data available does not allow more than speculation on this question.

obviously elders, attending. They were elders; they were also cell leaders. In response to the two questions relating to the settlement of a village dispute, those attending noted that the elders would be consulted in both situations, and in the first situation, a dispute within the village, that the cell leader would also be consulted.[56]

In the areas I studied most of the cell leaders were elders, although this was truer in Sindeni than in Marungu. Moreover, when the cell leaders were not in fact the elders of the village, they performed in the village political system as the elders had in the past. My findings also suggested that the cell leaders in the villages studied here were a combination of the elders and the young, educated, and party-oriented men. There was no hard line between traditional and modern village leader. Generally, there was a fusion of traditional and modern within the village political system and, in most cases, in the person of the cell leader himself. He was the primary link between the village and intermediate political systems. Nevertheless, he was still first and foremost a villager.

In most cases one leader in each village emerged formally or informally as the spokesman for the village. In Maranzara, this man was the very individual who was headman in the village before leaving in 1940 to participate in the cash economy outside the district. Upon returning in 1960, he was again headman, and after this system was abolished, he became the cell leader. Because of the small size of Maranzara the emergence of the cell leader who was first among equals was essentially simple. In Kwamkono the principal leader was the "Mayor"; in Kwamsala, he was the chairman of the communal farm. Because of the relatively compact geographic nature of the Marungu Ward, there was less need for individual village spokesmen to emerge there. The ward leadership—the TANU chairman, the village executive officer and the district councilor—were able to provide day-by-day leadership of the villages through the media of individual cell leaders, even though they did not themselves live directly in two of the villages.

[56] Interviews at Kwamkono, March 15, 1968.

The Cell Leader as Headman

The role of cell leader in contemporary Tanzania and that of headman during the colonial period are similar.[57] In 1949, Max Gluckman wrote, "Many district officers have described the village headman as the invaluable non-commissioned officer of native administration."[58] If we substitute "cell leader" for "headman" and "government" for "native administration," the statement holds true today for the areas studied here. The duties of the headman as described by Gluckman below are also similar to the official duties of the cell leader as described by the political party representative.

The headman is a key official, if usually unpaid. . . . For example, he has to report suspicious deaths and illnesses and strangers, and he has to see that his villagers keep the village clean, hoe paths, use latrines, follow agricultural and veterinary regulations, pay tax, etc.[59]

Lloyd Fallers writing of the village to government relations in Uganda similarly noted in 1956:

Civil-servant chiefs delegate numerous other duties to the village and sub-village headmen. The collection of taxes, the apprehension of minor criminals, the enforcement of public health regulations and the spreading of propaganda in favour of improved agricultural technique, all of which are formally the responsibility of the civil-servant chiefs, are in fact largely carried out by the headmen.[60]

The civil-servant chiefs have since been abolished in Uganda as they have been in Tanzania. If, however, the title divisional executive officers is substituted in the above quotation for civil-servant

---

[57] See the survey treatment of the headman in Max Gluckman, "The Village Headman in British Central Africa: Introduction," *Africa*, XIX (1949), reprinted in Max Gluckman, *Order and Rebellion in Tribal Africa* (New York, 1963), pp. 146–152. Also see the excellent particular treatment in Lloyd A. Fallers, *Bantu Bureaucracy* (Chicago, 1965), ch. 7.

[58] Gluckman, *Order and Rebellion*, p. 146.   [59] *Ibid.*, p. 152.

[60] Fallers, *Bantu*, p. 174.

chiefs the functions of the headman have remained unchanged in the particular cases studied here.

While these primary functions of the institution of headman/cell leader persist, the structure has taken on additional meaning in the context of independence. The post of cell leader in the eyes of government officials is first a political party position. And in a single-party system, a party position by definition becomes a government position. Thus, the cell leader not only has to carry out the duties of the traditional headman; he also has party duties. By and large the nature of the party organization of the cell system has meant that there is additional manpower to carry out the duties formerly performed by the position of headman. Where there was probably one headman per village, there is theoretically in Tanzania today one cell leader for every ten houses.

Village officials in contemporary Tanzania shared with the headmen of colonial vintage other characteristics to which Gluckman and Fallers paid special attention. While the cell leader was first and foremost a member of a village political system, he was also involved in the ward, the division, and the district political systems. And, in the final analysis, he was a part of the national political system. Thus the cell leader was subjected to demands that he perform a function in each of these systems. Inevitably, conflict between the differing roles emerged.[61]

Fallers has pointed out the conflict inherent in being the hereditary leader of a village while also in practice being the local agent of the national government.[62] All village and ward-level officials in this study including the cell leaders, the district councilor, and the ward chairman of TANU, were expected to perform as agents of the external governments, both district and national. At the same time, all of these officials were elected by the people of the cells and wards. Technically, only party members were supposed to vote for the cell leaders and the chairman of the ward; in practice this

[61] Gluckman, *Order and Rebellion*, p. 151.   [62] Fallers, *Bantu*, p. 175.

means all people who were interested in participating.⁶³ It is not necessary to depict these leaders as traditional suffice it to say that they were a product of a particular locality, and representative of that locality. As locals, they might find themselves in conflict with the values, objectives, and methods of the external political systems whose agents they are intended to be. To perform the duties expected and demanded of them by the external political systems would almost surely alienate them from the localities. They had to choose between alienating local constituents or suffering the wrath of the higher officials, and they usually maintained their position by remaining passive to national objectives most of the time, with well-calculated moments of sound and fury during visits of higher officials to their area. The isolation of most of Tanzania's villages made this technique possible.

Fallers also discussed what he described as the "headman's dilemma," noting that the headman in Uganda had given up traditional sources of income without receiving new ones. He suggested that without some source of income beyond his own fields, the headman could not maintain a standard of living and entertainment requisite to his traditional role in the society. In some ways, the headman in Fallers' view was in worse straits than the ordinary peasant since he had duties which the ordinary peasant did not have. Fallers' comment on the loss of traditional sources of income has some relevance to the cases studied here, since from the ward downward in the hierarchy only the village (later ward) executive officer received a salary. It is difficult to determine what was traditional in Tanga and Handeni because of the history of disruption of traditional patterns. It is clear, however, that leadership must have compensation—traditional or otherwise—for its efforts. For cell leaders, the increase in status might be sufficient. No data were available that indicated that they received any tribute from their

---

⁶³ For similar findings in Sukumaland, see Maguire's excellent study *Toward 'Uhuru,'* p. 370.

people. For the village leaders who emerged above the cell leader, it was likely, though again unproved, that the leader may have had potential claim on resources by virtue of his leadership role. Ward-level officials were able to acquire resources from the community because of their position, particularly from the ubiquitous general store, the *duka*. If, as seems inevitable, the *duka* was owned and operated by an Asian or Arab, the claim of the ward-level official was strengthened merely by the fact that the shop owner was a minority in the ward and often a not very popular one at that. In each ward studied here the *duka* also provided the means of transportation, a pickup truck, for the leadership. It was inconceivable that the shopkeepers would deny ward leaders their requests as long as these requests remained within tolerable bounds. Even when these demands were excessive, the shopkeeper who sought relief from higher officials might have to submit to the demands of division- and district-level leaders, and these would become even more expensive. The shopkeepers were likely to avoid such an escalation of the quasitribute system. In my view, it would be inaccurate to label this activity of the ward leaders as corruption or blackmail. While the data were extremely hard to come by, it appeared that some such activity was a norm at the ward and village levels.

Almost any leader, be he cell leader, ward chairman, or other, could requisition resources from the community for community projects such as welcoming a visitor, building a road or well, or assisting the leader in times of need. He might receive special prices for the items he bought. It would be of little value to label such activity as traditional or modern. It is important to note, however, that it was relatively open activity at the ward level. Just how open may be revealed by the contents of a letter I received when I was an agent and duly certified representative of the government [64] from a ward-level official. The letter, in part goes:

[64] Research in Tanzania is conducted only with written approval of the office of the Second Vice President.

My request to you is, please help me with 50 shillings so that I can pay my workmen who work for me in my farm, as I will be associated with you for five months. I will pay you back at the end of March.

I am not asking you as a government request, but I ask you as from your kindness if possible from your friendship.[65]

This letter called attention to Fallers' remark that the duties of the headman, or any leader, prevented him from giving his full attention to agriculture. In a subsistence economy this is an extremely important consideration. The duties of village leadership, and, especially ward leadership, were very time consuming. While it is true that in the subsistence economy time is not at a premium, during the peak seasons of the year it is unlikely that a man has time for much else than his fields. As noted, no ward-level officials were paid except for the village executive officer, who received a fulltime salary of 152 shillings (about $22.00) per month *if* he collected a satisfactory percentage of the ward's taxes. The district councilor from the ward received an allowance for the days of meeting, which probably met his expenses. The ward chairman did not receive a salary. Nor was there any salary for the cell leaders. Thus at the ward level and below there was no formal compensation for the leadership efforts of the elected officials. There can be little doubt that these officials neglected one or the other of their responsibilities—agriculture or leadership—under those circumstances.[66]

[65] From a letter received in 1968, translated from Swahili.

[66] The problem of uncompensated village leadership was particularly acute in such special development projects as village settlements, where a greater effort in the fields *and*, by definition, a greater political effort was demanded. The chairman of one of these projects was constantly tardy in his own work on the scheme, in part at least, because of his leadership duties. He eventually was detained for forty-eight hours by the area commissioner because he was derelict in his work duties. When district-level technical officers discussed the question of how to make the village development committees more effective, some noted that the members of the VDC's expected to be paid for their efforts since other government officials were paid. Because they were not paid, they were less than energetic.

In summary, the role of the headman under the colonial government was taken up by the village cell leaders and the ward officials. The conflicts that confronted the headman seemed to confront the village and ward leaders. In fact, the conflict might be even greater since the national and district leaders were making an all-out effort to mobilize the people for development.

The village can be accurately conceived as the most local political system. It performs to a greater or lesser degree the functions performed by any other political system; in so doing, it inevitably strives to maintain itself as a system. In this effort, it may steadfastly resist the efforts of other political systems to direct the behavior of the participants in the village system. In this process, the village political system may increase its capacity to deal with intrusions into its domain—it may develop politically. The development of the village political system may play havoc with the plans of the national political system for social, economic, and political progress in the nation. The following chapter will examine the interplay between the political systems from district to village around the issue of rural development.

CHAPTER VII
Village and State: Systems in Action

President Nyerere closed his speech presenting the Second Five-Year Plan to the TANU Annual Conference in 1969 with the words, "To Plan is to choose. Choose to go forward."[1] Mwalimu, or teacher, as Nyerere is known by his people, thus signaled the close of the first decade of Tanzanian development efforts. Two crucial choices were made during this decade—a decision to push independent, self-reliant development and a decision to place the major emphasis of the development effort in the rural areas.

The effectiveness of developmental policy depends upon whether the choices made in the nation's capital will be accepted and acted upon in the hinterland. This acceptance is dependent, in part, upon the intermeshing of political systems—immediate, intermediate, and national. The foci of my analysis of these systems are three: (1) the sharing of political functions between these systems, (2) the intersystem conflict of roles, and (3) the intersystemic inputs-outputs that are exchanged between the political systems. This assessment of linkages is incomplete, since it centers primarily only on those linkages relating to the rural development effort.

Sharing of Functions

The four categories of political functions suggested as guides to this analysis were: (1) the maintenance of order; (2) communi-

[1] *The Second Five-Year Plan,* p. xxiii.

cations; (3) political socialization; and (4) extraction/mobilization. An assumption upon which the study was based is that at any time these four categories of political functions are shared by all the political systems impinging upon the individual. While the field work concentrated on the linkages between village and district headquarters, attention was also paid to the presence of the regional and national political systems where their sharing the performance of political functions was observed and was relevant.

The conception of a series of political systems from the most local to the most distant from the individual suggests that the objectives of these systems, aside from the ultimate goals of survival, may differ. Thus the extent to which the political functions are performed by one system or the other and the extent to which the goals of these political systems are the same suggest the nature of the sharing of the political functions. The nature of this sharing will also indicate the extent to which the goals of the political systems, in this case, rural development, will be achieved. If, for example, there is not general consensus between systems upon common goals, the resources of the respective systems will be utilized, not in achieving these secondary goals for the respective communities, but in the primary pursuit of survival of the political systems. Thus, the extent to which the political systems share any of these functions is determined in part by the degree to which they accept common objectives.

The Maintenance of Order

Clearly, in the effort to promote rural change, the maintenance of order was not of highest priority, and thus I have not stressed this function. However, certain tentative conclusions about the maintenance of order may be suggested.

The continuing isolation of the village community from the rest of the society meant that the major problems requiring political action to maintain order have been confronted and resolved in large part by the most immediate political system, the village. The vast majority of disruptions of order in the villages were reconciled by the village elders and the cell leaders. If, however, the dispute couldn't be handled by the village political system, the dispute followed the traditional pattern of political conflict and was expanded beyond the boundaries of the immediate political system.[2] A marriage-divorce-dowry dispute in Sindeni Ward illustrated this expansion of political conflict. This dispute expanded to the district office, where it resulted in the imprisonment of the bride's father. Later the dispute was again taken up at the ward and village level in search of a way of removing the father from the order-maintaining processes of the district political system. In the areas studied here most problems of order originating at the village level did not have to do with developmental efforts, and most did not involve representatives from the ward, division, and district in attempts to solve the dispute, as this one did.

The first specialized institution for maintaining order, the police station, was most often found at the district headquarters, although in the more developed and thickly settled areas of Tanga there were substations, usually at division headquarters. There were no such substations in Handeni. The police forces, however, were seldom employed in the maintenance of order in the district. They were more important in the extraction/mobilization function discussed below. If widespread violence occurred at the village, ward, or division level the police mobile field force unit might have been called into the area to reestablish order, although this was rare.

In addition to the police, another institution, the youth wing of the political party, began to emerge at the ward level and functioned intermittently to maintain order. Of the two districts studied here, the TANU Youth League (TYL) was most active in Tanga District. Although a TYL organization existed in Marungu Ward, and was evident at public meetings, I saw no evidence that it took

---

[2] See a statement of this principle relating to the American context in Elmer E. Schattschneider, *The Semi-sovereign People* (New York, 1960), pp. 10 ff.

action to reestablish order. In Sindeni Ward, Handeni District, the TYL was nonexistent at the ward level and efforts to organize the league were met with the question, "Do we get paid?" Nevertheless, individuals at the ward level in both Marungu and Sindeni called themselves members of the Youth League and served a kind of patrol activity especially during public meetings.

At a ward development committee meeting in Sindeni, one individual wore the green shirt of the TYL and circulated throughout the meeting as if to maintain order. He was also in charge of the tiny shed that served as the jail in Sindeni. Members of the community treated this individual as if he were of questionable mental balance, and he was accepted more than responded to. At Kwamkono, the chairman of the TYL, as he was called, was a man of respect and position in the village. He accompanied the "Mayor" on visits throughout the village and welcomed visitors. Positioning himself at central positions during public meetings, he maintained order in the meeting.[3]

Like the police, the youth league was most active in the mobilization and extraction function. In the two wards considered here the league was only sporadically active below the district system level, and then its action had primarily to do with the district political affairs in the subsystems. In Marungu, Tanga, the TYL was evident only at ward-level functions. In Sindeni, Handeni, a TYL structure existed in Kwamkono, the original location of a village development committee and at Kwamsala, which was a TYL-sponsored development project.

Communications

The communication function has been conceived as a necessary prerequisite to all other political activities. An analysis of communication *within* and *between* political systems reveals the prin-

[3] A particular disorder with which he dealt was the interruption of an important national official's speech by the village halfwit.

cipal structures performing this function in particular political systems and the institutions that perform intersystem communication.

The structures performing the communications function with the village, ward, and division political systems also performed the communication function for the district system as it communicated throughout each of the subdivisions of the district. The principal structural medium through which communications took place was the political party. When the analysis moved closer to the local level and to the individual, however, party and government became synonymous. From the ward upward the structures were dichotomous; usually, however, the individual performing the government role also had a party role to perform and *vice versa*. In the ward, the village executive officer, who is an official of the government, was also the secretary of the ward party organization. The chairman of the party at the ward level was solely a party man, but his functions were both governmental and party. The district councilor originated from the ward political system also. His role in the communications function was slightly different from those of the party chairman and the village executive officer. While the role envisaged for him by other officials higher in the hierarchy of the district system was basically one of communicating policies to his constituents, he, while accepting this role, sensed a responsibility for representing his people to the district system.

From the division level upward in the hierarchy, communication was performed by more differentiated structures. Within the two divisions studied here, person-to-person, word-of-mouth communication between the three top officials—the chairman of the party, the executive secretary of the party and the division executive officer—was most common. It is important to note that while the government and party were to a considerable extent fused at this level, there were different kinds of information being communicated to the division from different kinds of structures at the *boma* office. In fact, there had been cases of conflict between the chairman, a political figure, and the divisional executive officer, and other civil servants at the division level. The most notable example revealed here occurred in Tanga District.

The minutes of the finance committee for October 1967 reported that

> the work of the Field Assistants, Agriculture, in the villages was not successful. These civil servants who are concerned are found not working day to day and their programs of travel are not known. Most of them travel for their own benefit, and pretend that they are on the job. This can be proven by the TANU leaders in the villages, cell leaders, Division Executive Officers, but it is impossible to be proved by the District Agriculture Officer because he does not work with them in the villages. He only gets reports monthly from them which are not true. Moreover, while they are in the villages, the Division Executive Officers, being the head of the division should know what their work programs are.[4]

The meeting resolved that it should be explained to all civil servants in the divisions that the divisional executive officer "is the head of the Division" and that they must keep him informed of their actions and work schedules. Here, then, was a local example of the lack of effective communication between civil servants and the political figures in the district political system. The DDPC's and WDC's were being established to cope with this problem. A similar committee at the division level was also planned.

The communication problem at the local level, the ward and division, had been less serious in Handeni District than in Tanga District, partly because local relationships in Handeni were more intimate than in Tanga District or, indeed, at the district level in Handeni. Due to the sparse nature of settlement and the poor physical communications systems with other communities, the ward and division officers in Handeni—the civil servants, the chairmen, and the divisional or village executive officers—interacted more inten-

[4] Tanga District Council, Finance Committee, Minutes 16–18, October 1967.

sively and thus communicated more successfully simply because there were really few alternatives to intense relationships among themselves.[5] Nevertheless, the problem of communication between structures *within* the respective political systems still existed in Handeni as it did in Tanga District. It was particularly acute at the district level. There were therefore two primary channels of communication between the district *boma* and the villages. The one may be described as the party-government channel; the other as the technician or civil servant's channel.

President Nyerere, in discussing the role of the political party in 1962 noted that the nation's goals could be achieved by

a strong political organization active in every village, which acts like a two-way, all-weather road along which the purposes, plans and problems of government travel to the people at the same time as the ideas, desires, and misunderstandings of the people can travel direct to the government. This is the job of the new TANU.[6]

The structures of the political party were the most important links between the political systems in the districts studied here. While the fusion between party and government started at the district level, and extended into the division and ward systems, it became complete in the villages where the major political institution was the cell leader. The cell leader was first a creation of the political party, but at this level he was also of equal importance as a structure within the political system. Through the cell leader the district political system was able to communicate with the people in the villages. Considering the difficulties of the physical environment, the effectiveness of this system in the districts studied here

[5] See Godfrey and Monica Wilson, *The Analysis of Social Change* (Cambridge: Cambridge University Press, 1945), for the statement of this general idea. "Our hypothesis is that the total degree of dependence upon others, i.e., the intensity of relations is the same in all societies, but that it may be more or less spread out. Intensity in the narrower circles or relations necessarily diminishes as intensity in the wider circles increases." *Ibid.,* p. 40.

[6] Quoted in Rweyemamu, "Nation Building," p. 186.

was rather remarkable. Generally communication from *boma* to village went via the divisional executive officer, to the village executive officer, to the cell leaders. Strictly party affairs were communicated through the party structure at the division level and then to the VEO (now WEO), who was both party bureaucrat and government official at the ward level. The cell leader, the ward leaders, and the division leaders then functioned intermittently in performing the communications function in the district political system.

This analysis, however, describes only one-half of the function of the political party envisaged by President Nyerere. Communication of party and government plans and objectives to the people was fairly sophisticated at this point. How effectively the communication of the "ideas, desires, and misunderstandings of the people can travel direct to the government" was an open question. In fact, my findings suggested that the nature of the message determined whether it was communicated to another political system higher in the hierarchy. Those messages that might be most important for the effective performance of the district political system were in most cases the very messages the district system did not receive by its established channels.

There was, for example, considerable opposition in the villages to certain district and national development policies. It is inconceivable that the cell leaders were not aware of and did not participate in the articulation of this discontent; they were likely in some cases to express this discontent to the ward chairman and the village executive officer. They did this, however, only if they were convinced they could do so with immunity for themselves and their constituents. At some point in the chain of communication from village to the district and national political system the likelihood that protest or discontent would bring displeasure upon the head of the communicator tended to stifle the communications function. Considering only the village to *boma* communications here, it was most likely that alternative routes of communication would be used, or that the feelings would simply not be communicated beyond the village or perhaps the ward level. Both developments were evident in the two divisions and districts studied here.

A letter expressing opposition to compulsory planting measures in Handeni District was a vivid example of a clandestine communication of discontent. Signed fictitiously, this letter went to the ward officials in Sindeni Ward and ultimately found its way to the highest circles of the district political system.[7] The route this expression of protest took in reaching the district *boma* was of some interest. The letter was first given to an agricultural field assistant in the ward,[8] then passed on to the divisional agricultural officer, who took the letter to the district agricultural officer, who turned it over to the district chairman of TANU. The chairman then took the letter to the area commissioner. Since the district agricultural officer was ostensibly under the direction of the area commissioner, the reason for his handing the letter to the district chairman of TANU was only open to speculation.

A contrasting type of clandestine communication of dissent was a widely rumored network of informers initiated by the district and national political systems, who sought to determine those "who talk against the government."[9] The actual effectiveness of this network of informers in communicating what the people felt and thought to the leaders higher in the hierarchy was impossible to determine. However, the existence of this network or the belief that it existed caused villagers to be extremely reluctant to relate their views to anyone, especially to a stranger.

The role of the district councilor in the process of communicat-

[7] See a copy of the letter on p. 69.

[8] The agricultural field assistant was the lowest level staff member of the Ministry of Agriculture who worked at the village level.

[9] It is impossible to determine of course the validity of these rumors. There is no reason to doubt them, however, and sufficient reason to accept the existence of such a network as a fact. Local people generally felt that they had the informer spotted and could even give the license number of the Landrover used by these agents.

ing village views to the district political system must be noted (to be discussed in detail below). In contrast to the cell leader, the district councilor was relatively vocal in articulating the protests of his constituents even if they happened to violate established policy. In addition, he felt, as a general rule, that it was his responsibility to voice his people's opinions. It is plausible to suggest, if not possible to prove, that his greater daring in voicing dissent was due in part to the fact that the greater scope of his constituency made it much more difficult to pinpoint the particular source of protest.

A final share in the communications function was very effectively performed by the national political system through Radio Tanzania, the national broadcasting system. This communication was totally from the center, Dar es Salaam, to the villages. Nevertheless, this communication was the most direct and persistent relationship the villagers had with the national political community. At least one radio was found in every village studied here. In most villages, there were several.[10] The radio was a constant center of attraction of the whole community and almost instantaneously informed the inhabitants of the most remote village of the developments in Washington, Moscow, and Dar es Salaam.[11] More important, in terms of its impact upon rural development, was the fact that the national ethic of self-reliance and development was constantly being transmitted to the countryside. Undoubtedly, President Nyerere was listened to with great respect, even reverence, and the villagers received his messages with considerable attention.

While the major participant in this communication via radio

[10] The estimated number of radios in use in Tanzania in 1966 was 120,000. The total population at this time was over 12,000,000. There is reason to believe that the number of radios was greater than this estimate. See United Nations, *Statistical Yearbook 1967* (New York, 1968).

[11] In the spring of 1968 I learned of the late Senator Robert Kennedy's decision to challenge President Johnson for the Democratic party's nomination for president of the United States, while I was camping on the outskirts of Sindeni village. The message came by way of Radio Tanzania to the home of the village executive officer, who then brought me the message.

was the national political system, the district political system might also use the airways. In the spring of 1968, the Tanga District Council, for example, had its agricultural bylaw regarding hours of work in the fields announced over Radio Tanzania.[12]

In summary, the communication function *between* the political systems studied here was shared by institutions within the various systems. The most prominent structures performing this function in all the systems from the village to the district boma were those of the political party. The more closely the analysis shifts to the village community, the more important the party was as a means of communicating *to* the people. It was also at this level that the influence of the village system was most strong. The return flow of information to the officials of the division and district may have taken alternative routes, or it may not have occurred at all.

Political Socialization

The primary relationships most important for political socialization are those in the family and small peer groups, and these were dominant in the rural areas of Tanzania,[13] where the village community, which was as a rule heavily oriented toward kinship, played the most important role in the political socialization function. The socialization process favored those attitudes toward government and politics that prevailed in the village political system. While the village political systems instilled in new generations and reinforced in older generations a belief in witchcraft, the paternalistic ethic, and the compulsion syndrome, the national political system tried to gain access to and control over the socialization function in these villages in order to change attitudes toward community and nation and the individual's role in them. The district and national political systems directed their socialization efforts to two audiences

[12] Tanga District Council, Minutes 29 September 1967.
[13] For an excellent treatment of political socialization, see Richard E. Dawson and Kenneth Prewitt, *Political Socialization* (Boston, 1969) and for this point, p. 105.

—the youth and the leaders. Both were expected, in turn, to contribute to the socialization and resocialization of the people at large.

The most important effort to socialize the youth was through the educational system. The district political system, through the district education officer with a technical staff of two or three people, was responsible for the administration and general direction of education in the district under general guidelines laid down by the national system. In 1968, the district councils paid approximately 50 per cent of the teachers' salaries in Tanga and 30 per cent in Handeni District. The central government paid the rest, and this sum was determined by the varying abilities of these districts to finance their educational systems.[14] Most councils provided 50 per cent of the cost and were in constant arrears on payments of teachers' salaries. Finally, in early 1969, the central government completely took over the financing of teachers' salaries in the districts.[15]

Since independence, an effort had been made to revolutionize the educational system to fit it to the needs of rural development and self-reliance from the lowest levels to the university level. In 1967, President Nyerere, in a major policy paper, declared that the purpose of an educational system is "to transmit from one generation to the next the accumulated wisdom and knowledge of the society and their active participation in its maintenance or development." [16] The type of society Nyerere envisaged is indicated in his statement of the goals of the educational system:

It has to foster the social goals of living together, and working together, for the common good. It has to prepare our young people to play a dynamic and constructive part in the development of a society in which all members share and in which progress is measured

[14] See Penner, "Financing Local Government in Tanzania," ch. 3, p. 8.
[15] *Standard,* February 13, 1969.
[16] Julius K. Nyerere, "Education for Self-Reliance" in *Freedom and Socialism,* p. 268.

in terms of human well-being, not prestige buildings, cars, or other such things, whether privately or publicly owned. Our education must therefore inculcate a sense of commitment to the total community, and help the pupils to accept the values appropriate to our kind of future, not those appropriate to our colonial past.[17]

The President called for major reforms of the educational system aimed at bringing the content and form of the education in line with the realities of the nation's goals and potential. These reforms included a reemphasis upon agriculture as the livelihood of the great majority of the people for many years to come, and the revision of instruction in the classroom to include practical participation in farming and other projects on the school grounds. Of considerable importance was the schools' encouragement of self-sufficiency in food and services to inculcate the spirit of self-reliance. The course of study also emphasized the valued aspects of traditional society in an attempt to promote a "Tanzanian" content in the classroom. The President pointed out the many wisdoms of the elders in the villages and encouraged educators to wed these wisdoms to modern techniques and knowledge.

His paper concluded:

The education provided by Tanzania for the students of Tanzania must serve the purposes of Tanzania. It must encourage the growth of the socialist values we aspire to. It must encourage the development of a proud, independent, and free citizenry, which relies upon itself for its own development, and which knows the advantages and the problems of co-operation. It must ensure that the educated know themselves to be an integral part of the nation and recognize the responsibility to give greater service the greater the opportunities they have had.[18]

Following the enunciation of this policy, the principles of self-reliance were stressed in all schools, up to and including the University of Dar es Salaam. While the impact of the education process

[17] *Ibid.*, p. 273.   [18] *Ibid.*, p. 290.

on the socialization of the youth to accept the ideals of the new Tanzanian society was unclear in 1968, the potential impact of that process may be suggested by the fact that in a population of over 12 million, enrollment in primary schools in 1968 was something like 14 per cent of all the primary school-age children. Only about 50 per cent of the children eligible for entry into the first year of primary education in 1969–1970 were provided places in the schools. While these statistics may appear discouraging, they, in fact, represent a considerable achievement over the situation prevailing at independence in 1961. At that time about 486,000 pupils were attending primary schools with about 12,000 completing their primary education. In 1966, 747,000 were attending primary school and those completing primary education were 57,000. The numbers enrolled in 1969–1970 were 850,920.[19] Even though the impact of education was limited because there was considerably less than total enrollment of children in the education system, there was no question but that the rhetoric of the Arusha Declaration was known and used by the youth in even the most remote village studied here.

A second aspect of the socialization of the youth was the organization of branches of the TANU Youth League in all schools. TYL activity, organized at the district level, was directly aimed at the political socialization of the youth. During 1967–1968 there was an increased effort to organize the Youth League in the schools and to engage the young people in drilling in preparation for defense of the nation. The green and black uniforms of the TYL became more prominent in the schools of Tanga and Handeni districts and youth participated in patriotic ceremonies as a group. Again, recalling the limited numbers of youth who were actively participating in the education system, the influence of the youth league through the educational system was limited. There was no

[19] See Idrian N. Resnick (ed.), *Tanzania: Revolution by Education* (Arusha, 1968), p. 4, and *Tanzania Second Five-Year Plan*, I, 149.

way to determine the proportion of youth who participated actively in TYL programs.

After the Arusha Declaration there was an intensified effort to educate leaders to their responsibilities in developing the nation. During 1967–1968 there were many seminars for all varieties of leaders in the party, civil service, and elected governmental positions. TANU had been instrumental in this effort, and in each district, the process was initiated by special teams of party spokesmen from Dar es Salaam. The assumption was that the leaders would return to their villages and inculcate the values of the Arusha Declaration in their people.

In spite of these government and party efforts, the village family was still the most important instrument of socialization throughout Tanzania, and the acceptance of the rhetoric and ethics of the national elite did not necessarily lead to a change in behavior.

The Extraction and Mobilization Function

The ability of a political system to perform the function of extraction and mobilization is a key index of its socioeconomic progress and, indirectly, of successful rural development in Tanzania. Extraction in this discussion refers to the ability of the systems to tap material resources for consumption. Mobilization is, in effect, the extraction of human as opposed to material resources. If the district political system is able to utilize structures in the division, ward, or village political systems for these ends, these structures are functioning as a unitary system, the district political system. Similarly, if the national political system is able to direct the activities of the district system for nationally determined goals, the systems are in the same instance performing as a national political system. This hierarchical model of a political system of subsystems is not a total representation of reality, however. In theory, and in fact, the lower level political systems may be able to extract resources from the higher level political systems for the pursuit of their goals that may not complement national goals. This possibility, as pointed out by Colin Leys, in the case of Uganda, may place in grave jeopardy national development goals not to mention the sheer survival of the national political system.[20]

The major extraction in the districts of Tanzania during 1967–1968 was taxation. This taxation took two major forms—a direct payment by citizens and indirect payments, which were primarily taxes on the sale of produce. In both cases the district political system was responsible for extracting these taxes from the citizens of the district. Eugene Lee noted of Tanzania in 1965:

> As in many developing countries, it is only through the local governments that the bulk of the population is directly taxed. In Tanganyika, for example, 98 per cent of the citizens have virtually no direct contact with or knowledge of any Central Government tax. Only in the districts or towns is the average citizen brought face to face with the high cost of economic development.[21]

The direct tax, or head tax, on individuals was known as the local rate. Ideally, it was levied on all adult males, and an estimated 20 per cent of the total eligible population in the country paid it. In 1965 the local rate made up slightly less than one-half of the district council revenue.[22] Indirect taxes on the sale of produce, the cess, contributed roughly 10 per cent of total district council revenue in the same year. Together these two taxes accounted for close to 60 per cent of total district council revenue. The cess accounted for only 2 per cent of total revenue for the national political system, while the local rate accounted for 8.5 per cent of total revenue for the nation as a whole.[23]

The sharing of the extraction/mobilization function was greatest in the effort to collect the local rates. Until the law was repealed by the national government in 1969, the direct responsibility of collecting this tax lay with the district council, and the bureaucracy of

[20] Leys, *Politicians and Policies*.
[21] Eugene C. Lee, *Local Taxation in Tanganyika* (Berkeley, 1965), p. 2.
[22] Penner, *Financing Local Government*, ch. 4.   [23] *Ibid.*, p. 16.

VILLAGE AND STATE: SYSTEMS IN ACTION 201

the council found this to be its most demanding work. The district executive officer was directly in charge of this effort, with the divisional executive officer and the village executive officer under his direction; the latter, however, had the greatest immediate responsibility. While the line of authority had to this point stayed completely within the bureaucracy of the district council, at the village level, the VEO often turned to the cell leaders for collection responsibilities. Thus the extraction function was thrust upon the cell leader, the chief link between the village and the external world, the mediator of local disorders and the outermost extension of the national party organization.[24]

The response of the cell leader to these demands was varied. Where the geographical conditions and the settlement patterns were such as to make it virtually impossible for the VEO to make the collections himself, he was very dependent upon the cell leader. Sindeni Ward, Handeni, was an example of these difficult conditions. In Marungu Ward, Tanga, in contrast, the VEO had a relatively easy time making the contacts for collection of the tax since the inhabitants of the wards were more concentrated in settlements and the communications network was more highly developed than in Sindeni. In 1968, for example, the percentage of taxpayers per households was 31 per cent in Pongwe and 21 per cent for Chanika.[25] The higher percentages of taxpayers in Pongwe Division is misleading because the VEO of Marungu was not as energetic in his collection of the personal tax as was his counterpart in Sindeni of Handeni District. His immediate superior, the divisional executive officer, complained to me that the VEO had only collected taxes from five people in two months.[26]

[24] The *Standard* (August 8, 1968) reports that in some places in the nation the Youth League has been employed by the VEO for the purpose of collecting the local taxes.

[25] Calculated from *Preliminary Results,* and data gathered through interviews with the division executive officer, Pongwe, January, 1968 and the division executive officer, Chanika, February 27, 1968.

[26] Interview, Pongwe, January 1968.

If the VEO was unable to make all the collections on his own and could not enlist the cell leaders in this task of extraction, he might turn to the district political system for assistance from the police mobile Field Force Unit (FFU),[27] thus bringing representatives of the national political system into the effort. Everyone wished to avoid this rather drastic measure representing the ultimate in conflict between the village systems and the district political system. For, at this stage, the district political system was sharing its extraction function with the national political system—specifically the police. At this stage, the extent to which the village political system shared the extraction function was nil. In the various stages of village participation in the extraction function prior to the use of the coercive power of the district and national political systems, the hard-pressed cell leader actually used the threat of the coming Field Force Unit as a means of extracting taxes from his people. In the words of the Handeni district executive officer, the people of the village viewed the cell leaders "as their savior if he is able to keep the police landrovers away." [28]

A less drastic measure involved putting all male adults who could not show a tax receipt in jail for forty-eight hours as a warning to the immediate offenders and those outside of what might happen to them. Legally, the divisional executive officer had this power and he could enlist other members of the district council bureaucracy in this effort,[29] particularly the messengers, one or more of whom may be stationed at the division office. A tragic outcome of such an employment of persuasion was the death of thir-

[27] The mobile Field Force Unit was a well-trained and well-armed contingent of national police usually stationed in the district headquarters, capable of rapid deployment via Landrovers to trouble spots in the district. They were primarily concerned with internal disruptions of order.

[28] Handeni district executive officer, 28 February 1968.

[29] Ministry of Local Government, Ref. No. LG 12/01, 7 October 1964, LG Circular 39/64 "Responsibilities of Divisional Executive Officer to Arrest and Lock up People." See above p. 148, for additional comment.

teen accused tax defaulters due to overcrowded conditions in a division jail outside of Mwanza in May 1968.[30]

The relative significance of the personal tax as a source of district revenue had traditionally been less in Tanga District than in Handeni District, for in the former there were the alternative sources of revenue, in particular, the cess upon sisal sales.[31] Even in the extraction of the individual tax, however, the process was much easier in Tanga because of the greater numbers of salaried workers to be found there.[32]

The power of the district council to require the employer to deduct the personal tax from the payroll increased drastically the capacity of the district to extract funds from the society. All district councils were instructed in 1964: "Under section 103A of the Local Government Ordinance, councils are empowered to require an employer who carries on his business in its area, to deduct the rate payable to that council by giving the employer a written notice to this effect." [33] The importance of this power and the presence of salaried employees may be emphasized by noting in comparison that Tanga's extractive ability was roughly *thirty* times that of Handeni's. In two districts dominated by large sisal estates and one of which was Tanga, Penner notes:

The tax collectors could afford to rely largely on the taxes collected at source from the employees of the estates and other wage paying institutions. Little effort was made to collect even the basic rate from self-employed individuals. However, in most communities the wage earning proportion of the population is so small that they cannot

---

[30] *Standard,* May 1, 1968.

[31] For example, in 1965 the percentage of the total revenue from the produce cess in Tanga District was 16.3 per cent compared to roughly 10 per cent for the nation as a whole. Penner, *Financing Local Government,* ch. 4.

[32] See above, p. 17.

[33] Ministry of Local Government, Ref. No. LG 12/67/04; L. G. Circular 18/1964 "Local Rate Collection."

afford to rely on taxation deducted at source and a more intensive effort is essential.[34]

As the fusion between party and government has been emphasized in this analysis, it should be stressed here that TANU dues were also legally deducted from the salaries of employees.

The second major category of extraction performed in the districts until 1969 were indirect taxes, the most important being a tax on produce sold in the districts. The ministry responsible for local government could, after consultation with the district council, "impose a tax with respect to any agricultural produce, fish or livestock sold within, or exported from the district." [35] This tax, known as the cess, made up about 10 per cent of total revenue for the district councils in 1965.[36] Other indirect taxes composed from 5 to 15 per cent of council revenue in the same year.[37] These included court fees, such as those for marriage and divorce proceedings, and the sale of various licenses, including bicycle licenses and a wide variety of trading licenses.[38]

The administration of the produce cess varied from district to district. In most districts and in Handeni and Tanga, the cooperative societies were the sole legal outlet for the farmer's crops. During the time this study was conducted the societies withheld a cess on all the produce they sold and sent it to the district council. Originally organized for marketing, the cooperative societies also performed part of the extraction function within the district political system. The produce cess was only part of total extraction performed by the cooperatives. Deductions for other fees, for, example, costs of handling and of staff, were considerable, and the farmer actually received a price for his products much lower than he was able to get for the product by selling on the black market. Farmers were widely dissatisfied with this state of affairs. A report

[34] Penner, *Financing Local Government*, ch. 4.
[35] Lee, *Local Taxation*, ch. 4.
[36] Penner, *Financing Local Government*, ch. 4. [37] *Ibid.*, p. 20.
[38] *Ibid.*

prepared at President Nyerere's direction in 1966 articulated this dissatisfaction.[39]

A comparison of prices the farmer received for his produce revealed the basis for his dissatisfaction. One farmer complained to the Presidential Special Committee:

> It is absurd to believe that a bag of maize which the Board [National Agricultural Products Board which buys food crops from the cooperatives] buys for Shs. 22/– [$3.14] is worth Shs. 46/80 [about $6.70] immediately after it has been moved from a society godown [warehouse] to the Board's godown which is just about 200 yards away.[40]

In 1967 rice paddy in the vicinity of Mombo was being bought for Shs. 32/– per bag at the local cooperative society while the farmer could receive over Shs. 60/– (roughly $4.50 to over $9.00) for the same bag on the black market. In July 1968 copra, the major market crop for Marungu Ward, Tanga District, which was bought from the farmer by the cooperative society for Shs. 6/60 to 7/– ($1.00) per bag was sold in Tanga for Shs. 21/– ($3.00). At the same time the price of copra in Kenya was relatively high and there was no way of determining what proportion of the copra crop was being sold into Kenya via the black market. In Handeni District it was estimated that 10 per cent of the maize crop in that district found its way into the illegal trade.[41]

As long as the farmer sold his crops to the cooperative the extraction of the cess took place automatically. When the farmer refused to sell to the cooperatives and went to the black market, the extraction function being performed by the cooperative societies in the district was flaunted. Typically, the cooperative societies and

---

[39] United Republic of Tanzania, *Report of the Presidential Special Committee of Enquiry into Cooperative Movement and Marketing Boards* (Dar es Salaam, 1966). This document contains a good survey of the cooperative movement in Tanzania and a summary of the farmers' complaints; see especially pp. 3–5.

[40] *Ibid.*, p. 3.   [41] Handeni, 28 February 1968.

the district council bureaucracy turned to the coercive institutions of the district political system to attempt to control the sale of the farmers' produce. From time to time there were systematic searches of trucks and other means of transport in an effort to apprehend those involved in the black market operations. Occasionally, the police Field Force Units searched the villages for rice and other crops.[42]

Either effort to enforce this extraction against determined opposition by the peasants was a very costly undertaking in both men and materials. The effect of this cooperative marketing operation upon farmer incentive to increase productivity was obvious. One of the major complaints during village discussions and surveys was the state of the marketing system.

Officials in Dar es Salaam were not unaware of the detrimental impact of the use of the marketing machinery to extract resources at the local level, in addition to its relatively high expense. In June 1969 the collection of the cess on produce by the district political system was completely eliminated. The Minister of Finance, Mr. Jamal, announced in his budget speech to the National Assembly the decision of the national government to repeal the authority of the district councils to collect both the head tax as well as the cess. The result shifted capacity to extract from the immediate and intermediate systems to the national system and, in the same stroke, shifted the burden from the peasants to those living in the urban areas.

A "far reaching and complex sales tax . . . aimed at placing financial mobilisation on a new and more enduring plane," was to replace the cess and the head tax which was calculated by Mr. Jamal to be roughly Shs. 110,000 in one financial year.[43] The sales

---

[42] This account was given the researcher by a farmer and has subsequently been substantiated in the press. See *Standard,* November 19, 1968: "About 14 members of the police Field Force Unit were sent to Pare Areas between July and September 4. . . . The FFU people were sent to prevent smuggling of paddy and rice from the district."

[43] *Standard,* June 20, 1969.

tax "excluded basic food stuffs and certain other goods primarily consumed by peasants and low income workers."[44] The government calculated that the proposals would "reduce taxes on peasants by Shs. 57.5–62.5 million over a full year and thus . . . represent a significant lessening of the burden on the peasants." At the same time the measures would "put additional burdens of Shs. 85–90 million on people with salaries and other regular incomes, and those engaged in commerce and various professions." "This means," the minister of finance concluded, "that we are not only shifting a tax burden of about Shs. 60 million from rural citizens to urban and other salaried citizens, but we are also adding a further 25 to 30 million on this latter category."[45]

Thus the urban dweller and the salaried citizen were to be subjected not only to the demand for making up the deficit in government revenue resulting from the policy decision to reduce the extraction from the peasant but also to even increased taxation. In response to this shift in policy it was estimated that peasant farmers would pay taxes and fees equal to about 12 per cent of their income, whereas those citizens with wages and salaries, the urban self-employed, and the business community would be paying taxes ranging from about 17.5 per cent of income to approximately 41 per cent of income. The percentage would be progressive in proportion to the amount of income which one received. Or, put in different terms, the average peasant family of five would pay Shs. 0/40 a day in taxes while families earning Shs. 3,600/00 per year, or about Shs. 10/00 a day, would be paying Shs. 2/00 per day in taxes. In progression, families earning Shs. 10,000 a year or about Shs. 30/00 per day would be paying about Shs. 8/00 per day and those earning Shs. 20,000 per year or about Shs. 58/00 per day would be paying about Shs. 20/00 per day in taxes.[46] Thus the policy of placing the 80 per cent of Tanzania's citizens who are peasants at the center of government's development efforts became even more concretely expressed in the political systems' extrac-

[44] *Ibid.*   [45] *Ibid.*   [46] *Ibid.*

tion efforts. Not only was the major extraction shifted away from the immediate and intermediate political systems, but the total burden on the citizens in the rural areas was substantially reduced. This decision was in response not only to the relatively high costs in resources and opposition that the collection efforts in the local communities stirred but, ultimately, to the low returns that all efforts elicited. The central point for a study of rural development efforts and the relationship between political systems in Africa is that the burden upon the peripheral areas was being lowered even at the time that the commitment of the political systems to these areas was being increased.

The shift of extraction capacity to the national political system was not surprising since the central political system had always been responsible for the extraction of resources. Of the total revenue collected by all political systems in the nation in 1963–1964, central government collections accounted for 75 per cent of the total, while district collections accounted for 21 per cent of the total. The biggest single source of national revenue was import duties and excise duties, which accounted for 51 per cent of the total national collection in 1963. The one other major source of resources for the national political system was the income tax on corporate and personal income. This accounted for 23 per cent of national revenue but was collected from less than one per cent of the population in 1962–1963.[47] Ultimately, the burden of the import and excise duties might fall on the farmers in increased prices. There was no noticeable dissatisfaction at this time and, indeed, virtually no realization that this extraction was being performed. There was undoubtedly some smuggling across boundaries and along the sea coast. While efforts to control this type of evasion of the extraction function could conceivably involve the immediate and intermediate political systems, this was not the case in the areas studied here at the time this field work was carried out.

The task of mobilizing human resources for developmental tasks

[47] Statistics are derived from Lee, *Local Taxation,* pp. 16, 17, 31.

was dependent to a much greater extent upon the shared efforts of the political systems within the district. The primary instrument for mobilization was the political party. The party mechanism not only linked institutions within a particular political system but also linked the different political systems in the hierarchy. A major contribution of the national political system to the mobilization effort was the communication of an ideological theme to the villages. This theme was then seized with varying degrees of enthusiasm by the elites of all the political systems and employed in their efforts to mobilize the countryside to the tasks at hand. Ultimately, however, concentrated and long-term mobilization in the areas studied here was primarily the function of the village and ward political systems.

A tentative analysis of the nature of the sharing of the extraction/mobilization function does not indicate the total levels of either aspect of this function in the political systems considered here. In reality, the level of extraction and mobilization performed in the village political systems at the direction of, or by, the district and national systems was limited in the cases studied. Since the capacity of political systems to perform the extraction/mobilization function at high levels is one indicator of high levels of political development, the implications regarding the relative developments of the district and national systems are fairly clear. By the same token, the ability of political subsystems—here the villages and wards—to effectively resist the extraction from or mobilization of its people and resources from and by other political systems is one criterion of the development of these subsystems.

Intersystem Roles: The Question of Dominance

The interplay of political systems considered here is highlighted by those individuals whose roles in their society demand that they be actors in more than one of the systems. The conflict of roles that this suggests was clearly evident throughout my research. Dominance was determined in most cases by the circumstances at hand. It was quite easy, for example, for the cell leader in the village to fulfill the demands of his role in the national political system by communicating party directives to the village. To participate in the communications function did not conflict with, and might even complement, the demands placed upon him by his constituents in the village. On the other hand, for the cell leader to participate in the extraction/mobilization function of the district or national system in the village very definitely conflicted with the role that these same constituents saw for him.

Under the shadow of the visiting area commissioner, the ward chairman of TANU was a staunch defender of self-help projects and communally worked block farms. When the area commissioner was not around, the chairman was the person who requested assistance from the district headquarters and was not seen by his constituents or by himself as part of the district or national political system. Each of the political figures described in this research was confronted to some degree with the conflict of demands of roles suggested here. The source of stress on roles came either from the nation and the district *boma* (the latter having been described here as the peripheral outpost of the national political system) or from the immediate village and other intermediate political systems, that is, the wards and divisions. The extent of the pull between these two sources of demands was conditioned by two factors that stood out in this study. First was the source of recruitment into the political roles and second was the feelings concerning the particular issue in question.

The independent government of Tanzania had made a determined effort to control recruitment to political roles. All appointments in the national hierarchy at least down through the area commissioners placed actors in areas outside their tribal origin. All technical officers at the district level and often at the division level were posted outside their own locale.

Obviously the central government could not exercise complete control over the elective, representative posts. It was very unlikely in Sindeni and Marungu wards, for example, that an individual not born and raised in the locality would be elected to represent the village in ward, division, or, ultimately, district political affairs. Party control over elections consisted, it may be recalled, only of approving or disapproving candidates who were nominated by the local party organization.[48]

The role conflict was obviously great on those individuals who had first to fit certain national party criteria before being allowed to run for election and, second, at the same time fulfill certain local criteria if they were to be elected. The conflict of demands placed on these roles only began at the election, however, since the behavior of these actors had then to attempt to satisfy what might well become two masters. At this point the issue toward which behavior was directed determined whether conflict would ensue and what the results of the conflict would be.

Among the actors occupying the roles linking the political systems studied here there was no disagreement with the general principles of Tanzanian independence and development as enunciated by President Nyerere. When, however, active support for these measures would conflict with values held at the local level, the behavior expected by district and national elites was in most cases not forthcoming.

The desired behavior was most often realized when political systems higher in the hierarchy exerted pressure upon the actors in the subsystems. In effect, occupants of these roles in the subsystems were subject to constant threat in that they were held responsible by their superiors in the other political systems if the performance of the village, ward, or division was not in accordance with district goals. In the cases studied here, however, the pressures from the locality—village, ward, and division—were greater and more effective than the counterpressure from the political systems

---

[48] See *Report of the Presidential Commission on the Establishment of a Democratic One Party State.*

higher in the hierarchy. The relative extent of contact with actors in other political systems was of crucial importance in this consideration. When, for example, the village was isolated from contact with other villages or from the division headquarters, the cell leaders had minimal contact with actors from higher political systems and were almost entirely under the influence of the villagers.

Where the role was filled by a locally elected representative, and where the representative idea was strong in the minds of the politician and his constituents, the dominance of the locality demands over the demands of the external political systems was most likely. Within the villages the cell leader was the most prominent example of this type of role. This category of locality roles also included, however, the ward chairman of TANU, the district councilor, and ultimately the chairman of the district TANU. As the role moved further from the locality, the influence of the immediate political system's demands on the role decreased in proportion to the increased influence of systems higher in the hierarchy. It is clear that as the scope of the system of which the role was a part increased, the intensity of the demands placed on the role from the localities decreased.

The dominance of locality demands on roles was clear, even on appointed positions in the localities that were filled by individuals from outside the immediate locality. A good example of such an individual was a rural development assistant who lived in one of the wards studied. He participated in the promotion of the developmental process most actively when under the surveillance of superiors from the division or district office, and during other times settled into a role of coexistence with the locality. A second prominent example was the contrasting performances of the village executive officers in Marungu and Sindeni. The VEO at Marungu was from the ward in which he lived, and among his constituents his reputation as a leader was very good. His performance as a collector of taxes and organizer of communal self-help projects, in the view of the divisional executive officer, was very poor. In contrast,

VILLAGE AND STATE: SYSTEMS IN ACTION 213

the VEO in Sindeni Ward was a Zigua, but he came from another division. His efforts to collect personal taxes were much more strenuous than his Marungu counterpart, although the hostile terrain plus the absence of an employer withholding of taxes made him less successful in monetary terms in this effort than the Marungu VEO.[49] The influence of the locality upon the behavior of the VEO's was indicated in an address of the Tanga area commissioner to the district council in 1966. Though not in reference to Marungu, the area commissioner noted that "some of the VEO's are traditional headmen so they don't bother the advice of leaders of the district. Some even have no time to deal with the Chairman of TANU."[50]

The divisional executive officer in both Chanika, Handeni, and Pongwe, Tanga, were from outside the division where they were stationed. The divisional executive officer of Chanika was of a different tribe. Both men were very closely tied to the district political system and their role in the district political system dominated their role in the divisions and the localities.

The District Councilor: Perceptions of Roles

As I have already described the district council as an example of a local institution of government particularly susceptible to central and district government control, the question of conflict of roles as perceived by the members of the district councils is of interest here. Locality influence upon the district council was great for several reasons. First, the contact of the councilor with the district political system was extremely irregular. During one year, the meetings numbered four at the most, although the coun-

[49] On two different occasions, I accompanied the Sindeni VEO on trips to meetings called by him for the discussion of ward affairs only to find, to my consternation, that, except for a few old men and some children, the villages were empty.
[50] Tanga District Council, Minutes 21 December 1966.

cilor might attend one or two committee meetings. The councilor's constituency, the ward, was a relatively constricted locality and there were no persistent demands that the councilor actively perform his roles in the district and national political systems. While the councilor was lectured and scolded during meetings with the district executive officer and the area commissioner, this pressure lasted but one day, after which the councilor returned to the sanctuary of his ward. Nevertheless, the district councilor was among the most prominent representatives of a local community in the district and the national political process, and I expected that he would be a good example of the conflict of roles, torn on the one hand by the expectations of his constituents and on the other by the demands of the central authorities for participation in the nation-building effort. I studied the role of the district councilor in some detail by considering the councilor's perception of his role as a councilor and his perception of the role of the dictrict council as an institution. Using a questionnaire distributed to each councilor in Tanga and Handeni districts during 1968, I asked each councilor what he saw his work as a councilor to involve and what he saw the most important work of the council to be.[51]

In both districts, the questionnaire had the support of a letter of introduction from the respective district council/district TANU chairmen.[52] The use of such a letter, absolutely necessary for any attempt to conduct research in contemporary Tanzania, accounted in part for the respectable response of councilors to the question-

[51] The questionnaire, and specifically the questions considered here, are patterned after similar questions employed in John C. Wahlke et al., *The Legislative System* (New York, 1962). The wording of the questions has been adapted to the context of the Tanzanian district council. The concept of role has of necessity been used here at a fairly low level of sophistication. The writer has been influenced in particular by the use of role analysis in Samuel J. Eldersveld, *Political Parties: A Behavioral Analysis* (Chicago, 1964), see especially ch. 10.

[52] These two posts, one in the district council, the other in TANU, the single political party, are by law held by the same person in contemporary Tanzania.

naire. Fourteen out of eighteen (78 per cent) of the Handeni councilors returned the completed questionnaire; while thirty-three out of a total of thirty-eight (87 per cent) of the Tanga councilors did so.[53] The responses to each questionnaire were anonymous, and official endorsement of the project did not appear to have dimmed the frankness with which councilors spoke their minds.

Councilor Perception of Individual Role

The district councilor's perception of his role as a member of the district council was sought by a consideration of the responses to the following questions: "What is the most important work of a district councilor? What are the most important things you do?" Since the questions were open-ended, some councilors gave more than one type of role that they saw themselves fulfilling in the council. An analysis of the responses suggests, however, four major categories of response. The largest proportion of councilors from both Tanga and Handeni councils suggested the role as one of communication between their people and the "government." While caution in analysis is essential because of the small numbers of councilors involved, I will use percentages here to contrast the responses of the Tanga councilors to those from Handeni. Twenty-seven per cent of the Tanga councilors' responses to this question suggested that the work consisted of "taking people's problems to council." Likewise, 27 per cent of the Handeni councilors' responses suggested this category as the most important work of the councilor. For the other side of the communication function, that of "taking the resolutions of the council to the people," 18 per cent of the Tanga responses and 27 per cent of the Handeni responses indicated this to be among the most important work.

A second major category of role perceived by the councilors was

[53] The questionnaire was mailed to the members of the Tanga district council on May 11, 1968. The final tabulation was made on June 26, 1968. The questionnaire was mailed to the Handeni councilors on June 19, 1968, and the tabulation was concluded on August 31, 1968. The questionnaire and virtually all the research was conducted in Swahili.

that of promoting development in their districts. Twenty-one per cent of the responses from Tanga spoke of the general area of encouragement and promotion of development efforts, while 23 per cent of the Handeni responses fell in this category.

The third major category perceived by the councilors was the "representation" role, including the mediation, negotiation, and representation function. Only 18 per cent of the Tanga responses and 17 per cent of the Handeni responses suggested that the role of councilor included this function.

The frustration that the Handeni councilors felt for the obviously very limited role they played in the destiny of their district was suggested by the episode of a young councilor who, upon finding during a meeting that the cooperative officer to whom his complaints about marketing conditions should have been addressed was absent, threw his hands into the air and exclaimed, "We're talking to the air." The Tanga councilors, while they might actually have had no more influence on government policies in the district, did feel more involved in council activities and thus might have felt less need to perform the actively representative role.

A final group of responses could be categorized as "governmental," which would include references to taxes, bylaws, and peace-keeping. Fourteen per cent of the Tanga responses fell under this general heading, while only 7 per cent of the Handeni responses could be clearly described as governmental. Among those included as giving "governmental" as a response were 9 per cent of the Tanga councilors' responses specifying that their work had to do with the taxing or income responsibilities of the council,[54] while none of the Handeni councilors responded in this fashion.

Significantly, only two councilors from Tanga and none from Handeni perceived their work as having anything to do with the provision of social services such as education, health, and roads, when, in fact, this had been the primary tangible activity in which

[54] They were "encouraging people to pay taxes" and "look for ways of increasing council's income."

the district council and the district political system had been involved. It may be suggested, in view of this finding, that these matters were so controlled by the council civil servants that the councilors themselves had little contact with or knowledge of these activities. Further observation seemed to confirm this proposition. For example, the councilors' perception of the council as an institution, to be discussed below, included as the second largest category of responses in Handeni and the largest single response in Tanga the provision of social services as the most important work of the council as an institution.

The councilors' perceptions of their role did not appear to be significantly affected by length of service or by their occupation.

The length of service in the council was divided into a "pre-1965" category and into a "1965 and after" category.[55]

Three of the Handeni councilors responding to the questionnaire had been in the council before 1965. Of the Tanga councilors, on the other hand, thirteen of the thirty-three (39 per cent) responding to the questionnaire had been in the council before 1965. These two percentages may be compared favorably to the statistics of the local council elections of October 1966, which found 36 per cent of all councilors retaining their seats; and these would also probably have been in the councils before 1965, the date arbitrarily chosen as the dividing point for this analysis.[56] While the small size of the populations dealt with limited the generalizations that might be made, the responses to the questionnaire come so close to the total group of councilors in each case that some cautious analysis may be suggested.

If length of service of membership is one indicator of institu-

[55] The year 1965, in addition to being at the approximate midpoint between the birth of the councils in 1962 and the time this research was conducted in 1968, is also the year Tanzania became a statutory one-party state. Councils and councilor behavior do not appear to have been appreciably affected by the formalization of single party rule.

[56] Computed from statistics found in Hardwick, "Local Government Elections," p. 130.

tionalization, then Tanga's council was more institutionalized than Handeni's.[57] General impressions supported this contention. For example, the Tanga councilor was identified at the meeting by a formal nameplate on the table in front of him. There were none in Handeni. There was a formal meeting hall in Tanga, but not in Handeni. The mechanics of record keeping in Tanga were rather formalized and efficient compared to the procedure in Handeni. A Tanga councilor's perception of his role as councilor did not, however, appear to be affected by his greater length of service or by the related condition of the higher level of institutionalization of his council.

In this study, councilor occupation was simply divided into farmer and nonfarmer. Since at least 85 per cent of the citizenry were engaged in subsistence agriculture, this distinction seemed adequate. The distinction, it should be noted, was made by the respondent and not by the researcher. Sixty-four per cent of the Handeni councilors described themselves as farmers; while 73 per cent of the Tanga councilors did so. There appeared to be no distinction in perception of individual councilor role due to the farmer-nonfarmer distinction.

On the basis of these data, supplemented by the writer's general observations, it was clear that the councilors generally saw their individual role in the district political system as primarily that of performing the function of communication between the villages that they represented and the government. The councilors apparently made no clear distinction between the district government and the central government. This blurring of distinction between central

---

[57] See Huntington, *Political Order,* pp. 13 ff, for the suggestion that chronological age is one indicator of institutionalization. The other indicators of institutionalization suggested by Huntington, including more than one generational age, complexity, autonomy, and coherence, are sorely lacking with the district council. It might be contended that seven years is too short a period for much institutionalization to take place. It might also be suggested that an increase in institutionalization is related to other factors such as the amount of power an institution is able to exercise.

and district authority was a highly accurate representation of reality. While there were a few notable exceptions, most councilors come close to viewing themselves as part of the administrative arm of the government.

Councilor Perception of Institutional Role

A second question aimed at determining how the councilor perceived the role of the district council as an institution and whether his perception of his own role as councilor was significantly different from his perception of the council as an institution. The question was: "In your view what is the most important work of the district council in this district?"

Forty-seven per cent of the Handeni responses viewed the most important work of the council to be the encouragement of farming, while only 20 per cent of the Tanga councilors shared this view. This perception of council role must be considered in terms of the fact that the central government had undertaken an intensive campaign to promote development throughout the countryside. Since February 1967, this campaign stressed rural development in particular.[58]

The task of encouraging and running development projects was mentioned as being an important work by 20 per cent of the Tanga responses, while no Handeni councilor saw this as important work of the council.

The provision of some form of social services for the people of the district was indicated as most important by 25 per cent of the Tanga responses, while 20 per cent of the Handeni responses cited this activity. The rather vague encouragement of development was mentioned in 10 per cent of the Tanga responses, under the general phrase "to encourage improvement in standard of living." Seven per cent of the Handeni responses contained a similar phrase.

---

[58] This emphasis is presented in President Nyerere's Arusha Declaration and subsequent elaborations thereon. See "The Arusha Declaration" in Nyerere, *Freedom and Socialism,* pp. 231–251.

Thirteen per cent of the Tanga responses and 7 per cent of the Handeni responses cited the most important work of the council as "to collect taxes."

The categories of responses may be summarized into two major functional areas. Under the first, "Promotion of development," were included those perceptions of council role most directly related to the promotional function. Those responses that stressed vague developmental goals—"fights poverty, illness and illiteracy"—and those that specifically state the objective of encouraging farming or development were included in this area. The second major grouping was labeled simply "governmental functions." Those responses that specifically referred to services or to some aspect of organizing for accomplishing an objective were placed in this grouping. If we keep these two major areas of responses in mind, we see a distinct contrast between the perceptions of institutional role held by the Handeni councilors and their Tanga counterparts. Sixty-seven per cent of the Handeni councilors gave responses categorized as promotional, while only 38 per cent of the Tanga response could be clearly labeled promotional. Conversely, responses that were clearly governmental in nature were mentioned in 63 per cent of the Tanga responses and in 34 per cent of the Handeni responses. Among the "governmental functions" were specified such duties as collecting taxes and providing social services. Supplementary participation, observation, and surveys of the available documents in the two districts indicated that these responses reflect the work of the two councils. For example, discussions at council meetings in Tanga tended to be much more governmental—that is, they stressed how to maintain order and carry out projects—while in Handeni there was a tendency to spend much of the meeting listening to the proposals and demands of the district executive officer and responding to them.

As in the consideration of councilor perceptions of individual roles, the councilor's length of service in the councils and his occupation did not appear, on the basis of the data at hand, to have had an appreciable affect upon his perceptions of the role of the council as an institution.

The District Council: The View from the Center

Since independence in 1961, considerable efforts had been made to educate local officials for the role that the central government perceived for them in national development. This educational program had been particularly intense since 1967, when the Arusha Declaration signaled an increased emphasis upon rural development. In view of this effort, it was useful to compare the councilors' perceptions of their role to that perceived for them by officials of the center. Since the councils were themselves relatively undeveloped institutions, the comparisons of the role perceptions might be important indicators of the central government's success in instilling the national development goals in local institutions, as well as an indicator of the success of the institution's performance in the development effort. While it was impossible to quantify central government officials' view of the proper role of the councilors, it was possible to glean from the public records an idea of what these officials perceived the work of the councilors to be.

Central government officials apparently saw no clear distinction between the role of councilor and of the council as an institution such as appeared in the perceptions of role held by individual councilors. There was virtually no comment on the role of the councilor until 1965. In February of that year, the district executive officer in Handeni advised the finance committee of the council that many people in the district were not paying their taxes and that it would be a "good procedure for councillors to work together with the Village Executive Officer in seeing that every person in his place has paid tax as he may know much more than the VEO." The VEO was the village-level council bureaucrat whose primary responsibility was to collect the head tax and TANU dues.[59] The ineffec-

[59] Handeni District Council, Finance Committee, Minutes 26–27 February 1965, National Archives (304/L5/8B/29). There is little doubt that

tuality of this attempt to solicit the councilor as a tax collector was best indicated by the fact that there had been little emphasis upon the councilors' responsibilities in this area before, and there has been little since. Only 5 per cent of the Tanga responses and none from Handeni referred to this task as part of the work of the councilor.

Concern with the work of the councilors grew after the Arusha Declaration emphasized rural development efforts. After 1967, central officials increasingly articulated the proper role of the district council in these efforts. In the presence of the regional commissioner, who is the top political and governmental official of the region, the chairman of the Tanga district council and TANU urged "that the councillors should have meetings in the villages and explain the policy of the council and the party so that people will understand the advice which they receive regarding agriculture." [60]

In February 1967 the district executive officer of Handeni discussed "The Task of the District Councillor" in some detail with the council. He explained during the meeting that the councilors were the council itself, and as such represented the district:

> They are the representatives of the citizens to the District Council and they are working for the citizens and presenting their opinions. Councillors are the Authority which is to arrange all programs for the District. . . .
>
> The Council has to run all activities by means of money and thus people have to pay taxes and cess, etc. It is the job of the councilors to briefly explain to the citizens they represent all problems of the

---

the councilor knew much more than the VEO, since the councilor was chosen from and by the local people, while the VEO, a political appointee of the district council leadership, was in the cases studied here from outside the area in which he worked. His major purpose was to collect taxes (his salary of 152 shillings per month, about $21.00, depended upon how successful he was in this effort) and TANU dues (6 shillings, or slightly less than $1.00 per year) and to mobilize local participation in development projects.

[60] Tanga District Council, Finance Committee, Minutes 6–7 April 1967.

VILLAGE AND STATE: SYSTEMS IN ACTION

resolutions passed by the council and present to the council the problems and opinions of the people. . . .

Councillors have to relate with the employees (civil servants) in a good manner as it is their job to see that employees are doing a good job and they have to insist on explaining to the people the policy of the council and how the job should be done.[61]

The core function of communication between the people and the government that the Handeni district executive officer stated here is the same function that the councilors stressed, in almost precisely the same terms, in their responses to the relevant questions in the questionnaire. Later in this same meeting, the chairman of the council hinted that perhaps the communication was not as satisfactory as he would like by asserting that every councilor had to follow government policy and that if he did not then he was "violating this responsibility." [62]

During this same period, the Tanga area commissioner addressed the councilors on their responsibilities and called upon them "to go to the Village Development Committees and decide with them which ways can be followed so that a person who has no shamba [farm] would be able to get one, and those who have shambas may increase them." The area commissioner then pointedly called attention to the fact that each one of the councilors owed his position as councilor to the fact that the party, TANU, had made it possible for him to be a leader. At this same meeting, the district chairman also reminded the councilors that "they had been elected through TANU." [63]

In June 1967 the area commissioner of Tanga lectured the councilors on their responsibilities to pass bylaws that might not please their constituents. He told the councilors that their job was to pass bylaws that would annoy some of the citizens; however, the result would be for their own good because they would have crops

---

[61] Handeni District Council, Minutes 17 February 1967.   [62] *Ibid.*
[63] Tanga District Council, Minutes 23 February and 16 March 1967, "Appendix B, Address of the Chairman of Council."

from their farms. These bylaws might cause the councilor not to get votes from citizens next election, but it was not good for them to worry about the votes for their own benefit, for they should be worried about the welfare of the citizens.[64]

In two addresses to the council, the Handeni chairman lectured the councilors on their duty to explain and educate the people as to council policy. He reminded the councilors "of their responsibilities in explaining to citizens the resolutions of the District Council and the Arusha Declaration." [65]

Two months later the chairman asked the councilors to explain to the people how they should use their time. "It's our duty to explain to citizens that they should work hard and expand crops." [66]

During early 1968 the proper role of the district council in the total development effort was publicly discussed by President Nyerere himself. After criticizing the reluctance of cooperative officers to go into the rural areas and serve the farmers, the President noted that the same criticism applied to local councils: "They do not send representatives to stir the minds of people within their areas to work hard and therefore build the councils' stable self-reliance. As a result many councils have failed to run themselves although the Government has assisted in paying some of their staff." [67]

The party newspaper, the *Nationalist,* commented editorially on the role of the councils under the general heading, "Rural Development." Prior to independence, the editor wrote:

Institutions such as the local councils or as they were called then "native authorities" existed purely for the purpose of collecting taxes

---

[64] Tanga District Council, Minutes 1 June 1967, Appendix A, "Address of the Area Commissioner."

[65] Handeni District Council, Minutes 27 July 1967, Appendix A, "Chairman's Speech."

[66] Handeni District Council, Minutes 26 September 1967, Appendix A, "Chairman's Address."

[67] *Standard,* January 3, 1968.

which were used chiefly for the benefit of the "bwanas" [colonials in this context]. . . .

With independence things have changed. These institutions must now not only serve but be seen to serve the best interests of the hitherto colonized people—the masses of Tanzania. The district councils . . . cannot remain content with merely collecting taxes from the people even though these revenues we know, are utilized for development. The councils must do more . . . emphasis now must be on development rather than administration. . . .

The councils should . . . initiate development projects on the land in order to enable the peasants to be productive throughout the year.[68]

In a negative fashion the comments of officials indicated that they did not see the representative role as being a particularly important one for the council and councilors. In fact, they saw the efforts of councilors to "represent" to be downright troublesome. For example, the Minister for Local Government and Rural Development reportedly warned the councilors of Shinyanga District Council in April 1968 "to stop intriguing and undermining workers of the council." The minister addressed the councilors at the end of a visit to the district and "told them that the responsibilities of a councillor involved looking for ways and means of solving the problems of his people and not undermining employees of the council of which he is a member." [69]

There were several comments in the records of both Handeni and Tanga districts referring to the "interference" of the councilors with the work of the government officers in the districts. The significance of these comments was indicated not by their relative scarcity but by the fact that they appeared at all.

The Tanga district councilors were warned shortly after the organization of the council "about interfering with the civil servants job in their offices by letters," and the chairman of the council proclaimed to the members: "The problem we have in this council

[68] *The Nationalist,* January 31, 1968.
[69] *The Nationalist,* April 1, 1968.

is that some of the Councillors do not know their responsibility and how to explain to people what is to be done. There are some Councillors who interfere with the jobs of civil servants, and this is not good." [70]

The chairman of the Handeni District Council called attention to a similar problem. In an address to the council in June 1965, he noted: "Citizens should remember that it is the government's aim to promote self-reliance and people have to pay their taxes and TANU subscriptions. He added that some councillors did the opposite of what the government wanted. He asked that this be stopped." [71]

From these admonishments of government officials, it was fairly clear that these officials perceived the proper function of the district councilors to be the communication of government and council decisions to their constituents and the encouragement of adherence to these decisions. The councilors themselves shared this view, stressing in both councils studied here that one of the most important duties of a councilor was to communicate government's plans to his constituents and to encourage participation in development projects. In addition, however—and this is a function which the officials did not mention—the councilors felt that they should communicate their "people's problems to the council." Taking "people's problems to the council" embodied the kernel of the representative function. A second category of councilor perception of role was even more actively representative in that it contained the idea of argumentation of the people's interests. Included in this category were such responses as "to negotiate," "to discuss and defend the people to the council," "to look after the people's money," and "to get people results." This category of response was mentioned in less than 20 per cent of the responses in both Tanga and Handeni districts. This did not mean that even these councilors were actively engaged in behavior that represented their constituents

[70] Tanga District Council, Minutes 26–27 October 1962 (304/L5/9A).
[71] Handeni District Council, Minutes 23 June 1965 (304/L5/8A/29).

VILLAGE AND STATE: SYSTEMS IN ACTION 227

even in a verbal sense. In fact, in the cases studied here it was the exception rather than the rule when a councilor represented his people verbally before the council. When he did engage in such active representation of constituency views he most often found himself "talking to the air," as the expression went.

The questionnaire included a series of statements aimed at determining the sense of legislative efficacy in the two councils.[72] These items, to which the councilors responded in an "agree," "disagree," or "don't know," pattern, provided a five-point scale of legislative efficacy for each councilor. From these scales an index of legislative efficacy was established for the two councils. If the index of legislative efficacy was computed for the entire council, the contrasts in efficacy between Handeni and Tanga was rather marked. On an index of efficacy ranging from complete efficacy indicated by a composite score of 1.0, to complete nonefficacy, indicated by a score of .00, the Handeni council had an efficacy score of .45, while the Tanga council had a score of .65.[73] When,

[72] The statements in the order most-to-least efficacious are as follows:
  1. "So many people want so many things that it is often difficult to know what stand to take."
  2. "Many of the resolutions are so detailed and technical that I have trouble understanding them."
  3. "There is so little time during a council meeting to study all the resolutions and problems that sometimes I don't know what I'm voting for or against."
  4. "My ward includes so many different kinds of people that I often don't know just what the people there want me to do."

These statements, to be answered by "Agree," "Disagree," or "Don't know," are adapted from Wahlke *et al., The Legislative System*, see especially pp. 474–475. The coefficient of reproducibility for the Tanga council is 0.909. For Handeni, two coefficients of reproducibility have been computed. The first, 0.91, assigns the "Don't knows" at the cutting points in the "Disagree" category (n = 4). The second, 0.82, places these "Don't know" responses in the "Disagree" category. For all the responses from Tanga councilors, there were only three "Don't knows"; while there were a total of ten "Don't knows," responses from the Handeni councilors.

[73] The index of legislative efficacy is adapted from Wahlke *et al., The Legislative System*, pp. 474–475. Briefly, the procedure multiplies the high

however, the index of efficacy was controlled by separating out the nominated members from the Tanga council, the two indices of efficacy were markedly similar: .45 for Handeni and .47 for Tanga. Handeni, it will be recalled, had no nominated councilors. The nominated members of the Tanga council, separated from their elected counterparts, had an efficacy score of .71.

The intent of appointing members to the council in 1966 was to increase the competence of the council, and these data suggested that the process of nomination had in the councils studied here at least increased the sense of efficacy held by the council as an institution.[74] The contrasts between the two districts that have been noted suggest caution in drawing any more conclusions from what appeared to be the marked contrast in council attitude toward its role provided by the presence of nominated members.

To sum up this discussion of the conflict of roles between political systems, the demands were greatest upon those who occupied party roles. The method of recruitment to party positions was highly directed and controlled by the district and national political systems. At the same time, however, the occupant of these roles was ultimately responsible to the local party apparatus. Those officials down through the division chairmen of the party were assisted by an executive secretary of the party bureaucracy who was appointed by and responsible to the Central Committee of the national party organization.[75]

In the areas I studied, there was no question that the district councilor had the only role at the level of the district headquarters that ultimately was dominated by local interests. All other roles in the district system were dominated by the demands of the district

---

scorers by a weight of 1.0, medium scorers by 0.5, and low scores by 0.0. The values thus derived are added and averaged, yielding index scores ranging from one to zero.

[74] See Hardwick, "Local Government Elections."
[75] Constitution of TANU, Article IV, B 2.

system. For example, all government employees down through the VEO were under constant pressure to behave as their role in the district political system demanded. They had to collect taxes and organize self-help projects or explain to their bureaucratic superiors why they had not. The district demands in Handeni and Tanga were virtually identical with the demands made by the national political system. For all intents and purposes the district roles other than those of the district councilors were national roles. Even for the district chairman of TANU the twin responsibilities of government and party together with the fact that the chairman's relationships were dominated by district and national actors meant that the role of district chairman was effectively dominated by the district and national conceptions of how that role should behave. In turn, the quality of the chairman's leadership abilities was appraised in terms of how effectively he could persuade his constituents throughout the district that they, too, should adopt national goals as their own. Essentially, the same pressures and expectations were placed upon the member of the National Assembly elected from the area. In both cases, effective leadership tended to ensure security of tenure, while ineffective leadership—defined as the failure to strike the tenuous balance of minimal satisfaction to both constituents and superiors—meant loss of position.

Intersystemic Inputs and Outputs

The input-output formulation is commonly used in the analysis of political phenomena to direct attention to those functions being performed within a particular political system. As a major concern of this study is with the linkages between political systems and subsystems, the input-output formulation is used here to focus attention more directly on the exchanges between these political systems. While each political system studied still converts inputs into outputs in the environment in which it exists, the primary concern here is not with those exchanges within a particular political system and its total environment, but with those exchanges that cross the boundaries of one political system into another.

These exchanges consist of two types. One type is composed of the system outputs which are directed toward and become inputs, as demands or supports, into another political system. An example of this type of input is the Sindeni Ward Development Committee's request for district assistance in the building of a TANU office at Sindeni.

A second type of exchange is the input of an individual or institution into a political system higher or lower in the hierarchy that bypassed the most immediate political systems. For example, there were cases where an individual made a demand upon the district political system as an individual, for example, for relief from an oppressive village executive officer, and thus bypassed completely the village political system. At this point the individual was acting as a part of and within the district political system. Others might act directly as members of the national system in a similar fashion. In the event that *all* inputs bypassed the local political system and went directly into the district or, conceivably, the national political system, it could be concluded that full integration of subsystems had been achieved.[76]

Our major concern here is with the outputs of one system or subsystem that became part of the input of another and thereby *linked* the two systems. Inputs into another system might be broken down into demands on and supports of that system. The decisions and actions of the authorities of that system, on the other hand, were viewed as the outputs of the system.

Demands might be further classified as demands for: (1) the allocation of goods and services, (2) regulations of behavior, (3)

---

[76] Theoretically, this is possible, but it is impossible to foresee in reality. In this eventuality the political functions would no longer be shared between political systems but would be performed by the political system that is the focus of the full integration.

participation in the system, and (4) communication and information from the political system. Types of supports were subclassified as: (1) material supports, (2) obedience to laws, (3) participatory supports, and (4) attention paid to government communication.

Outputs might be subclassified into: (1) extractions, (2) regulation of behavior, (3) allocations or distributions of goods and services, opportunities, honors, statuses, and so on, and (4) symbolic outputs.[77]

My application of the concept of system-to-intersystemic linkages requires us to keep in mind that for each political system upon which we focus—village, ward, division, district, or national—the demands and supports as elaborated above are emerging and being dealt with from *within* the boundaries of each political system. Of greater interest for our consideration of linkages between systems, however, is the case where the political system under consideration *also* is encountering inputs—demands and/or supports of varying nature and quantity—from other political systems *external* to the political system under our focus. Likewise, the outputs of the political system which has our attention—in the forms elaborated upon above—will contribute to the maintenance of the system under our consideration by coping with the stresses provided by the inputs. In addition, however, some of these outputs may become inputs into other political systems.

The key consideration here is the extent to which authoritative decisions—that is, decisions which people accept because they think they must, either because the decisions are just or because they will suffer some deprivation if they do not—are made within the abstraction of the political system under our consideration. The concept of political system is an abstraction which is useful for ordering political behavior and, hopefully, aiding our understanding of it. The fact that authoritative decisions apply in different ways and for different ends is a fact, however, which any reader can understand. Any town has rules, written and unwritten, which the

[77] See above, p. 34.

citizen knows about and breaks at the risk of punishment. The extent to which the citizen's life is directed by the rules will suggest the degree to which the various political systems control the individual's behavior. The variation is great in Tanzania and other developing nations where the strength of the national systems is still relatively weak. My study here attempts, through the application of these ideas to the problem of promoting rural development in Tanzania, to reveal some of the intricacies of the relationship between village and nation in that society. Since the major impetus for rural development came from the central political system and the district was the most distinct outpost of the national system, it is appropriate to continue this analysis by focusing on the district political system and by assessing its inputs and outputs with other political systems.

The District Political System: Inputs

Inputs into the district political system arise from four possible sources. They may come from within the district system itself, from the environment of the district system, from the immediate and other intermediate political systems, and, finally from the national political system. Since our major concern here is with the linkages between political systems, attention is directed primarily to those inputs which originated from other political systems. The inputs from the immediate, other intermediate, and the national political systems into the district system formed, *ipso facto,* part of the outputs of these systems. In turn, the outputs of the district system that were directed to the national, immediate, and other intermediate systems were *ipso facto* the inputs linking these systems to the district. This focus on the inputs/outputs of the district into the national and subdistrict political systems, then, simultaneously fixes attention on the inputs/outputs of other systems that formed part of the intersystemic linkage with the district.

The inputs into the district system were divided into demands and supports. In turn, each category of input was examined as it originated from both the national political system and the political systems subordinate in the hierarchy to the district. Here the subordinate political systems were the villages, which I have labeled immediate political systems, and the much more fledgling ward and division political systems, of which only the villages and divisions were significantly involved in authoritative decisions in the areas studied here.

It was surprising to discover in surveying the public record and my field work that virtually *no* concrete demands were directed toward the district political system from the national political system. Although there was considerable exhortation to work harder, to grow more crops and to engage in nation-building projects, these demands were relatively general and were translated into concrete demands by the district system with considerable flexibility.

Any national demand for goods and services from the district political systems was virtually nonexistent, since the bulk of national resources were collected through the efforts of the national system from what in reality were national sources. The national regulations that forcefully impinged upon the district system were few and generally accepted by the district actors. Demands for regulation of behavior placed upon the district system were not stringent; they centered around the symbolic celebration of special holidays and of preparing welcomes for national officials. The greatest single type of national input into the district system was communication and information and every district office was full of written directives and regulations from Dar es Salaam. The district response to these directives and regulations was indicative of the input of the district system into the national system and will be treated below.

The absence of concrete demands by the center on the districts was related to two conditions. First, for all intents and purposes, the district political system was composed primarily of representatives of the center who embodied the general demands and goals of the national political system. If concrete demands were placed on the inhabitants of the district or upon other more local systems within the districts, these demands were articulated by district-level actors who were part of the national system. They embodied in their goals and techniques national goals and ethics. The one major exception to the general conclusion that the actors in the district *boma* were in reality national actors was the district councilor. The district chairman of TANU, though a second possible exception, was essentially a member of the national system.[78] Most of the district actors, that is, the office of the area commissioner, the technical officers, and the council bureaucracy, were directly linked to some part of the national political system, and their behavior was most directly determined by this relationship. The frequent transfer of district staff further promoted this national over district orientation. Even so, district policy was very much a product of the personalities, the talents, and the ecological restraints of the district. National policy, especially as enunciated by President Nyerere, encouraged local flexibility along general policy themes; indeed, considering the diversity of the country this was the only realistic position.

The second condition contributing to the lack of concrete demands by the center on the district political system was the fact that as of 1969 the national political system had been virtually incapable of demanding and enforcing a response from the peripheral areas. The national political system did not have the manpower and material resources to mount a campaign for enforcing national edicts on the countryside. Also, the resources upon which the center maintained itself had been derived from the center, not from the periphery. Thus policy had stressed exhortation rather than demands threatening the ultimate use of force.

---

[78] While considerable effort has been taken to show the democratic nature of the one-party state in Tanzania by describing how members of the TANU-controlled National Assembly have lost their seats to challengers from the localities, a more meaningful indication of internal democracy might be the consideration of turnover of district chairmanships.

The immediate and intermediate political systems were the second source of intersystem inputs into the district system. Surprisingly, the demands of these systems that were articulated to the district political system were also few. At the village level there was a great desire for social services. The most important of these was for some form of medical care, but of those demands that were felt relatively few were articulated to the district system. The very notable exception to this rule were the special development projects. Within these projects the participants very forcefully articulated their demands. In some cases the participants articulated their demands directly to Dar es Salaam and thus bypassed all other systems.[79] Otherwise, although village surveys indicated that the peasants were aware of the potential use of the village development committees and the village executive officer as channels through which their demands could be made, on the whole, Handeni and Tanga villagers seldom articulated their needs to the district political system.

As a case in point, the walls of the well in one of the villages in Marungu Ward, Tanga District, were collapsing, destroying the source of village water supply and creating a hazard for the small children of the village. Although the villagers wanted the well repaired, they expressed their concern only to division officials during my visits to the village with these officials. Otherwise, the people did not request, in any way, that the district authorities repair the well. The villagers did not even consider requesting help from the ward or village system.

Demands for material assistance from the district authorities came primarily in times of food shortage. During these times, which have been particularly acute in Handeni, the cell leaders asked village executive officers to secure food; the VEO's took the demand to the divisional executive officer, who took the case to the district

[79] These observations are based on my study of a village settlement scheme, a village irrigation scheme, and a cattle-coconut scheme. See Chapter IV above.

executive officer.[80] The district authorities, usually the district executive officer and the agricultural officer, assessed the seriousness of the food shortage and, if the famine merited relief, responded by sending food to the area. By the nature of its urgency, no case was known in which the district political system had not responded to such a request and the information available indicated that the district response to this demand had been virtually automatic.[81]

The demands of the localities to the district system for regulation of behavior were very few. In most cases the local village system regulated its own behavior. If a dispute involved two villages or if it could not be solved by the village system, the next level of state authority—the VEO and/or the ward chairman of TANU—acted as mediator and judge. In either case, the individual occupying these positions also had a position in the district political system. He might be occupying this position, however, because of his status in the village or other local system. The district system was then involved in the regulation of behavior because it had itself co-opted certain positions of the local systems into its own system.

If the regulation of behavior involved the use of force then the district system would make use of the police stationed at the district headquarters. Though not a common practice, the most prominent demand for such action would be situations where clashes between different ethnic groups led to bloodshed. In these cases the district political system employed the force devolved to it by the national political system to regulate behavior in the localities, and, in effect, the national system itself was regulating behavior in the local system. As mentioned earlier, the TANU Youth League might get involved in the regulation of behavior.

The demand for participation in the district system from locals was virtually nonexistent. Local leaders might feel a sense of par-

[80] In recent years there were food shortages in 1947, 1950, 1952, 1958, and 1962.

[81] Based on interview with the district executive officer, Handeni, 28 February 1968.

VILLAGE AND STATE: SYSTEMS IN ACTION 237

ticipation in their contact with the district system, but this participation was primarily symbolic and had little meaning as far as the actual making of decisions was concerned. If a district notable was to visit a village, the local people participated to the extent of preparing the arrangements, and attending the meeting, but this degree of participation was more a participation in the affairs of the village system than in the district system.

The local demand upon the district political system for information and communications was limited and was primarily associated with demands for social services and material assistance. The possession of information as to how to secure either of these was crucial to successful demands upon the system, and the communications process was central to such success.

The second half of the input dimension is support. The material support of the district system by the national system was considerable. With the exception of the district chairman of TANU, the district councilors, and some of the council bureaucracy, all members of the district government and party structure were paid by the central government. During this field work at least 50 per cent, and in some cases 70 per cent, of all teachers' salaries in the districts were paid by the central Ministry of Education and this percentage has subsequently run to 100 per cent. The major proportion of roads in the districts were in the care of the central government, and for the roads maintained by the districts, 50 per cent of the cost came from Dar es Salaam. The national input into the district and subdistrict systems was substantially increased in 1969 and, at the same time, national control over government services was increased in similar proportions. In his budget speech to the National Assembly in June 1969, the Minister of Finance indicated this trend rather clearly. He noted that

account has been taken of any additional commitments which Government has accepted as being in the national interest. In this connection, there is first the decision to pay the full salaries of what are known as category A and category B primary school teachers from revenues of the Central Government. Then there is the continuing takeover of District roads by the Central Government for maintenance at a level far higher than Shs. 400/– per mile which the District Councils were barely able to do. Furthermore, the rural health centers are now to be administered by the Central Government and their future expansion and maintenance is to be Central Government responsibility. Rural Water Supply is another service for which the Central Government will assume full responsibility in the coming year.[82]

At the subdistrict level, the bureaucracy was split in its dependency; some upon the center and some upon the district. The extent to which the staff financed by the national government in Dar es Salaam would be supplemented by staff supported by the district depended primarily upon the resources available to the district. Not only salaries, but transportation and equipment, were provided by the center. Attempts to determine precisely the sums involved in Tanga and Handeni proved to be fruitless. District officers did not know the total budgets for their offices.

Virtually all this material support originated at the center, since the revenue that the districts contributed to the central government coffers was inconsequential. In fact, the only direct contribution to the central government revenue was through income taxes and as of 1963 only 0.21 per cent of the total population had their income taxed.[83] Thus, it may be concluded that the governmental apparatus at the district office and below was almost completely dependent upon the material support of the national political system.

Of the three remaining classes of supports, obedience to laws, participation, and attention paid to government communication, only the last could ever be conceived as a support to the district political system from the national political system. While the na-

[82] Interviews, Handeni, January 29–31, 1968. The precise data provided for Handeni District is that there were 2,250 miles of roads in the district under the care of Comworks, the central government, and 172 miles of roads to be maintained by the district council with a support of 50 per cent of the cost from the center. The budget speech is found in the *Standard*, June 20, 1969.

[83] Lee, *Local Taxation*, p. 31.

tional political system did respond to communications from the district political system, it did so primarily in times of emergency, the most notable example being the presence of famine conditions in Handeni District. The greatest support provided by the national political system for the district was in the supplying of resources—financial, personal, and material. In view of the national goal of integrating all areas into the national political system, this support for the district system was not surprising.[84] In part because of these same goals, the national political system had been particularly sensitive to communications of emergency, such as famine, from the district.

A second source of support for the district system were the immediate political systems, the villages. The support that the village political systems gave the district political system was limited and grudgingly given. Using the types of support suggested in the conceptualization employed here, it must be concluded that the local systems did offer limited support in the categories of material resources and in the attention paid to government communication. There was only meager support in obedience to district laws and in participation.

The most important material support was the payment of personal taxes, a support generally offered only under some threat of duress. As stated in the earlier discussion of extraction/mobilization it was estimated in 1967 that only 20 per cent of the eligible taxpayers actually paid the tax. A 1964 statistic on this percentage had 18 per cent of the total male population paying taxes in Handeni while 24 per cent of the same population in Tanga District were paying taxes in that year.[85]

A second type of material support for the district political sys-

[84] While it was not the case in either Handeni or Tanga districts and was not noticeably the case in any district in Tanzania, it is theoretically feasible to conceive of a national political system that embodies elements which for tribal, economic, or other reasons direct support to the regions or subsystems within the national system, thereby enabling that subsystem to better maintain itself vis-à-vis the national system.

[85] See Dryden, *Local Administration*, p. 140.

tem coming from the villages were those self-help projects that contributed in some fashion to the district political system. Roads, bridges, and, possibly, school buildings were most directly supportive of the district system. Other projects such as dispensaries, community centers, and well-building projects enhanced the district political system, but my findings suggest that their short-run enhancement of the district system's ability to maintain itself had been small.

As stated above, the populace did respond to communications emanating from the larger political systems, and when President Nyerere articulated the national political ethic at the national level, it was echoed at the district and regional levels. Generally, the peasant accepted the ethic itself and, while many citizens verbalized this composite of ideas, this verbal acceptance had not yet resulted in significant changes in the behavior of the villagers to make the ethic a reality. Furthermore, the state was not yet sufficiently developed to enable the political system to secure through coercion or persuasion the change desired and demanded in order to achieve these developmental goals.

Obedience to laws is another support for the political system, but laws of the district political system impinging upon the villager were minimal. The fate of the tax laws has already been discussed.

A second group of laws which villagers encountered directly were the agricultural bylaws requiring certain acreages of specified crops. The vigor with which the district authorities had attempted to enforce these bylaws in Handeni had increased the degree of obedience to the law, but it had not increased the willingness of the villagers to obey the law. It might, in fact, have increased their resistance.

A final supportive input from the immediate political systems to the district system is participation. Participation might be expensive in terms of time and resources or it might be inexpensive. Expensive participation in the district systems was low in Handeni and Tanga. Participation in an inexpensive fashion may have been considerable. Time, for example, in a peasant society may be the most abundant resource. The most notable participation in the district political system by the villages was likely to be the response to visits by district and national officials. It was relatively easy for the locality to put forth a warm welcome and some type of affair; usually in the form of an *ngoma* (dance). These affairs were generally arranged by the VEO, the ward chairman of TANU, and the cell leaders. The VEO was an employee of the district government organization and the others participated because of their party position and affiliation. Beyond this point, participation was very low.

The District Political System: Outputs

The outputs of the district political system can be ordered into three classifications—outputs that become inputs into the local systems, that become inputs into the national system, and, finally, those that become inputs into the district system itself. We may assume that the outputs of the district system will tend to support the maintenance of the district system. Furthermore, if the political socialization of either of these three levels of political systems successfully directs the attitudes and goals of the actors of the other systems, these systems are then poised to perform the remaining political functions—extraction/mobilization, the maintenance of order and communication—as unitary systems. This level of consensus could only be reached in the abstraction of theory and could only be held momentarily to a particular issue. Here we focus our analysis on those outputs of the district system, viewed here as an intermediate system, that link the district to the local political systems and to the national political system.

The first category of output to be considered is that of extractions. The district system extracted material and human resources from both the local political systems and from the national political system. The district extraction of resources from the localities has already been considered under the perspective of locality inputs into the district system. The district political systems' efforts to extract from the localities were their most difficult and most demanding activities.

Structural reorganization and differentiation of structures at the subdistrict level during the time of my field work aimed at extracting resources more efficiently. Restructured bodies such as the division development committee, the ward, the ward development committee, the ten-house cell system, and the reorganization of the office of the divisional executive officer into a party position—all were instigated at the direction of the national political system and carried out by the national agents who were part of the district system.

Extractions of the district system from the national political system have already been considered as part of the inputs from the national system. Material extractions of the district system from the district and the localities contributed to only an inappreciable degree to the support of the national political system. Moreover, the district headquarters was overwhelmingly dependent upon the support of the national political system for its existence and for its ability to extract even to a very limited extent from the localities. The actors and institutions that existed at the district level were at the behest of the national system. Significantly, however, the capability of the national system to direct the actions of the district system was limited, and a major finding of this study was that while the district actors were very much dependent upon the central political system, they were also able to perform independently as a political system unto themselves.

One must question whether the material support of the district by the central political system is not in danger of becoming, in effect, an extraction by the district system from the national system. The data needed to show the total extent of district reliance upon the central government were simply not available. National expenditures, for example, were not dichotomized into those which go for the support of a ministry's work in the districts and those that applied directly to the work of the central government in the capital city alone. The frame of mind that does not request such an accounting was another indication of the extent to which the district political system was assumed to be part of central government.

Although the data that would be needed to demonstrate the full extent of district reliance upon the central government are simply not available, the national inputs into Handeni District during 1967–1968 far outweighed the district's contribution to the nation. While the Handeni contributions to the nation's coffers were closer to the norm for the nation as a whole, the contributions of Tanga District to the nation's resources were considerable, primarily because Tanga had industry and cash cropping to provide a source for tax on exports, which in turn contributed substantially to the nation's revenue. While this support came from a relatively small proportion of the economy, Tanga as a geographic and administrative area did make a considerable contribution to the nation's development and satisfied demands made upon it by the national political system much more readily than did Handeni. Ironically, this condition took the pressure off the individual villager and, in fact, may have encouraged a situation where the villager in Tanga contributed relatively less in the way of material and physical resources to the nation-building effort than did the villager in the much poorer Handeni District. In effect, therefore, greater pressure was placed upon the individual peasant in Handeni than in Tanga because he was the chief source of support for the district system. When there were alternative sources of support, as in Tanga, the demands of the nation and the district could be met with less stringent extraction from the individual peasant.

The extent of national involvement in the material support of the district systems is suggested by a consideration of the sources of district council revenue and the main items of district expenditure. While there was no definitive way of knowing what proportion of material support for the district came from the coffers of the district council, it was almost certain to be less than half. Thus it should be noted that if only the sources of revenue for the district council, a relatively minor institution in the governmental structure, are considered, roughly one-third come by way of the education grant (see Table 4) which, together with certain other forms of grants, formed a major direct extraction of resources from the national system by the district council.[86] The principal sum of the grants was eliminated in February 1969, when the central government announced that henceforth teachers on the mainland would be paid their salaries by the central government rather than by the district councils.[87]

The radical tax reforms in 1969, including the abolition of the personal tax and the produce cess, and the subsequent central government takeover of all responsibility for teachers' salaries drastically reduced the need for the district political system to depend upon its own extraction efforts to secure revenue from the localities for its support. Instead, the national political system shouldered the responsibility of providing an even greater share, approaching 100 per cent of the district's support. A central point for this study is the fact that while the burden upon the peripheral areas was being lowered, the commitment of the national government to these areas was being increased. Having taken over the funding responsibility for the districts, the national political system might have placed itself in a better position to resist district extraction from the nation. For example, R. G. Penner has written specifically of the tendency in 1968 for a council to so order its affairs that the central government would be compelled to bail it out of financial difficulties. Writing of the grant system for the support of education, Penner noted that "the equalization element of the grant structure is administered informally. The Ministry is most likely to be generous with councils in financial trouble, it is quite possible that it got that way by overindulging itself with extravagant educational

[86] See Penner, *Financing Local Government,* ch. 4.
[87] *Standard,* February 13, 1969.

Table 4. The district council's main sources of revenue, in per cent

District	Personal rates	Produce cess	Education grants	Other
Tanga				
1962	44	—	30	26
1963	30	20*	19	31
1964	34	30	11	25
1965	37	16.3	19.7†	
Handeni				
1962	35	—	46	19
1963	44	—	30	27
1964	44	4	24	28
1965	35.5	4	36.9†	
1967	45	5	34	14
All districts			Licenses, fees, etc.	
1961	48	10	38	2
1962	46	6	23	23
1963	40	8	33	18

Sources: Data for Tanga and Handeni 1962–1964 are adapted from Table B, "Main Sources of Revenue Tanga Region," in Dryden, *Local Administration,* p. 138. The Handeni and Tanga 1965 figures are from Penner, Table, "Revenues of Local Government, 1965." Data for 1967 are based on Handeni District Council, Finance Committee, Minutes 28 April 1967. Data for "All Districts" are from the Republic of Tanzania, "Local Government Report, 1963," Appendix H, "District Council Finance," mimeographed. Columns 3 and 4 for "All Districts" are tabulated from different sources than the data for Tanga and Handeni and therefore are not directly comparable.

* Tanga District's high percentage of revenue from the produce cess is due to the high concentration of sisal estates in the district, and the district administration has been able to collect a cess on every ton of sisal sold.

† Penner's figures for grants covers *all* grants, not only grants for education as the other sources have. The difference in total grants is very small, as indicated.

expenditures. Thus the Ministry could well be supporting councils who showed a lack of prudence by attempting to educate more students than they could afford." [88]

Table 5. Main items of district expenditure, in per cent

District	Administration	Social service	Development	Other
Tanga				
1962	24	49	16	12
1963	25	45	11	19
1964	20	44	18	20
1965	18.5	45.8*	—	—
Handeni				
1962	24	55	.003	20
1963	26	46	1	19
1964	21	61	1.5	17
1965	16	53.6*		
1967	16	68	6	10
All districts				
1961	32	37	15	14
1962	28	46	12	12
1963	29	53	4	11

Sources: Data for Tanga and Handeni 1962–1964 are adapted from Table C, "Main Items of Expenditure Tanga Region," in Dryden, *Local Administration*, p. 138. The 1965 data are from Penner, Table, "Expenditures of District Councils 1965." The 1967 data are based on Handeni District Council, Finance Committee Minutes 28 April 1967. The data for "All Districts" is from Republic of Tanzania, *Local Government Report, 1963*, Appendix H. "District Council Finance," mimeographed. The source for the "All Districts" data provides a breakdown different from those of previous sources; therefore columns 3 and 4 are not directly comparable.

* The figures under Social Service for 1965 taken from Penner's study are limited to educational expenditure alone. It is clear from comparing the 1965 figure to the data for other years that education constitutes a major proportion of district expenditure.

[88] Penner, Financing Local Government, ch. 3.

The second category of outputs—the regulation of behavior—has also been considered as among the inputs into the district system from the local and the national political systems. Regulation of some forms of behavior has been conceived as either demanded by the latter two systems or as given in the form of obedience to behavior demanded by district authorities. The regulation of individual behavior was found to have been primarily an output of the village political systems. Outputs of the district political system in this area were primarily centered around the rural development effort. A combination of coercion and persuasion emanating from the district *boma* regulated to some degree the activities of the localities as they related to rural development. In the cases studied here this regulation was most evident in the pressure from the *boma* to till certain acreages and through the use of the forty-eight-hour detention law by the Handeni area commissioner to enforce these rules.

In either case, the regulation of behavior that the district political system was able to produce was based on its persuasive abilities in the villages and the national capital and upon its ability to regulate behavior through coercive techniques. The latter was effective only in the villages and was directly dependent upon the national system's contribution of resources to the district. In the two cases studied here, as in any situation, the line between coercion and persuasion was impossible to distinguish. In both Handeni and Tanga, the ability of the district to apply coercion was very limited both by the resources available and by the physical environment.[89] The technique of persuasion was being applied primarily through the structure of the political party. There was considerable support of the party efforts via the radio, which was the most important means of communication.

[89] For an assessment of the ecological determinants of policy in Handeni, written by a former colonial officer who returns to the district after ten years, see David Brokensha, "Handeni Revisited," *African Affairs*, LXX (April 1970), 159–168.

The ability of the district to regulate the behavior of the national system was primarily a negative ability. The district could simply consume national resources *without* a corresponding contribution to the achievement of national goals, as apparently Handeni did. It was widely rumored that President Nyerere had made references throughout the nation to the laziness of the Zigua of Handeni.[90] While on tour in Handeni during February 1969, the President "expressed his disappointment when he saw people 'leaning against the walls instead of improving their village or farms.' On the same tour, he told the residents of Kwamkono, one of the villages considered in this study, that "it was not exploiters who retarded the progress of the people as in colonial days, but lazy people." [91]

Under famine or other crisis circumstances the districts may actually have been able to regulate or at the least, affect the behavior of the national system. This potential draining of the national political system by the local and intermediate political systems has been discussed by Colin Leys with regard to local politics and development in Uganda.[92]

The third category of output was the allocation or distribution of goods and services, of opportunities, honors, statuses or anything material or symbolic that might be held in value. Here the output of the district political system was considerable. For the villager, the district *boma* was the source of food in time of famine, of assistance in time of emergency, natural or otherwise. Here also one's complaints and demands might be heard and, here, the capability to satisfy these complaints and demands lay. Control over food stores, over the marketing process, and over the educational process, and all other aids to individuals lay in the district headquarters. In most cases applications for employment in the govern-

---

[90] Although the researcher has heard the Zigua scolded in public by district officers, and heard this comment credited to President Nyerere, the precise citation of the comment is not available.
[91] *Standard*, February 12, 1969.   [92] Leys, *Policies and Politicians*.

ment and for entry into certain types of advanced education had to be supported by the area commissioner or by other district officials. Access to the national officials also lay through the district *boma*.

Although the demand from the localities for goods, services, and honors was constant, the supplies of both were very limited. Thus, for every assistance provided or every cell leader honored, others were slighted. If the allocations of goods and services could have been used solely as a reward for good performance in the rural development effort, this output from the *boma* would have contributed to the development process. In fact, however, the allocation of goods and services was always under some duress—flood, famine, or some sickness. Thus the district political system's outputs in this category were almost always, even before independence, in response to a necessity rather than a reward for good performance. Under these conditions no precedent had been established for reward for self-help. The district outputs of goods and services that became inputs into the national system were nil. As we have seen, the relationship was very much in the opposite direction. The national political system's outputs in this area were the primary source of the district system's support.

A final category of output from the district system was the symbolic output, and its nature and composition was most difficult to determine with precision. Undoubtedly, villagers looked with pride upon the flag, the presence of an African in the position of area commissioner (81.9 per cent of the senior- and middle-grade civil service positions were held by Tanzanian citizens by 1969) [93] and the role of the political party in the new nation. Parades in the district headquarters and visits of national figures from Dar es Salaam all lent color and excitement to what may have been a rather uneventful life. How much the increased demands placed upon the villager in conjunction with these symbolic rewards lessened the

---

[93] United Republic of Tanzania, *The Economic Survey and Annual Plan, 1970–71* (Dar es Salaam, 1970), p. 87.

value that the villager placed on these intangibles is, at this point, an unanswerable question. The symbolic output of the district political system into the national system was very minor, if it existed at all.

CHAPTER VIII

The Village, the State, and Rural Development

Clearly the links between village and state in Tanzania are changing. While the comparisons of the two districts and the villages within them have accentuated the diversity and complexity of political structure and action in this East African country, some concluding generalizations relating to rural development and center-periphery relations may be drawn. The cluster of ideas contained in the Arusha Declaration and subsequent elaborations of this document form the basis of the Tanzanian ethic for development. Its central theme—self-reliant development of the rural areas—had been elevated to the level of a national ideology, and by 1969, President Nyerere's articulation of this doctrine had become the central focus of government action throughout the countryside and peasants in Handeni and Tanga districts seemed to have accepted the ideology as legitimate.[1]

Many observers have described the acceptance of a general body of beliefs as being a primary step in the creation of a nation.[2] The

[1] Legitimacy is used here in the following fashion: "Legitimacy is the foundation of such governmental power as is exercised both with a consciousness on the government's part that it has a right to govern and with some recognition by the governed of that right." See "Legitimacy," in *International Encyclopedia of the Social Sciences.*

[2] Most students of nationalism ascribe to this view in some degree. Rupert Emerson notes, for example, that "the simplest statement that can be made about a nation is that it is a body of people who feel that they are a nation." *From Empire to Nation* (Boston, 1969), p. 102. A developmental view of nationhood is stated by Almond and Powell. Nation build-

emergence of a sense of Tanzanian nationhood with the developmental ethic at its core was an accomplished fact in the areas studied here. This could be attributed in good measure to the charismatic leadership of President Nyerere, the wide use of Swahili, and the absence of a compelling fear of tribal dominance from any single tribe. While the nation-building stage in Tanzanian development was significantly under way, there was considerable question, however, about the capacity of the nation to implement developmental policies through the apparatus of the state. The interpretation and implementation of the development ethic is primarily the task of the intermediate and immediate political systems, and it is at this level that the task of modernization faces its most severe test.

The task belongs primarily to the actors in the district political systems and sorely tests their ability. Social scientists often discuss the gap between center and periphery in the non-Western world, but in the cases studied here, the gap occurred most distinctly between the district and the subdistrict levels. Ultimately, the ability of the national system to direct, first, the interpretation of the national ethic at the district level and, second, the district's implementation of the ethic in the villages is the final test of the center's capacity to rule and to direct the society's resources to national goals.

---

ing, in their view, "refers to the process whereby people transfer their commitment and loyalty from smaller tribes, villages or petty principalities to the larger central political system." *Comparative Politics*, p. 36. The trying question was to what extent the broad commitment to abstract ideals guided everyday behavior in the particular. (Consider Prothro and Grigg, "Fundamental Principles of Democracy," *Journal of Politics*, XXII (1960), 276–294, for the point in a Western setting.)

That the populations of Handeni and Tanga districts accepted the ethic is based on my general impressions and on highly similar responses received to the questions, "What is this nation's biggest problem?" and "What are the things you are proudest of in this nation?" The responses to both questions, while unquantifiable, were impressive because of their marked similarity to the statements of the national leadership, even to the point of exact replication of phraseology.

The Interim Result: Accommodation, Acquiescence, Withdrawal

Individuals and institutions may react in three ways when the intermediate political systems attempt to implement policies that require changes in behavior that people are neither enthusiastic about nor willing to oppose openly. Most likely the peasant's first, and minimal, reaction to the intrusions of the external political system into his established patterns of life was accommodation. In these districts accommodation generally meant little more than appearing for political meetings and overtly expressing the developmental ethic to government officials. As a high-level civil servant, himself a Zigua from Handeni stationed elsewhere in Tanzania, noted to me, "The Zigua have learned how to say, Yes! Yes!; when they don't mean yes at all. They mean, No!." [3]

Political systems under stress, as well as individuals, also accommodate. This was true—perhaps even especially true—for the district. Some district political systems invented mythical development projects and successes. In July 1968 I made several attempts to visit an ujamaa village, which had been described as having been set up for one hundred and twenty families in Tanga District.[4] After setting up several appointments with government officers to visit the village, I was discreetly informed that the village did not yet exist. In Handeni District, I discovered that a well-building project which officials had extolled as one of the most successful self-help projects in the district had been built during the time of British colonial rule and subsequently *repaired* by the self-help project. In Handeni during 1969 it is reliably reported that a local party official literally created an ujamaa village from nothing solely for a pending visit by President Nyerere after which it was to, and

---
[3] Discussion, January 2, 1968.
[4] The account was in the *Standard,* July 1, 1968.

did, disappear.[5] One cannot know how many other achievements on the records in the capital of Dar es Salaam or the district headquarters throughout the countryside do not exist. Political systems under pressure from the center to produce solid development results were likely to exercise their own form of accommodation. The most common form of accommodation to date had been simply to pass false or inflated accounts of development results to superiors who were out of touch with local conditions.

As the district political system became capable of securing greater compliance to policy goals due to increased coercion or will, a second possible reaction was acquiescence. For the peasant, acquiescence was a temporary coping measure. Such was essentially the case in the Handeni cassava campaign of 1967–1968 discussed in Chapter III. In the districts studied here the capability of the district political system to maintain a permanent acquiescence to its demands simply did not exist.

If the external system were able to place unrelenting pressure on the localities to ensure compliance with their demand, a third reaction might occur. The individual peasants might merely withdraw physically from the penetration of the external political systems into their immediate political system.

In view of the poor state of communications, infrastructure, and the high percentage of involvement in subsistence agriculture, withdrawal was not only a feasible alternative to government pressure for change, it was a likelihood.

This study revealed only a few instances of withdrawal in Handeni and Tanga since to date the external systems had not yet sought to implement persistent demands upon the localities. One instance of withdrawal took place in Handeni when peasants, after initially moving close to the all-weather road crossing the district and running from Dar es Salaam to Tanga, moved away from it in order to resist the easy access of government tax collectors.[6]

[5] The incident has been reported in Seth Singleton, "Tanzania since Arusha," *Africa Report*, XVI (December 1971), 11.
[6] I learned this from discussions with government officials and peasants

Open resistance on the part of the peasant as a means of coping with government intrusion was not only almost certainly technically impossible; it was not yet even necessary. Environmental considerations, as mentioned above, made selective withdrawal from contact with the external political systems an easy process. Because of different physical environments, withdrawal in Handeni was much easier than in Tanga. Ironically, the relatively more developed economy in Tanga District allowed the political systems to secure resources with greater ease and released some of the pressure for extraction from the individual peasants in Tanga, whereas they bore the major brunt of such extraction in Handeni.

The ease of withdrawal at this stage of development in Tanga and Handeni Districts suggested that any sustained effort to enforce external demands upon the peasant was almost certainly doomed to failure—hence the basic logic of President Nyerere's statement playing down the use of force to promote development efforts in his address presenting the Second Five-Year Plan to the National TANU Conference in 1969. He noted that when political officers had tried to use force in the past to get people to produce certain amounts or to plant certain acreages, they had found that "the people cultivate the required area for the first year but that the crop is surprisingly small, and then when the second year comes along the peasants have moved further into the bush to get away from the officers of Government!" [7]

In Handeni and Tanga the ability of the central government to force policy through the intermediate political systems was limited. Initially, as documented in Chapter IV, increased efforts were made to employ the technique of force in the development efforts. This was true, in part, because the elite in the district systems had become reconciled, indeed committed, at this stage in Tanzania's de-

---

in the area. On the other hand, there was an increase in total settlement along this road. For an example of withdrawal in another setting see David Hapgood, "The Politics of Agriculture," *Africa Report*, XIII (November 1968), 11.

[7] *Tanzania Second Five-Year Plan*, p. xvi.

velopment efforts to use compulsion.[8] The capacities of the systems, however, while sufficient to secure acquiescence to their immediate demands, were not sufficient to prevent withdrawal in the face of increased pressure. Such efforts were almost certain to be futile in the long run.

In the face of this reality, the decision was made in October 1968 to decentralize the authority for the planning and the enforcement of rural development efforts to the immediate political systems, the villages. Withdrawal from one's own village was unlikely, as Vice President Kawawa was quoted in the *Standard* as he explained the purposes of decentralization of authority to villages: "When the projects were approved the residents all have to implement them as they would have legal force. . . . The villages were not places where the lazy people could hide themselves." [9]

The assumption, as yet unproved, was that the central political system could establish its authority in developmental matters by persuasion and thereby be able to guide and direct the immediate political systems to take up rural development efforts. The proof of this assumption lay largely on two considerations. First, would the peasant accept the development ethic as his own national objective? This study suggested that was largely accomplished. Second, was there sufficient institutional development to facilitate effective linkage between the state and the villages? Throughout this study, I have stressed the numerous examples of restructuring of old and the attempted creation of new institutions aimed at more effective implementation of national development policies in the villages. This process was most noticeable at the subdistrict level. While this institutional experimentation—resulting in part in a decentralization of decision making—had been under way, a centralization of functions was also noticeable. Principal among these

---

[8] Consider the insightful comments on this phenomenon in Aristide R. Zolberg, "The Structure of Political Conflict in the New States of Tropical Africa," *American Political Science Review*, LXII (March 1968), 70–88.
[9] *Standard*, February 17, 1969.

was the almost total nationalization of the extraction function, which had the ultimate effect of making the intermediate and immediate political systems even more dependent upon the national system for resources. This process indicates the complexity of the relationship between political systems as the process of linking village to state proceeds. The major institution through which the total effort was being made in Tanzania was the political party, TANU. The ultimate effectiveness of the party in directing the will and efforts of the Tanzanian villagers to particular developmental tasks was still in question.

The Center-Periphery Nexus: An Assessment

The government intended that the formal structures linking village and state in each administrative and geographical subsystem be similar to those at other levels of the hierarchy and to those in other geographic locations at the same level. Although the extent to which these structures actually existed and functioned varied a great deal from village to village, some generalizations may be made.

During the 1960's, for the vast majority of peasants the primary political system was the immediate political system. Even though the villages were isolated from external political systems, the linkages which did exist between the village and the intermediate political systems and, ultimately, the national system were based on the developing structure of TANU, the ruling political party. While the way individuals performed their party roles was often considerably short of what national party leaders might have wished, the party as a governing institution through the cell leaders was an accepted fact at the village level.

Of the three intermediate political systems—the ward, the division, and the district—the district was the most institutionalized and was the most important external influence on the lives of individuals in the village. The district headquarters was the most substantial representation of the central political system in the peripheral areas. This is explained, first, by its overwhelming dependence upon the central government—appointments, promotions, and resources were determined by the central government and the maintenance of the district system was dependent upon the grace of the central government. Villages had only limited representation and influence in the district. The high rate of turnover in key positions in the districts also helps to explain the continuing national orientation of district actors.

The actors brought together at the district headquarters were there for the task of governing and developing the peoples and villages of the district in accordance with the center's will. This task, plus the tradition surrounding the *boma* as seen both by those occupying these roles and those toward whom their efforts were directed, set in motion behavior that was systematic in nature and that aimed at preserving the prerogatives and privileges characteristic of the actors in the district system. Although the national orientation of most of the district actors and their inclination toward self preservation might tend to maintain the district system, the success of the district system and, ultimately, that of the national system depended upon how successfully the district political system could establish linkages with the villages. The gap between center and periphery was most pronounced at the subdistrict level, and the contact of the district system with the villages, either directly or indirectly through the ward or division structures, was extremely intermittent.

The ward and division political systems were in a state of flux, and it was unclear as to what extent these intermediate systems would be subservient to the systems higher in the hierarchy and at the same time to be able to establish and exercise authority over the villages.

The Development of Subsystems: A Threat to National Direction?

A major proposition that I have pursued in this study is that in the process of national development and modernization the attempt on the part of the national political system to increase its capacity to maintain itself gives rise to a similar capacity on the part of political subsystems to maintain themselves in the face of increasing pressure from external systems. This development can increase the subsystems' capacity to defend themselves from external intrusion—the extreme form of which would be resistance—or it may be turned to securing the actions desired by the elites of the external systems. In the latter case the systems would be moving toward a condition where the localities and the nation are performing as a single system.

My findings in Handeni and Tanga Districts suggested that some such development had occurred within the district and subdistrict political systems of these two districts. For the district systems the development had taken place along with substantial, even increasing, commitment to the national political system. At the subdistrict levels political development had also occurred and was most evident in the increased differentiation of political structures intermediate between the village and the district. While these systems were substantially committed to the nation in the abstract sense, they were also embryonic institutions that could cushion the demands of external systems on these subsystems.

The potential conflict between center and periphery that was evident and that might increase would occur when the wards, divisions, and finally, the villages were expected to implement developmental policies and other tasks whose specifics were determined by authorities external to these systems, a task performed in the cases studied here by the district political systems.

Tanzanian leaders seemed to lessen the potential for conflict between center and periphery by the revolutionary step of decentralizing the authority for decisions on the specifics of policy and the responsibility for implementation of these policies to the ward, the second most local political system. They appeared to assume that the broad commitment to the nation and its leadership in the countryside would be sufficient to guide these subsystems to take the actions necessary to further national development. The leadership had not chosen to leave this assumption unsupported, however, and they had bolstered it by centralizing the extraction of resources in the national system and thereby enabling the center to exercise greater control and direction over the nation's resources.

The paradox facing Tanzanian leadership was a severe one. They could not govern and promote modernization in this impoverished land without more developed institutions in the numerous subsystems throughout the rural areas. At the same time, however, the increased capacity of these periphery institutions increased the potential of these subsystems for turning the resources of the nation to their own ends and to thus jeopardize national objectives. This paradox had been raised and faced in the 1960's, Tanzania's first decade of independence and the decade of nation building. The decade of the 1970's would determine whether the resources of the rural areas would be turned successfully to the objectives of the nation through persuasion rather than force, and whether the decade of nation building could be followed by a decade of state building and modernization and a better life for Tanzania's people. These developments would determine whether the Tanzanian nation could itself survive the strains of periphery demands upon national goals.

Selected Bibliography

GENERAL

Articles

Ashford, D. E. "Bureaucrats and Citizens," *The Annals,* 358 (March 1965), 89–101.

———. "The Last Revolution: Community and Nation in Africa," *Annals of the American Academy of Political Science,* 354 (July 1964), 33–45.

———. "Patterns of Consensus in Developing Countries," *American Behavioral Scientist,* IV (April 1961), 7–10.

Befu, Harumi. "The Political Relation of the Village to the State," *World Politics,* XIX (July 1967), 601–621.

Bible, Bond, and Cary McNabb. "Role Consensus and Administrative Effectiveness," *Rural Sociology,* XXI (March 1966), 5–14.

Binder, L. "National Integration and Political Development," *American Political Science Review,* LVIII (September 1964), 622–631.

Bohannan, Paul. "Extra-Processual Events in Tiv Political Institutions," *American Anthropologist,* LX (February 1958), 1–12.

Brierly, T. G. "The Evolution of Local Administration in French-speaking West Africa," *Journal of Local Administration Overseas,* V (January 1966), 56–71.

Buchanan, W., *et al.* "The Legislator as Specialist," *Western Political Quarterly,* XIII (September 1960), 636–652.

"Centralization and Decentralization," in Sills, David L. (ed.). *International Encyclopedia of the Social Sciences* (New York: Macmillan, 1968).

Eisenstadt, S. N. "Bureaucracy, Bureaucratization and Debureaucratization," *Administrative Science Quarterly*, IV (December 1959), 302–320.

Eulau, H., Wahlke, J. C., et al. "The Role of the Representative: Some Empirical Observations on the Theory of Edmund Burke," *American Political Science Review*, LIII (September 1959), 742–756.

Fesler, J. W. "Approaches to the Understanding of Decentralization," *Journal of Politics*, XXVII (August 1965), 536–566.

Glickman, Harvey. "Dilemmas of Political Theory in an African Context: The Ideology of Julius Nyerere." In Jeffrey Butler and A. A. Castagno, *Boston University Papers on Africa*. New York: Frederick A. Praeger, 1967. Pp. 195–224.

Gorvine, A. "The Utilization of Local Government for National Development," *Journal of Local Administration Overseas*, IV (October 1965), 225–232.

Greenwood, A. F. "Ten Years of Local Government in Ghana," *Journal of Local Administration Overseas* (January 1962), 23–28.

Hanna, William John. "The Cross-cultural Study of Local Politics," *Civilizations* (Brussels), XVI (1966), 8–96.

———. "Image-Making in Field Research in Tropical Africa," *American Behavioral Scientist*, IX (January 1965), 15–20.

Hassinger, Edward. "Social Relations Between Centralized and Local Social Systems," *Rural Sociology*, XXVI (December 1961), 354–364.

Henderson, K. M. "Charting a New Terrain: Comparative Local Administration," *Public Administration Review*, XXVII (June 1967), 142–147.

Hoselitz, Bert F. "Levels of Economic Performance and Bureaucratic Structures." J. G. LaPalombara (ed.), *Bureaucracy and Political Development*. Princeton, N.J.: Princeton University Press, 1963. Pp. 168–199.

Huntington, Samuel P. "Political Development and Political Decay," *World Politics*, XVII (April 1965), 386–411.

Jacobson, E., et al. "The Use of the Role Concept in the Study of Complex Organization," *Journal of Social Issues*, VII, no. 3 (1951), 18–27.

Kalleberg, A. L. "The Logic of Comparison: A Methodological Note on the Comparative Study of Political System," *World Politics,* XIX (October 1966), 69–83.

Kellstedt, L. "Atlanta to 'Oretown'—Identifying Community Elites," *Public Administration Review,* XXV (June 1965), 161–168.

Lewis, A. B. "Local Self-Government: A Key to National Economic Advancement and Political Stability," *Philippine Journal of Public Administration,* II (January 1958), 54–57.

Loomis, Charles P. "Systemic Linkage of El Cerrito," *Rural Sociology,* XXIV (March 1959), 54–57.

Lyden, Fremont, J. "Role Consensus and Organizational Effectiveness," *Public Administration Review,* XXVII (March 1967), 60–61.

Mair, L. P. "Representative Government as a Problem in Social Change," *Rhodes-Livingstone Journal,* No. 21 (1957), p. 17.

Meek, C. A. "A Practical Experiment in Local Government," *Journal of African Administration,* II (3) (July 1950), 21–28.

Parsons, T. "Social Structure and Political Orientation," *World Politics,* XIII (October 1960), 112–128.

Patterson, Samuel C. "Characteristics of Party Leaders," *Western Political Quarterly,* XVI (June 1963), 332–352.

Riggs, Fred W. "Bureaucrats and Political Development: A Paradoxical View." In J. G. La Palombara (ed.), *Bureaucracy and Political Development.* Princeton, N.J.: Princeton University Press, 1963. Pp. 120–168.

———. "Economic Development and Local Administration: A Study in Circular Causation," *Philippine Journal of Public Administration,* III (January 1959), 86–146.

———. "The Theory of Developing Politics," *World Politics,* XVI (October 1963), 147–172.

Sady, E. J. "Improvement of Local Government and Administration for Development Purposes," *Journal of Local Administration Overseas,* I (July 1962), 135–148.

Silverman, C. "The Legislator's View of the Legislative Process," *Public Opinion Quarterly,* XVIII (Summer 1954), 180–190.

Simpson, Richard L. "Sociology of the Community: Current Status and Prospects," *Rural Sociology,* XXX (June 1965), 127–150.

Starr, B. W. "Levels of Communal Relations," *American Journal of Sociology,* LX (May 1955), 125–136.

Steward, Julian H. "Levels of Sociocultural Integration," *Southwestern Journal of Anthropology*, VII (Winter 1951), 374–390.

"A Survey of the Development of Local Government in the African Territories since 1947—Tanganyika," *Journal of African Administration*, IV (April 1952), 13–24.

Wahlke, J. C., et al. "American State Legislator's Role Orientation toward Pressure Groups," *Journal of Politics*, XXII (May 1960), 203–228.

——. "The Political Socialization of American State Legislators," *Midwest Journal of Political Science*, III (May 1959), 188–206.

Whitaker, C. S., Jr. "A Dysrythmic Process of Political Change," *World Politics*, XIX (January 1967), 190–218.

Zentner, H. "The State and the Community: A Conceptual Clarification," *Sociology and Social Research*, XLVIII (July 1964), 414–427.

Zolberg, Aristide R. "The Structure of Political Conflict in the New States of Tropical Africa," *American Political Science Review*, LXII (March 1968), 70–88.

Books

Adu, A. L. *The Civil Service in New African States.* New York: Frederick A. Praeger, 1965.

Alderfer, H. F. *Local Government in Developing Countries.* New York: McGraw-Hill, 1964.

Almond, Gabriel A., and G. Bingham Powell, Jr. *Comparative Politics: A Developmental Approach.* Boston: Little, Brown, 1966.

Apter, David. *The Political Kingdom in Uganda.* Princeton, N.J.: Princeton University Press, 1961.

Ashford, D. E. *National Development and Local Reform.* Princeton, N.J.: Princeton University Press, 1967.

——. *Perspectives of a Moroccan Nationalist.* Totowa, N.Y.: Bedminster Press, 1964.

Buell, R. L. *The Native Problem in Africa.* New York: Macmillan, 1928.

Burke, Fred G. *Local Government and Politics in Uganda.* Syracuse, N.Y.: Syracuse University Press, 1964. An abridged form of "The Development of Local Governments in Uganda: A Comparative

SELECTED BIBLIOGRAPHY

Approach," unpublished Ph.D dissertation, Department of Political Science, Princeton University, 1958.

Clark, Colin, and M. R. Haswell. *The Economics of Subsistence Agriculture.* 2d ed. London: Macmillan, 1966.

Deutsch, Karl W. *The Nerves of Government.* New York: The Free Press, 1966.

Easton, David. *A Framework of Political Analysis.* Englewood Cliffs, N.J.: Prentice-Hall, 1965.

———. *A System's Analysis of Political Life.* New York: John Wiley and Sons, 1965.

Eldersveld, S. J. *Political Parties: A Behavioral Analysis.* Chicago: Rand McNally, 1964.

Etzioni, Amitai. *Political Unification.* New York: Holt, Rinehart and Winston, 1965.

Fallers, L. *The King's Men.* London: Oxford University Press, 1964.

Furse, Sir Ralph. *Aucuparius.* London: Oxford University Press, 1962.

Geertz, C. (ed.). *Old Societies and New States.* New York: Free Press, 1963.

Gluckman, Max. *Order and Rebellion in Tribal Africa.* New York: The Free Press, 1963.

Gourou, Pierre. *The Tropical World: Its Social and Economic Conditions and Its Future Status.* 4th ed. Trans. S. H. Beaver and E. D. Laborde. London: Longmans, 1966.

Gross, Neal, Ward Mason, and Alexander McEachern. *Explorations in Role Analysis: Studies of the School Superintendency Role.* New York: John Wiley and Sons, 1958.

Harlow, Vincent (ed.). *History of East Africa.* Vol. II. Oxford: Clarendon Press, 1965.

Helleiner, G. K. (ed.). *Agricultural Planning in East Africa.* Nairobi: East African Publishing House, 1968.

Hicks, Ursula K. *Development from Below.* London: Oxford University Press, 1961.

Jacob, D. E. and J. U. Toscano (eds.). *The Integration of Political Communities.* Philadelphia: J. B. Lippincott Co., 1964.

Janowitz, Morris (ed.). *Community Political Systems.* Glencoe, Ill.: The Free Press, 1961.

Kilson, M. *Political Change in a West African State: A Study of the*

Modernization Process in Sierra Leone. Cambridge: Harvard University Press, 1966.

Lewis, W. Arthur. *Politics in West Africa.* Toronto: Oxford University Press, 1965.

Leys, Colin. *Politicians and Policies.* Nairobi: East African Publishing House, 1967.

Maas, A. (ed.). *Area and Power.* Glencoe, Ill.: Free Press, 1959.

Maddick, H. *Democracy, Decentralization, and Development.* London: Asia Publishing House, 1963.

Middleton, John, and E. H. Winter (eds.). *Witchcraft and Sorcery in East Africa.* London: Routledge and Kegan Paul, 1963.

Mitchell, C. *Tribalism and the Plural Society.* London: Oxford University Press, 1960.

Richards, A. I. (ed.). *East African Chiefs.* London: Faber and Faber, 1960.

Steward, Julian H. *Area Research: Theory and Practice.* Bulletin 63, Social Science Research Council, 1950.

—— (ed.). *Introduction and African Tribes. Contemporary Change in Traditional Societies,* Vol. I. Urbana: University of Illinois Press, 1967.

United Nations, Department of Economic and Social Affairs, Director for Public Administration. *Decentralization for National and Local Development.* New York: United Nations, 1962.

Vidich, A. J., and J. Bensman. *Small Town in Mass Society.* Princeton: Princeton University Press, 1958.

Wahlke, J. C., et al. *The Legislative System.* New York: John Wiley and Sons, 1962.

Wilson, G. and M. *The Analysis of Social Change.* Cambridge: Cambridge University Press, 1945.

Winans, E. V. *Shambala: The Constitution of a Traditional State.* Berkeley: University of California Press, 1962.

Worsley, Peter. *The Third World.* London: Weidenfeld and Nicolson, 1964.

Wylie, L. *Village in the Vaucluse.* Cambridge: Harvard University Press, 1957.

Zolberg, A. R. *Creating Political Order.* Chicago: Rand McNally, 1966.

SELECTED BIBLIOGRAPHY

TANZANIA

Articles

Austin, Ralph A. "The Official Mind of Indirect Rule. British Policy in Tanganyika 1916–1939." In P. Gifford and W. P. Louis (eds.). *Britain and Germany in Africa.* New Haven: Yale University Press, 1967.

Bates, Margaret L. "Tanganyika: Changes in African Life 1918–1945." In Vincent Harlow (ed.), *History of East Africa,* Vol. II. Oxford: Clarendon Press, 1965. Pp. 625–641.

Baxter, H. C. "The Religious Practices of the Pagan Wazigua," *Tanganyika Notes and Records,* XVII (1943).

"Blueprint for a One-Party Democracy," *African Report,* October 1965, pp. 19–29.

Cliffe, Lionel. "Reflections on Agricultural Development in East Africa," *East African Journal,* II (November 1965), 26–30.

Cory, H. "Reform of Tribal Institutions in Tanganyika," *Journal of African Administration,* XII (April 1960), 77–84.

Dryden, S. "Local Government in Tanzania—Part I," *Journal of Administration Overseas,* VI (April 1967), 109–122. Part II, *Journal of Administration Overseas,* VI (July 1967), 165–179.

Dudbridge, B. J., and J. E. Griffiths. "The Development of Local Government in Sukuma-Land," *Journal of African Administration,* III (July 1951), 141–146.

Dundas, Hon. C. "Native Laws of Some Bantu Tribes of East Africa," *Journal of the Royal Anthropological Institute* (1921), 217–278.

Eberlie, R. F. "The German Achievement in East Africa," *Tanganyika Notes and Records,* LV (September 1960), 181–214.

Ehrlich, Cyril. "Some Aspects of Economic Policy in Tanganyika, 1945–1960," *Journal of Modern African Studies,* II (July 1964), 265–77.

Gerlach, Luther P. "Nutrition in its Sociocultural Matrix: Food Getting and Using Along the East African Coast." In David Brokensha (ed.), *Ecology and Economic Development in Tropical Africa.* Berkeley: Institute of International Studies, University of California, 1965. Pp. 245–268.

———. "Traders on Bicycle: A Study of Entrepreneurship and Culture Change among the Digo and Duruma of Kenya," *Sociologus,* 13, no. 1 (1963), 32–49.

Glickman, H. "One-Party System in Tanganyika," *The Annals,* CCCLVII (March 1965), 136–150.

Gluckman, Max. "Psychological, Sociological and Anthropological Explanations of Witchcraft and Gossip: A Clarification," *Man* (London), III (March 1968), 20–34.

Harris, Belle. "The Tanzanian Elections 1965," *Mbioni* (Monthly Newsletter of Kivukoni College, Dar es Salaam) II, No. V (special election edition, n.d.).

Henderson, W. O. "German East Africa: 1884–1918." In Vincent Harlow (ed.), *History of East Africa.* Oxford: Clarendon Press, 1965. II, 123–163.

Ingham, Kenneth. "Tanganyika the Mandate and Cameron 1919–1931." In Vincent Harlow (ed.), *History of East Africa.* Oxford: Clarendon Press, 1965. II, 543–594.

Kayamba, H. M. T. "Notes on the Wadigo," *Tanganyika Notes and Records,* XXIII (1947), 80.

Kingdon, Z. E. "The Initiation of a System of Local Government by African Rural Councils in the Bungue District of Tanganyika," *Journal of African Administration,* III (October 1951), 186–191.

Klerruu, W. "Whys and Wherefores of TANU Cell System," *Mbioni* (Monthly Newsletter of Kivukoni College), III (June 1966), 3–11.

Lemarchand, R. "Village by Village Building in Tanzania," *Africa Report,* X (February 1965), 11–13.

Liebenow, J. Gus. "The Chief in Sukuma Local Government," *Journal of African Administration,* XI (April 1959), 84–92.

———. "Some Problems in Introducing Local Government Reform in Tanganyika," *Journal of African Administration,* VIII (July 1956), 132–139.

Lonsdale, John. "The Tanzanian Experiment," *African Affairs,* LXVII (October 1968), 330–344.

McAuslan, J. P. N. B. "The Republican Constitution of Tanganyika," *International and Comparative Law Quarterly,* XIII (1964), 502–574.

Mackenzie, W. J. M. "Changes in Local Government in Tanganyika," *Journal of African Administration*, VI (July 1954), 123.

Mawhood, P. N. "Choosing the Town Councillor," *Journal of African Administration*, XIII (July 1961), 131–139.

Miller, Norman N. "The Rural African Party: Political Participation in Tanzania," *American Political Science Review*, LXIV (June 1970), 548–572.

Mohiddin, Ahmed. "Ujamaa: A Commentary on President Nyerere's Vision of Tanzanian Society," *African Affairs*, LXVII (April 1968), 130–144.

Montague, F. A., and F. H. Page-Jones, "Some Difficulties in the Democratization of Native Authorities in Tanganika," *Journal of African Administration*, III (January 1951), 21–27.

Morgenthau, A. S. "African Elections: Tanzania's Contribution," *Africa Report*, X (December 1965), 12–17.

Mwakawago, D. N. "Changing Patterns in Tanzania," *Mbioni* (Monthly Newsletter of Kivukoni College) II, No. IX, 36–40.

Pierard, R. V. "The Dernberg Reform Policy and German East Africa," *Tanzania Notes and Records*, LXVII (June 1967), 31–38.

Raum, O. F. "German East Africa: Changes in African Life under German Administration 1892–1914," in Vincent Harlow (ed.), *History of East Africa*. Oxford: Clarendon Press, 1965. II, 163–209.

Sady, E. J. "Community Development and Local Government," *Journal of African Administration*, XI (October 1959), 179–187.

Tanner, R. E. S. "Law Enforcement by Communal Action in Sukumaland," *Journal of African Administration*, VII (October 1955), 59–65.

Tordoff, W. "The General Election in Tanzania," *Journal of Commonwealth Political Studies*, IV (March 1966), 47–54.

———. "Regional Administration in Tanzania," *Journal of Modern African Studies* (Cambridge), LII (May 1965), 63–89.

Warrell-Bowring, W. J. "The Reorganization of the Administration in Tanganyika," *Journal of Local Administration Overseas*, II (October 1963), 188–194.

Winnington-Ingram, C. "Reforming Local Government in a Tanganyika District," *Journal of African Administration*, II (No. 2), 10–15.

Books

Bastin, E. *La décentralization administrative et l'évolution des structures politiques en Afrique orientale Britannique: Éléments d'une étude comparative.* Liège: Faculté de droit de Liège, 1958.

Beidelman, T. O. *The Matrilineal Peoples of Eastern Tanzania.* London: International African Institute, 1967.

Bienen, Henry. *Tanzania: Party Transformation and Economic Development.* Princeton, N.J.: Princeton University Press, 1967.

Burke, F. G. *Local Governance and Nation Building in East Africa: A Functional Analysis.* Occasional Paper No. 9. Syracuse, N.Y.: The Program of Eastern African Studies, Syracuse University, 1964.

———. *Tanganyika: Preplanning.* Syracuse, N.Y.: Syracuse University Press, 1965.

Cairns, J. C. *Bush and Boma.* London: John Murray, 1959.

Cliffe, Lionel (ed.). *One Party Democracy.* Nairobi: East African Publishing House, 1967.

Cole, J. S. R., and W. N. Denison. *Tanganyika: The Development of Its Laws and Constitution. British Commonwealth and the Development of Its Laws and Constitution,* Vol. XII. London: Stevens, 1964.

Dryden, Stanley. *Local Administration in Tanzania.* Nairobi: East African Publishing House, 1968.

Dundas, C. C. F. *African Crossroads.* London: Macmillan, 1955.

Guillebaud, C. W. *An Economic Survey of the Sisal Industry of Tanganyika.* 3d ed. Welwyn, England: James Nisbet and Co., 1966.

Hyden, Goran. *Political Development in Rural Tanzania.* Nairobi: East African Publishing House, 1969.

Ingham, Kenneth. *A History of East Africa.* New York: Praeger, 1962.

Lee, Eugene C. *Local Taxation in Tanganyika.* University of California Institute of International Studies, research series, No. 6. Berkeley, 1965.

Liebenow, J. Gus. *Colonial Rule and Political Development in Tanzania: The Case of the Makonde.* Evanston: Northwestern University Press, 1971.

Maguire, G. Andrew. *Toward 'Uhuru' in Tanzania: The Politics of Participation.* Cambridge: Cambridge University Press, 1969.

Mitchell, Philip. *African Afterthoughts.* London: Hutchinson, 1954.

SELECTED BIBLIOGRAPHY

Mochiwa, Anthony. *Habari Za Wazigua.* London: Macmillan, 1954.
Nyerere, Julius K. *Freedom and Socialism.* Dar es Salaam: Oxford University Press, 1968.
———. *Freedom and Unity.* Dar es Salaam: Oxford University Press, 1966.
Penner, R. G. *Financing Local Government in Tanzania.* Nairobi: East African Publishing House, 1970.
Prins, A. H. J. *The Central Tribe of the North Eastern Bantu.* London: International African Institute, 1953.
Ruthenberg, Hans. *Agricultural Development in Tanganyika.* München: Ifo-Institut für Wirtschaftsforschung (Afrika-Studien, N. 2, 1964).
——— (ed.). *Smallholder Farming and Smallholder Development in Tanzania.* München: Ifo-institut für Wirtschaftsforschung (Afrika-Studien, N. 24, 1968).
Symers, Sir Stewart. *Tour of Duty.* London: Collins, 1946.
Tordoff, William. *Government and Politics in Tanzania.* Nairobi: East African Publishing House, 1967.
Wenner, Kate. *Shambaletu.* Boston: Houghton Mifflin, 1970.
Wood, Alan. *The Groundout Affair.* London: The Bodley Head, 1950.
World Bank Report. *The Economic Development of Tanganyika.* Baltimore: Johns Hopkins University Press, 1961.
Young, R., and H. A. Fosbrooke. *Smoke in the Hills: Political Tension in the Morogoro District of Tanganyika.* Evanston, Ill.: Northwestern University Press, 1960.

Government Documents

Note: I have surveyed the accessible records of Tanga and Handeni Districts; the most important of these are the district books from each district and the official minutes of the district councils and district council committees. I have also read the government files pertaining to problems of rural development and local government for the districts. Most of these are in the National Archives in Dar es Salaam. Since the material in the National Archives has not been fully indexed and is scattered in many offices throughout the city, there is no way of determining the extent to which this research is complete. These official records, most of which are unpublished, are not cited in the selected bibliography of government documents below. Instead, I have cited them in footnotes where relevant.

Great Britain

Hailey, Lord. *Native Administration and Political Development in British Tropical Africa.* London: H.M.S.O., 1940–1942.

Report of the East African Royal Commission, 1953–1955 (Cmd 9475) London: H.M.S.O., 1955.

United Republic of Tanzania (Tanganyika)

African Census Report, 1957. Dar es Salaam: Government Printer, 1963.

Hill, J. F. R., and J. P. Moffett (eds.). *Tanganyika: A Review of Its Resources and Their Development.* Dar es Salaam: The Government Printer, 1955.

Ministry of Economic Affairs and Development Planning, Central Statistical Bureau. *Preliminary Results of the Population Census Taken in August, 1967.* Dar es Salaam, December 1967.

Moffett, J. P. (ed.). *Handbook of Tanganyika,* 2d ed. Dar es Salaam: Tanganyika Government Printer, 1958.

Report of the Presidential Commission on the Establishment of a Democratic One Party State. Dar es Salaam: The Government Printer. 1965.

Report of the Presidential Special Committee of Enquiry into Cooperative Movement and Marketing Boards. Dar es Salaam: The Government Printer, 1966.

Tanga District. *The District Book.* Microfilm, National Archives, Dar es Salaam and Syracuse University Library.

Tanga Region. "The Provincial Book" (Regional).

Tanganyika Five-Year Plan for Economic and Social Development 1st July, 1964–30th June, 1969. Vols. I and II. Dar es Salaam: The Government Printer, 1964.

Tanzania Second Five-Year Plan for Economic and Social Development 1st July 1969–30th June 1974. Vols. I and II. Dar es Salaam: The Government Printer, 1969.

University Dissertations and Papers

Georgulas, Nikos. "Structure and Communication: A Study of the Tanganyika Settlement Agency." D.S.S. dissertation, Syracuse University, 1967.

Liebenow, J. Gus. "Chieftainship and Local Government in Tanganyika: A Study of Institutional Adaptation." Ph.D. dissertation, Northwestern University, 1956.

Miller, Norman N. "Village Leadership and Modernization in Tanzania: Rural Politics Among the Nyamwezi People of Tabora Region." Ph.D. dissertation, Department of Government, Indiana University, August 1966.

Mwensasu, Bismarck. "T.Y.L. Settlement Schemes: The Whys and Wherefores of Success and Failure—An Impressionistic View." Kivukoni College, September 9, 1966. Mimeographed paper.

Njohole, B. "The TANU Cell System." Dissertation, Department of Political Science, The University of East Africa. Also published as Political Science, Paper 6; Dar es Salaam, March 1967.

O'Barr, Jean Fox. "Ten-House Party Cells and Their Leaders: Micropolitics in Pare District, Tanzania." Ph.D. dissertation, Department of Political Science, Northwestern University, 1970.

Rweyemamu, A. H. "Nation Building and the Planning Process in Tanzania." Ph.D. dissertation, Department of Political Science, Syracuse University, 1965.

Yeager, Rodger D. "Micropolitics and Transformation: A Tanzanian Case Study of Political Interaction." Ph.D. dissertation, Department of Political Science, Syracuse University, 1968.

Newspapers

The Nationalist (Dar es Salaam), May 1967–July 1968.
The Standard (Tanzania), May 1967–June 1971.

Index

Africa: agricultural productivity, 15; economic development, 14-15; paternalism, 91; political ideology, 13; poverty, 12; rural development, necessity of, 11, 16; unemployment, 13-14
African socialism, 5-8, 15
Africanization, 249
agricultural field assistants, 88-89, 166, 190, 193
agricultural ordinances, 46, 65-71
agriculture, 10-11; basis of development 5, 9, 11-16, 197; marketing, 204-206; nature of society, 4-5; subsistence, 39
akida, 109-111
Arab colonization, 39, 108-110
area commissioner, 114-116, 132, 210; in Handeni, 70, 116, 136-137; powers, 69, 114-117, 119-120, 140; in Tanga, 116, 137, 223
area secretary, 117-118
Arusha Declaration, vii, 1-7, 16, 101, 198, 221-222, 251

baraza (general meeting), 36-37
black market, 204-206
block farms, 66-71, 121
boma (district offices), 113-122, 145
British colonial period: agricultural ordinances, 46, 63-65; compulsion, 44, 72-73; district commissioner's team, 120; estate agriculture, 43-46; government, 107, 111-113; indirect rule, 47, 111-112, 122-123; paternalism, 90-92; special schemes, 43-44
bylaws, 223-224, 240; *see also* agricultural ordinances

cassava, 63, 65, 68
cattle-coconut schemes, 53-56
cell leader: compensation, 181-182; duties in TANU constitution, 171-172; as elder, 176-178; as headman, 179-182, 184; maintenance of order, 173, 177; role in communication, 172, 191-192; tax collection, 164, 172-173, 201-202; traditional-modern dichotomy, 175, 178; on village development committee, 155, 158-159; as village leader, 75, 174, 212
center-periphery relationships, 244, 251-252, 257-259
Central Intelligence Division (CID), 118
centralization, 29
Chagga, 59, 107
Chanika Division, 148
chiefs, 61, 86, 90-91, 108, 111-112, 145, 148, 179
chiwili (farming together), 75-76
civil service, 118; Africanization, 249; conflict with politicians, 117-118, 120-122; financial support, 238; recruitment, 210

communal farms, 68, 75, 102; see also block farms
communal labor, 71-72, 74-75
communal self-help, 74, 76, 157, 240
communication, 25-26; clandestine, 193; of discontent, 193; in the district, 192; effectiveness of, 191, 193, 195; role of the district councilor, 193; role of the national political system, 194; stifling of, 192
compensation, 181-183; for precolonial leaders, 181; for village and district leaders, 183
compulsion: British period, 44-47, 63-65, 72; comments by Nyerere on, 97-100, 102-104; German period, 41, 72; independence period, 62-63, 65-67, 94-97, 100-102, 121, 193, 247, 255-256
Cooperative Movement and Marketing Boards, Report of the Presidential Special Committee of Enquiry, 204-205
cooperative societies, 204-206
cotton, 41
culture, political, 26-27

Dar es Salaam, University of, 13, 98
decentralization, 102-103, 130, 154, 256, 260
decision-making, democratic, 99
detention, forty-eight-hour, 148-149, 202-203
Digo, 147, 168
district commissioner, 74, 119-120; in Handeni, 67, 91; in Tanga, 63, 65
district councils, 122-131, 244-246; committees, 128-129; councilors' view of their role, 193-194, 213-221, 226-228; dependence upon central government, 131, 237-238; election of, 124-125; government officials' views of council, 129, 221-226; history of, 113, 122-123; ineffectiveness, 128-130; legislative efficacy, 227-228; modification of, 130; nominated members, 125-126; powers, 65, 96, 123-124, 129-130, 196, 200-201, 205-206; TANU's role in, 124-126
District Development and Planning Committee (until 1967, District Development Committee), 68, 75-76, 117, 138-142, 155
district executive officer, 126-128, 141
district government, 113-116, 142-143; civil servants in, 120-122; expenditures, 242-246; preindependence, 110-113; revenue, 241-245
District Magistrate, 119
district officers, 120-121; conflict with area commissioner, 120-122; frequent transfers, 121; use of force, 121
district political system: demands, 233-237; inputs, 232-241; outputs, 241-250; supports, 237-241
"district team," 138-139
division, 145-154, 187, 189-190
division development committee, 146, 151-153
divisional executive officer (after 1969, divisional executive secretary), 148-154, 158-159, 179-180, 189-190, 192, 202-203
divorce, 25, 187
duka (general store), 107, 160-162, 165, 167, 182

education, 196-198, 244-246; district council support, 196, 244-246; enrollment, 198; Ministry of Education support, 196, 237; political influence in, 119; for self-reliance, 7, 196-198; traditional values in, 197
elders: independence period, 151, 156, 159, 163, 175-178; precolonial period, 108
expatriates, 44, 48, 53-54
extension efforts, 59-60
extraction, 200-202; ideology in, 209; resistance to, 209; role of cooperative societies, 204; role of FFU,

INDEX

extraction (*continued*) 206; role of TANU, 209; shifting of burden, 206-207; shifting of capacity, 206; TANU dues, 204

famine, 46-47, 61, 63-64, 70, 91-93, 239, 249
Field Force Unit, 69, 164, 202, 206

German colonial period, 40-42, 109-111; agricultural ordinances, 46-47; compulsion, 41, 72-73, 94; estate agriculture, 41; government, 107, 110-111; response to infanticide, 87
Ghana, 11
Groundnut Scheme, 43

Handeni District, 16-17, 243, 248, 254-255, 259; block farms, 67-72; communication in, 190-191; district council in, 196, 215-218; expenditures, 246; famine, 63-65, 235-236, 239; infanticide, 86-87; population, 17, 82-83; precolonial period, 108; rainfall, 61, 79-82; revenue, 245; soil, 82; witchcraft in, 86-89
headman (*jumbe*), 90-91, 110, 112, 179-181, 183-184

indirect rule, 47, 111-113
infanticide, 86-87
input-output, 34-35, 185, 229-250
institutionalization, 127, 218
intersystem roles, 31-34, 185, 209-229

Jamal, A. H., 206
jumbe, 110; *see also* headman

Kawawa, R. M., 51, 134, 171, 256
Kenya, 14, 205
kiboko (whip), 102
Kivukoni College, 133
Knox County, Tennessee, 79-80
Kwambilu, 161-162

Kwamkono, 160, 162-163, 167, 174, 178, 188
Kwamsala, 168, 178, 188

leadership, 99, 112-113
League of Nations, 1
legislative efficacy, 227-228
Local Government Services Commission, 126, 149
locality, 10

maize (corn), 61, 81-82, 205
Maji Maji Rebellion, 40, 94
Maranzara, 55, 166-167, 174, 178
Marungu (village), 158-159, 167, 174, 178, 212
Marungu Amani, 158, 168
Marungu Ward: composition of, 158; organization of, 158, 166; political functions in, 187-188, 201, 212-213, 235; population, 158; villages in, 166-168
messengers, 118, 202
Migombani, 158, 168
Minister of Finance, 206, 237
Ministries: Agriculture, 53, 59, 71, 166; Education, 237, 244, 246; Home Affairs, 66; Local Government and Rural Development, 97, 104; Regional Administration and Rural Development, 117
modernization, 16
Mombo Village Irrigation Scheme, 52-53

National Agricultural Products Board, 205
National Assembly, 75, 124
national political system, 233-234, 239-240
National Union of Tanganyika Workers (NUTA), 135
Native Authority, 47, 64, 67, 73, 111-112, 122-123, 224
Nigeria, 14
Nyerere, J. K., vii, 1, 6, 54, 90, 194, 211, 252; on compulsion, 97-100, 102-104, 255; on development, 2-11, 39; on district councils, 224;

Nyerere, J. K. (*continued*)
on education, 196-197; on laziness, 248; on political party, 6, 191; on poverty, 7; writings of, 3-10, 196-197

paternalism, 61, 90-94; in Handeni, 92-93; in Tanga, 93-94
peasants, 2, 4-5, 12, 39, 47-50, 52-53, 55-56, 58-60, 102, 207, 255
"Peoples Plan," 62
Peters, Carl, 40
police, 187-188, 202, 206, 236
political development, 28-32, 169, 184, 209, 252, 256-257, 259-260
political functions, sharing of: communications, 25-26, 188-195; extraction and mobilization, 27-28, 188, 199-209; maintenance of order, 24-25, 186-188; socialization, 26-27, 195-199
political seminars, 122, 133, 199
political socialization: education system, 196-197; family, 195; TANU Youth League, 198; village, 195
political systems, 19-20, 231-232; immediate, 20-21, 23-24, 235, 257; intermediate, 21, 23-24, 235, 257-258; national, 22-24, 234, 237-239; system-to-system linkages, 22-31, 34-35, 153, 185-186, 191-192, 201, 229-230, 257-258
Pongwe Division, 146-147
provincial commissioner, Tanga, 45, 72
provincial office, Tanga, 47, 64

Radio Tanzania, 194-195
rainfall, 79-82
regional administrative secretary, 115
regional commissioner, 100, 115-116, 119, 150, 222
regional government, 115-117
research techniques, 35-38, 214
roles: conflict in, 209-213; of district council, 219-221, 224-229; of district councilor, 215-219, 221-224;

local demands, 212, 214, 228-229
rubber, 41
rural development: British efforts, 42-48, 63-65; district council role in, 65-66, 215-216, 219-220; German efforts, 40-42; imperative of, 11-16; "improvement" approach, 50, 59-60; opposition to policies, 192-193; peasant role in, 60-63; postindependence efforts, 48-63, 65-71, 76; special schemes, 50-57; "transformation" approach, 50; World Bank Report, 49-50

self-reliance, 3-4, 9, 77, 92, 197
Sindeni (village), 161-163, 167, 178, 213
Sindeni Ward, 160, 166; composition of, 160-161; organization of, 160-162; political functions, 162-166, 188, 201, 212-213; population, 161; villages in, 166-167
sisal, 41, 107, 119, 158
slavery, 40
soil, 82
special development schemes, 43-44, 50-58
state building, 24

Tanga District, 16-17, 45, 63-66, 72, 93-94, 243, 253-255; communication in, 190-191; district council in, 196, 215-218; population, 17, 82-83; precolonial history, 108; rainfall, 79-81; soil, 82
Tanganyika African Parents' Association (TAPA), 135
TANU (Tanganyika African National Union), 2, 114-116, 189, 257; branch conference, 124; branch secretary, 146, 151; bureaucracy, 132-134; central committee, 125; district chairman, 115, 126, 132, 136, 229, 234; district executive committee, 115-116, 124, 134-135; district executive secretary, 115, 132; district secretary, 114, 132; district working committee, 116, 135-136;

INDEX

TANU (*continued*)
divisional chairman (branch chairman), 146; divisional executive secretary, 115, 149-150; divisional secretary, 146; elected officials, 134-136; independence movement, 74; leaders' code, 6; national executive committee, 169; regional chairman, 115; regional development committee, 115; regional executive committee, 115; regional executive secretary, 115; regional secretary, 115; role in district, 126, 131-132; role in elections, 124-125, 211; ten-house cell, 169-171; ward chairman, 146; ward secretary, 146

TANU Youth League (TYL), 68, 162-164, 174, 187-188, 198-199

Tanzania, United Republic of: agricultural productivity, 58; Arab colonization, 39-40, 108-109; British colonial period, 42-48, 111-113; economics, 237-238; education in, 196-198; German colonial period, 40-42, 109-111; independence movement, 48-49, 59-60; political organization, 115-116, 146-147; population, 1, 82-83; postindependence history, 1-2, 77-78; poverty in, 12, 15, 58-59

taxation, 200-208, 244, 254; burden on urban and salaried citizens, 206-207; cess, 204-206; direct, 200; district collections, 208; excise duties, 208; German period, 110; head tax, 124, 130, 172-173, 200-203, 221, 239; import duties, 208; indirect, 200; national collections, 208; payroll deductions, 203-204; proportional, 207; reduction on peasants, 207; sales tax, 206-207; use of force in collection, 202

technicians, *see* district officers
ten-house cell, 169-171

traditional values, 8, 11, 71, 75-76, 103, 122, 157, 197
tribalism, 108-111

ujamaa villages, 8-9, 97-98, 157, 253-254
Union of Tanzania Women (UWT), 135
United Nations, 42
United States, 25, 33

village, 2-3, 107-108, 164, 166-184, 192-193; dissent in, 192-193; government in, 178; isolation of, 186, political system in, 184, 186-187, 192-193, 195; preindependence period, 109-111; response to national government, 239, 241
village development committee (VDC), 103, 152, 155-157, 162, 171
village executive officer (VEO; after 1969, ward executive officer), 150, 156, 161-166, 183, 189, 192, 201-202, 212-213, 221
village irrigation schemes, 52-53
Village Settlement Agency, 50
village settlement schemes, 50-51

ward, 147, 154-166, 180-181, 183, 212-213
ward development committee (WDC), 103-104, 156, 158-159, 171; in Marungu Ward, 158-159, 175-176; in Sindeni Ward, 162-163
ward executive officer, 150
witchcraft, 85-89
World Bank Report, 43, 49-50
World War I, 42
World War II, 42-45

Zanzibar, 77, 108
Zigua, 63, 75, 86-87, 92, 108, 165, 248, 253
Zigua Tribal Council (*Ufungilo*), 73-74

*From Village to State
in Tanzania*

Designed by R. E. Rosenbaum.
Composed by Vail-Ballou Press, Inc.,
in 10 point linotype Times Roman, 3 points leaded,
with display lines in Corvinus Medium.
Printed letterpress from type by Vail-Ballou Press
on Warren's No. 66 text, 60 pound basis,
with the Cornell University Press watermark.
Bound by Vail-Ballou Press
in Columbia book cloth
and stamped in All Purpose foil.

Library of Congress Cataloging in Publication Data
(For library cataloging purposes only)

Ingle, Clyde Reid, date.
    From village to state in Tanzania.

    Bibliography: p.
    1. Local government—Tanzania. 2. Tanzania—
Politics and government. 3. Tanzania—Rural conditions.
4. Tanzania—Economic policy. 5. Villages—Tanzania.
I. Title.
JS7697.2.I5   320.9'678'04   72-4570
ISBN 0-8014-0733-8